Growing Up Religious

Also by Robert Wuthnow

AFTER HEAVEN

*Spirituality in America
Since the 1950s*

LOOSE CONNECTIONS

*Joining Together in America's
Fragmented Communities*

POOR RICHARD'S PRINCIPLE

*Recovering the American Dream
through the Moral Dimension of
Work, Business, and Money*

GOD AND MAMMON IN AMERICA

SHARING THE JOURNEY

*Support Groups and America's
New Quest for Community*

Robert Wuthnow

Growing Up Religious

Christians and Jews
AND THEIR
Journeys of Faith

Beacon Press
BOSTON

Beacon Press
25 Beacon Street
Boston, Massachusetts 02108–2892
www.beacon.org

Beacon Press books
are published under the auspices of
the Unitarian Universalist Association of Congregations.

03 02 01 00 99   8 7 6 5 4 3 2 1

This book is printed on recycled acid-free paper that contains at
least 20 percent postconsumer waste and meets the uncoated paper
ANSI/NISO specifications for permanence as revised in 1992.

Book design by Boskydell Studio
Composition by Wilsted & Taylor Publishing Services

Library of Congress Cataloging-in-Publication Data

Wuthnow, Robert.
Growing up religious : Christians and Jews and their
journeys of faith / Robert Wuthnow.
p.   cm.
Includes bibliographical references.
ISBN 0-8070-2806-1 (cloth : alk. paper)
1. Religious biography—United States.   2. United States—
Religious life and customs—Case studies.   I. Title.
BL2525.W865   1999
291.4′2′0973—dc21   98-27780

"Got to feed the soul just like you feed the body. I'm taking the children, too, the Lord willing. Good Book say, 'Raise a child in the way he should go and he will not depart from it.'"

"That's what it say. Sure is what it say."

Maya Angelou
I Know Why the Caged Bird Sings

Contents

Preface   ix

Introduction   xv

PART I

The Sacred at Home

1   Family Rituals   3

2   Home for the Holidays   25

3   Generations in the Spirit   44

PART II

Going to Services

4   Houses of Worship   69

5   The Ties That Bind   85

6   Learning to Be a Leader   106

PART III

Moving Away

7   Points of Departure   123

8   Remembering the Past   141

9   The Move to Spiritual Practice   162

PART IV

E Pluribus Unum?

10   Bridging Diversity   197

11   Seeing with Four Eyes   219

Notes   237

Preface

ONE MORNING I was sitting by a secluded lake, watching the sunrise. I was alone except for an early-rising flock of wild geese. Although it was Easter, I was feeling neither the thrill of spring nor the joy of resurrected life. As I mused, a car approached and pulled into the parking area. The car was old and dirty, an inexpensive model suffering from a bad case of New Jersey rust. The driver was a young woman, probably in her late twenties. Her clothes, like her car, signaled someone who was barely surviving financially. She was accompanied by another woman, who, by appearance, was her sister. In the backseat were two preschoolers, a boy and girl, the latter sporting a new bonnet.

"You wait here with Auntie," the driver instructed as she got out and went around to the trunk. After rummaging for a while, she lifted out a sack of plastic eggs and two brightly colored baskets. Then she headed for a clump of bushes where she began hiding the eggs. Suddenly the children could wait no longer and ran to join her. Laughing at their impatience, she handed them their baskets, and they ran off in search of hidden treasure. Within a couple of minutes all the eggs had been found and the children were back. The little boy was crying because his sister had gotten more than her share. The mother evened the score, and soon both children had opened their eggs and were consuming the jelly beans hidden inside. Before they left, Auntie made them pose, pose again, then pose for a third time; when she finally had them configured just right, she took a single snapshot to commemorate the day.

Later that morning, I attended church with my family. The luxurious flower arrangements overwhelmed me. The speaker's homily about the risen Christ calling us home to a place of warmth and safety reassured me. The huge crowd that packed the building impressed me. The nationally acclaimed organist, playing Widor's Toccata Symphonie no. 5, inspired me. And as I sang the last verse of "Jesus Christ Is Risen Today," embellished with descant and *trompet extraordinaire*, my eyes momentarily filled with tears. But the tears were of gratitude to that poor woman by the lake for the simple love she had shown her children—and me—that Easter morning.

I think often of that day, wondering about its meaning and what it may reveal about spirituality in our time. Was this woman aware that she was doing something deeply spiritual that morning? Is it important that she was or was not aware? Did her children see love that morning, or were they unwitting participants in the commercialization of a sacred day? Were they growing up religious? Would her act have evoked thoughts of spirituality in me had I not attended church a few hours later? Would church have evoked the sacred if I had not observed her a few hours earlier?

We cannot know the answers to most of these questions. But they are emblematic of the ways in which our thinking about spirituality is now being refocused. The very next Sunday my church was devoid of flowers. Attendance had dropped by three quarters. The clergyman who had delivered a fine homily the week before was taking a vacation. His substitute thanked congregants for the money that had been raised at the annual rummage sale. A guest speaker pleaded for volunteers to help with a tutoring program in the inner city. Another speaker announced that the yoga class would meet on Tuesday instead of Wednesday.

The next day a reporter called from Florida to ask if I could help him understand why Scott Peck's *The Road Less Traveled* was near the top of the *New York Times*'s bestseller list year after year. The reporter wondered whether we were in the midst of a spiritual awakening. He had just spoken to the author of another bestselling book, who told him the American people were becoming more spiritual because they were undergoing a metaphysical alteration of consciousness. What did I think?

A few days later I asked the same question of a man whose job puts him in daily contact with clergy, religious leaders, and researchers who study

American religion. "The one thing I'm sure of," he replied, "is that things are changing profoundly—and the clergy don't have a clue that it's even happening."

This book is my attempt to find out what *is* happening. I am interested in the childhood experiences that give us clues about the nature of spirituality. Talking with adults about their religious upbringing has convinced me that spirituality is much more deeply rooted in our personal histories, in our families and congregations, than in anything else. If we are to understand it, one way of doing so is by paying close attention to these life histories.

During the preliminary phase of my research, I designed several national surveys that were conducted with the cooperation of the Gallup Organization and reanalyzed other Gallup, Harris, and National Opinion Research Center surveys in order to compare people who had experienced religious training or involvement while they were growing up with those who had not, and to make comparisons among other subgroups of the U.S. population. I also examined biographies and published articles for stories about growing up religious and for theoretical and empirical treatments of religious socialization and related topics.

The interviews were conducted over a three-year period. Each interview lasted at least two hours, and many took five, six, or seven hours to complete. The interviewer asked semistructured questions about the respondent's life history, memories of the religious beliefs and practices of his or her mother, father, and grandparents, childhood religious beliefs and practices, both at home and in religious organizations, and related childhood customs involving holidays, celebrations, and ethnic traditions; requested a chronology of the respondent's involvement in religious organizations and a narrative account of his or her spiritual journey; and posed some retrospective questions about how major public events and social movements may have affected the respondent's faith, current devotional practices, current religious beliefs and understanding of spirituality, and current congregational involvement. Questions were pretested and modified several times and then adapted to suit different religious backgrounds, ethnic traditions, and age groups.

Because national surveys provided some representative evidence regarding religious backgrounds, subjects for the in-depth interviews were chosen by a system of quotas rather than randomly. I wanted to obtain information from a diverse group of people who had undergone relevant religious experiences while they were growing up. Target quotas included approximately equal numbers of men and women, approximately equal numbers of younger and older people, and substantial representation of ethnic and racial minorities, religious diversity, occupational and educational diversity, and geographic diversity. Individual respondents were chosen through a snowball technique: eight interviewers used personal and organizational contacts to identify initial respondents, who then referred the interviewers to other potential respondents.

The respondents ultimately numbered two hundred, 107 women and 93 men; their mean age was forty-six (21 respondents were in their late teens or twenties, 49 were in their thirties, 58 were in their forties, 31 were in their fifties, 23 were in their sixties, and 18 were in their seventies or eighties; the youngest respondent was eighteen and the oldest was eighty-seven). Respondents identified their primary denomination or faith tradition as follows (many of course had been involved in more than one specific tradition): 53 were mainline Protestants, 36 were evangelical Protestants, 42 were Catholics, 23 were Jewish, 3 were Eastern Orthodox, 5 were Muslim, 4 were Hindu, 17 were from other traditions, and 17 were eclectic. Among the Protestants, at least fifteen different denominations were included. Nearly all the respondents had grown up with some exposure to religion, but respondents varied considerably in how actively they had been involved in religion as children and in how much exposure to religion they received at home. Ethnically and racially, approximately 20 percent of the respondents were from nonwhite, non-Anglo backgrounds: 14 respondents were African American, 17 were Hispanic, 7 were Asian American, and 2 were from other backgrounds. (Among the European Americans there was a wide variety of ethnic origins.) Occupationally and educationally, respondents ranged from those who had advanced graduate degrees and were working in the professions to those who had fewer than four years of high school and were working in a variety of blue-collar and clerical occupations. While most considered themselves middle class, a substantial minority had working-class occupations, and there was wide variety among those who had middle-class occupations. Geographically, the respondents lived in eight states, including ones in the New England, Middle Atlantic, Southern, Midwestern, and Pacific regions; by origin, more than twenty-five states were represented.

Each interview was tape-recorded with the respondent's consent, and verbatim transcriptions were made of each tape. These transcripts ranged from fifty to more than two hundred pages in length.

My deepest appreciation goes to the two hundred men and women who agreed to answer questions about their upbringing, the values they learned as children, their parents' religious practices, how they celebrated holidays and attended religious services, how they matured, and where their spiritual journey has led them. They talked candidly about the pain in their lives, as well as the joys, on condition that their identities would not be disclosed. To this end, I have given them pseudonyms and disguised some of facts of their personal lives.

The research was conducted with the support of a grant from the Lilly Endowment. I am grateful to Craig Dykstra at the endowment for his oversight of the project. The interviews were conducted by a team of trained interviewers—Tara Bahrampour, Courtney Bender, John Evans, Robin Rusciano, Natalie Searl, Diane Winston, and Wendy Young—who had the relevant backgrounds themselves to talk intelligently with people from Jewish, Muslim, Catholic, and a variety of Protestant traditions. Natalie Searl also oversaw transcription of the interviews. Martha Sharp assisted with library research.

Work of this kind also heightens my appreciation of my own upbringing and thus my gratefulness to my parents and grandparents. I am also grateful to my wife, Sara, and my children, Robyn, Brooke, and Joel, who are responsible for my continuing education and personal enrichment.

Introduction

Growing Up Jewish

Ninety percent of Hal Meyerson's extended family died in the Holocaust. Growing up in the United States after World War II, Hal never remembers any of his family talking about it. "They just buried it," he says. "They tried to fit in and live like everyone else." But he is grateful that his parents took him to temple regularly, taught him Hebrew and Yiddish, and observed religious customs at home. "It gave me stability," he says. "I wasn't a ship just drifting in any direction. It was tradition. It had gone on since King David and it was going to go on forever. There was no question that this would go on forever."

Hal Meyerson, fifty-one, is a mountain of a man. At six feet two and weighing nearly 250 pounds, he looks a lot like Luciano Pavarotti. Seated in his den, he is surrounded by his hobbies and his work. On the wall are heads of several moose and pictures of himself fishing. The room is strewn with books about animals and with pictures of his pets. A sailfish adorns one wall. A live parrot sits in a cage. Animals are Hal's life. Across the driveway is the building that houses his veterinary practice. Toward the road is a large pond stocked with fish. Much of the fifty acres making up his estate is devoted to horse pastures and the rest is a wooded haven for wildlife.

When Hal was fifteen, his parents purchased the farm. His father, Samuel, had been given only a few months to live, so he wanted a secluded, peaceful place to die. But the doctors were wrong. Samuel occupied the farm for fifteen years before retiring to a warmer climate, and at eighty he is still going strong. Hal returned to the farm when his parents left, and this is where he and his wife raised their three sons, all of whom are now grown.[1]

As a child, Hal spent a great deal of his time at the synagogue his parents and maternal grandparents attended. It was a Conservative temple. Both sides of the family had been Orthodox for as long as anyone could remember. But Samuel had gone away to college during the Depression, served in the Coast Guard during World War II, and then become a prominent government contractor. He joined the Conservative temple, Hal thinks, "because it was more appropriate to society and his lifestyle."[2]

If they accommodated themselves to society in this way, Hal's parents nevertheless made sure he received an abundance of religious training. They sent him to Hebrew school three afternoons a week for an hour and a half after regular school. On Friday evenings the family lit candles and said the traditional blessings at dinner. "My father would say the hamotzi over the bread and my mother would say the blessing over the candles, my father over the wine," Hal recalls. Saturday mornings were always spent at the temple, as were Sundays. Hal especially remembers the Sunday ritual. It always began with a father-and-son breakfast of chocolate milk, bagels, and lox, and this was followed by Hebrew classes.

At home, Hal read voraciously (like his mother), including many books about religion; from his father he learned to pray. One day at Hebrew school, the teacher chided him because he was praying so vehemently. Later, the teacher realized that this was just the way Hal prayed. "My mother," he says, "always prayed just like everyone else, but my father and I prayed like we were the only ones there." He adds: "If you're going to pray and if it is going to mean anything, it has to come from your soul!"

This attitude carried over to his daily life. Every evening he knelt beside his bed with his mother and said his prayers. Every morning he put on te-fillin and tallis and said his prayers. He prayed about everything—his horse, his girlfriends, his homework, how he was feeling. When he was younger, he recalls, he had a mental image of God as a little old Jewish man writing down his prayers in a book. "If the pearly gates closed before you got enough prayers in," Hal says, "I figured you were just a goner." But another part of him was sure that God would not let that happen. He did not fear God, but thought of God as his protector.

Hal attributes much of his current interest in spirituality to the fact that his father took time to explain what everything meant while he was growing up. Like prayers. Hal says it would have been easy to read them in Hebrew and know the words but not understand why the prayers were important. For example, in reading the Amidah, Hal's father would say, "'Do you know what this means? Do you know why the martyrs said it while they were being tortured to death by the Spanish Inquisition or by the Russian pogroms? Do you understand what the mourner's Kaddish means?'" Hal says, "When I was a kid I used to think, 'Well, this is a prayer for dead people.' But it's not. It doesn't even mention the dead. So he would explain those things to me."

Religious upbringing was indistinguishable from family rituals and ethnic customs. Hal's parents both spoke Yiddish fluently and talked a lot about the stories they had heard of ancestors who had been rabbis or who had been persecuted in Russia during the pogroms. Hal's mother cooked ethnic foods, including ample bowls of chicken soup whenever he was sick. She made her own pickles, served chopped chicken liver on Jewish rye bread, and on special occasions brought out some of her mother's homemade gefilte fish.

The seders were especially important because they drew the wider family together. Hal recalls: "The seders were all celebrated with my father's family. And they were seders! They started at sunset and didn't finish until three or four o'clock in the morning. I remember how we used to meet in Aunt Minnie's apartment. There was a living room and a dining room, and the table stretched from the wall of the living room through both rooms to the wall of the dining room. Then there was a bathroom and two bedrooms. The coats were all piled in the bedrooms and literally nobody could move. Thirty or forty of us. All the aunts and uncles and cousins."

Growing up religious was thus a way to retain one's ties to the past. Many of the outward customs that had characterized Jewish ghettos in the past might be deemphasized, but religion could be performed in the relative safety of the family and at temple. Hal says his father was a deeply religious man but was also religious because of tradition. "His father took him to services; he was going to take me to services." He adds, "It was the thing to do to take me and it was an emotional high for him, too, to pray, to go to synagogue."

Following religious tradition also means linking oneself to a longer chain of customs. Still speaking of his father, Hal says, "His father sat shiva for his grandfather. He sat shiva for his father. I will sit shiva for him, and I will expect my kids to all sit shiva for me. I can trace that back to King David." The thought of losing this continuity disturbs him. "Now I'm not sure that that's going to happen," he laments, "because it seems like every generation gets further away from the central core of the religion."

The more he learns about the Holocaust, the more Hal believes it is essential for Jews to take their identity seriously. He thinks his ancestors probably took their faith for granted before the Holocaust but had to become more self-conscious about it after World War II. "The Holocaust sent an electric shock through the Diaspora," he says. "It's one thing to read in the books that this guy hated Jews or that in the sixteenth century there was a Spanish Inquisition. But to see the pictures of starving bodies of people just piled on top of each other and know that they were killed only because they were related to you has to have made a tremendous effect on the whole community." People need to understand their tradition and remember what happened.[3]

Saint Patrick's Girl

When Mary Shannon was in sixth grade, she thought everyone in the world was Irish. She and her eight brothers (four older and four younger) had grown up within a few blocks of Saint Patrick's Church, attended parochial school since kindergarten, and lived exclusively in an Irish neighborhood. Besides the Malloys (her maiden name), there were lots of Kellys, Kennedys, Brennans, and O'Sheas. Two of the families at church had different-sounding names—Morelli and Cuneo—but Mary assumed they were Irish, too. It was a close neighborhood in many ways. People lived in row houses that all looked alike. Everybody shopped at Morelli's grocery store, just down the block. And Mary remembers running in and out of her friends' houses, all of which seemed to be the same: crucifixes on the walls, holy water, little statues of Mary, shamrocks.[4]

A year later, Mary's innocence was shattered. Her father suffered a massive heart attack, causing him to lose his job and forcing the family to move to another community. The neighbors were now German, Polish, and Russian. Most were Jewish. "It was like being sucked out of something that had been your whole life and put into something that was totally foreign," she explains. Mary attended public school that year. The strain was almost too much. "I felt scared and there was a lot of sadness. I didn't feel accepted. I missed what had been such an integral part of our life. I felt very different, and up to that point I just felt like I just was like everybody else."

The following year the family moved again, this time to another Irish Catholic community. Mary went back to attending parochial school. After high school graduation, she attended a Catholic college. There she met Tom Shannon, whom she married at age twenty-two. By the time she was twenty-five, she had given birth to two daughters and a son. A few years later, she started teaching and commuted to another Catholic college in the area for a master's degree in school administration. Since then, she has taught for eight years at the elementary level and served for six years as a principal, all in Catholic schools.

Being Catholic is thus an integral fact of Mary's identity. As she reflects on the values she was taught as a child, she says instantly that "the church was the center of our life." She means this quite literally. Her paternal grandparents were Irish immigrants who lived nearby and made sure their grandchildren were receiving proper religious instruction. Her father had been forced to quit school in eighth grade in order to help support the family. Over the years he worked his way up the ladder at a local manufacturing company and was active in the union.

Her mother had worked before marriage and got a job at a bakery when the children were old enough to be in school. But with nine children, the family always struggled financially. They lived in a row house at first and eventually moved into a run-down twin house that her father rented cheaply in return for doing maintenance work. Mary remembers that the church pitched in on a number of occasions to bring food to the family and to supply presents for the children at Christmas. "The community was very tightly knit," she remembers. "When some were struggling, the others would help."

In return, the Malloys spent much of their free time contributing to the church. "My parents taught us to reverence and take care of the Sisters," she says. "We did a lot of housecleaning and stuff like that for them when they needed things to be done, ironing and laundry. We also helped at the rectory with the hosts. When they come, they're all joined together, so we would go to do the separating of them and preparing things for church. My mother also helped with cleaning the church."

Every Sunday everyone attended mass. During the week, attending Catholic school put the children in daily contact with the church. Each evening the whole family sat around the dining room table and did homework together. And before bedtime, Mary's mother read a Bible story, prayed with her, and sometimes sang a religious song with her.

Mary says her parents taught her that "the Lord lives in all of us" and that how people worship is their personal choice. Thus, she feels an affinity with other people who have a deep religious faith, whether they are Catholics, Protestants, or members of some other religion. How Mary understood God was deeply influenced by the dynamics within her family.

She reports: "God was loving, loved everyone, was forgiving. Growing up in that little house with a lot of people, there were often tiffs in the house. So forgiveness was an important part of keeping your family together, and disagreements and things of that nature. So my mom always taught us, and my dad, that we're to forgive. Somebody can drive you crazy, but that we're to forgive and accept one another. So that was who God was for us."[5]

Tarrying with Jesus

Jess Hartley has known few of the material advantages that Hal Meyerson and Mary Shannon have enjoyed. Jess grew up in a low-income housing development; his family was supported by the meager wages his father earned as a clerk at a toy store and, later, as an independent contractor doing janitorial work and polishing hardwood floors. Like Mary, Jess is also the fifth of nine children. He is a former high-jump champion and soccer star who enjoys singing in the church choir, eating his mother's fried chicken, and taking his daughter on outings to Chuck E Cheese. At thirty-seven, Jess is a muscular man with medium brown skin, hazel eyes, and a neatly trimmed beard, who stands six feet two and weighs about 180 pounds.

He has followed in his father's footsteps, taking over the floor polishing business when his dad went into semiretirement a decade ago. For the first ten years of their marriage, Jess and his wife lived in a "semi" (or duplex) located in an inner-city neighborhood just three blocks from an area infested with drug dealers. They considered themselves fortunate because they had purchased the duplex with a mortgage of $300 a month, which they paid by renting out the other half. Their daughter is now five years old and they have recently moved to a working-class community a few miles away in order to be in a better school district. Naturally gregarious, Jess enjoys meeting his customers, often engaging them in long conversations while he waits for a section of freshly waxed hardwood to dry.

When asked what sort of values he learned from his parents, Jess spontaneously emphasizes his religious upbringing. "I can remember we always had prayer in the home. One of the things we always learned was that God was the head of our life. It wasn't just that you have to do this or that. We always were reminded that whatever we had, it was because of God. God was the one that allowed us to have these things."

Jess says he learned from an early age the story about Christ's coming into the world and dying on the cross. He knew the story long before he had any idea what it meant. Gradually he learned that it was a privilege to receive Christ and that a person had to seek Christ with utmost sincerity for this to happen. The way to "fervently seek the Lord," Jess explains, was by "going to the altar and doing what we called tarrying." To tarry meant being in constant prayer and supplication, either during a service at church or at one of the many prayer meetings Jess's mother hosted in their living room. "One of the things I remember was over and over again we'd give thanks, 'Thank you, Jesus. Thank you, Jesus.' Just over and over again, I mean, even to the point where sometimes you'd get tongue-tied and you didn't know if the gift of the Holy Spirit came upon you and you spoke in unknown tongues or if your tongue was just all twisted!"

Jess's family belonged to the United Holy Church of America, a small denomination founded in North Carolina, by revivalist Isaac Cheshier, in 1886. By the time Jess was a teenager, the denomination numbered some sixty-five thousand members in nearly seven hundred congregations scattered from Georgia to New England, including approximately two hundred churches that split off to form their own denomination a few years later. The "tarrying" Jess experienced as a child was common to most of the holiness and Pentecostal denominations that emerged around the turn of the century and spread rapidly among both African Americans and European Americans in working-class communities.[6]

Jess's father had been reared in a different denomination, but when he started courting Jess's mother (as Jess tells it) the preacher told him, "You want to see one of our girls in our church, you're going to have to be coming to our church." He did, eventually serving on the deacon board, then as a trustee, and for a few years preaching part-time at a storefront church in another town. In retirement, Jess's father has become increasingly active in church work, now as a delegate to the denomination's regional convention.

The church was a pervasive influence in Jess's life from the time he was little. The Hartleys went to church every week, despite one or two of the children's being sick on any given Sunday, simply loading everyone into the battered family station wagon and driving the few miles to their house of worship. Generally the service began at eleven o'clock and ran until two-thirty, sometimes longer "if the spirit started moving." The Hartleys also attended Sunday school before the morning service, an afternoon service, and an evening service.

On Wednesday nights the whole church gathered for a revival meeting, and on Friday nights they met in homes for prayer. Jess remembers his father's favorite saying, "It's a poor frog who doesn't praise his own pond." His philosophy was to support the church wholeheartedly. "Why are you in it if you're not going to be in it fully?" Ushers meeting, choir, deacons, joint services with another congregation in the district: it didn't matter; Jess's father made sure the family was represented. "You belong to an organization, you support everything about it. You support it because it's your church."

Jess's own favorite church organization was the Young People's Holy Association (YPHA), which met every Sunday evening. The children were plied with cookies and games to secure their interest. In retrospect, it amuses Jess that his high school graduation gift was being sent to the denomination's national YPHA convention and, because the convention was held every four years, that his college graduation gift was also a trip to the convention. Four years later, he attended again, this time meeting his future wife, a young woman who already knew some of his friends because she attended a congregation about fifty miles away.[7]

Although they spent much of their time at church, Jess's family was also intensely religious at home. He feels that the basic religious principles were ones he learned at home and that these were simply reinforced at church, not the other way around. Whenever his mother held prayer meetings in the living room, the children were invited, indeed expected, to participate. They learned early how to pray and heard the petitions of their elders.

"They'd always start out by thanking God," Jess remembers. "'Thank you for what you've done, thank you for this day, thank you for health and strength. Now we ask you for these things, for protection, for our needs.'" Besides the family, the house itself was often an item for prayer. "We believed in praying over the front door to keep the power of the enemy from getting into the house; we believe that's how you prayed; it's like in the biblical days about putting the blood on the door, he passed over it."

In the evenings after supper, Jess's father usually sat in his easy chair and read the Bible to himself. He also read the Bible to the children. "We were taught that the Bible was sort of our map of life." During high school and college, Jess says he "wanted to get out there and experiment" with a different way of life, but there was always something tugging at his conscience. "I'm sure it was those prayers that kept any of us from going too far." Jess knows his father is enormously proud of having raised nine children, none of whom became involved with drugs or violent crime, despite the prevalence of both in their neighborhood.

As a child, Jess's conscience was closely intertwined with his understanding of God, whom he visualized as "a big face in the sky that was looking at everything and that had everything to do with everything." Jess's notion of God came mostly from hearing the people at church pray, asking God to "watch over us and protect us." When Jess wanted something tangible, he'd ask his parents, but when he wanted something bigger, like winning a game or not having it hurt when he went to the dentist, he'd ask God. Jess also believed God could cause bad things to happen to him if he deliberately did something he knew he shouldn't. "If I was hurting somebody or taking something that didn't belong to me, I felt that God could let me die and go to hell."

The voice of conscience can indeed tug powerfully when it carries the authority of God. Jess remembers how the boys at school used to tease him: "You're square, you don't curse, you don't party, you don't do anything. Come on, let me hear you say one of those words." One time Jess did. "I was in elementary school, playing ball, and I missed the ball and I said this word, the 's' word. I stopped and I looked around like I knew my mother was standing behind me with her hands on her hips! I was like convicted right there, like 'Oh, forgive me, Lord!' That's how I was."

Conscience may not be totally effective in corralling adventuresome youth, but the inner turmoil it creates can leave a powerful impression. As Jess grew older, he realized increasingly that his religious upbringing made him different from other young people. Especially in relating to the opposite sex, he felt inadequate and inexperienced. Despite the fact that he played three sports and was vice president of the student council, Jess had little interaction with girls during his first three years in high school. Then in his senior year he realized what he was missing and started dating a girl named Wanda.

Time came for the senior prom and Jess asked Wanda to go. The only problem was that Jess's church did not allow dancing, other than the gospel dancing and shouting that took place during the services. So Jess arranged to pick up his tuxedo at a friend's house and told his parents he and Wanda were just going to dinner. The plan worked: Jess and Wanda went to the prom, barely avoiding being seen by some people in the neighborhood who knew his parents, and then went to an after-prom party at another friend's house.

Unknown to Jess, however, his parents had discovered the truth by interrogating his sister, and when he arrived home at dawn the front door was locked and chained. Jess went directly to the floor cleaning job he had scheduled in order to postpone the inevitable confrontation with his parents. That evening when he came home his father said, "I have a question for you. Did you go to the prom last night?" Jess admitted he had, and to this day he remembers the disappointment on his father's face and what his mother said next: "You really hurt your dad. Not because you went to the prom, but because you lied to him, you really hurt him." Two decades later, Jess still feels that he betrayed his father's trust irrevocably that night.

When Jess went away to college on an athletic scholarship, his conscience followed him. Central to the holiness tradition in which he was raised was the idea that believers should try to "perfect" themselves, especially by keeping their bodies and minds as pure as possible. Dating was still hard for him, and he seldom went to a dance and never drank beer with the other guys. They called him "the choirboy," which indeed he was, because he spent much of his spare time singing in the gospel choir on campus.

Eventually he pledged a fraternity, and there he was exposed directly to all the evils his parents had taught him to avoid. The first smoke, the first drink, and the first puff on a joint of marijuana were all memorable transitions, yet in each case Jess found himself mildly amused because the thrill of the unknown was at best disappointing. "I guess I was like President Clinton," he muses. "I didn't inhale. I didn't even know how. The other guys said, 'Don't give him any more, he doesn't even know what to do.'"

If an active conscience like this could generate guilt in large doses, the same religious tradition nevertheless acknowledged the impossibility of humans' achieving perfection. Mrs. Hartley reminded Jess repeatedly that "it's one thing to sin, quite another to lie there and wallow in it!" She told him, "Just recognize that you did wrong, ask for forgiveness, and then get up and go from there." Using his prom experience as an example, Jess says he learned to forgive himself and move on. "You forgive and forget because that's what Jesus did for us. He forgave our sins. You put them in the sea of forgetfulness and go on from there."

For Jess, going "on from there" has meant staying involved in his denomination and continuing to pray, like his mother did, even when things don't go as planned. He and his wife suffered the anguish of a miscarriage and the death of a newborn, and they have struggled continuously to make ends meet. For the past five years they have attended a congregation of about 150 people who support each other in good times and bad.

The church remains true to its holiness roots, but Jess also values its openness and diversity. "I believe everybody has their own personal way of reaching God," he says. "You can serve God in your own way [at the church], rather than feeling cramped or being pushed into a mold." He's proud that the church includes both black people and white people and that there is genuine respect for one another among the parishioners. "Everyone has something to offer; it's a very free-spirited place."

Despite its flexibility, the church is striving to make a distinct difference in the neighborhood that surrounds it. "If I can quote from the Blues Brothers," Jess says, "we're on a mission. We have something we have to do, and we believe that God is going to get that job done, and it's going to get done with us or with somebody else. God will move us out of the way if he has to. We believe that God has put us there for the community, that the community will flock to it because the spirit of God is moving, and it's evident."

Right now, the church has so many people coming that it is sometimes hard to find a seat. "There's been Sundays when the Holy Spirit has moved so much in the church that people have come in and given their life to God, and afterwards they said there was just something about our church —the love they felt in our church, the togetherness, that's what drew them to our church. I felt good, because I was a part of it."

Mainline Protestant

Bruce Gallahue and his wife live in a two-story brick colonial house on a cul-de-sac in an upper-middle-class section of the "mainline" district of a large city in the Northeast. The house is decorated conservatively, its public spaces revealing little about the private lives of its occupants other than that they have a taste for order and a desire to belong. The walls are white, the living room furniture is beige, there is an accent chair in blue, and the mantle is dominated by a nautical clock and a large painting of several exquisite boat houses. Down the hallway toward the kitchen hangs a set of family portraits: under each of the children's and grandchildren's names is neat calligraphy explaining the meaning of his or her name. The silence is punctuated by the regular ticking of the clock.

Wearing corduroy trousers, a maroon sweater, white turtleneck, and Bass shoes, Bruce Gallahue is a man of understated accomplishment, graciously giving up a Saturday morning on the golf course to talk of his past. At sixty-four, he can look back on a childhood completed before World War II, an adolescence spent attending an exclusive preparatory school, college at an Ivy League university in New England, and a three-year stint as an officer in the Navy. Bruce married his high school sweetheart, whom he had met at his church's youth fellowship group, and immediately after leaving the Navy, joined his father's financial securities firm, working first as a sales trainee, then as an investment counselor, and eventually as a partner and senior vice president. He is a lifelong Presbyterian.[8]

When Bruce was a child, his father was generally quite busy with his work, and his mother, who had attended finishing school and college but was not employed, divided her time between looking after him and his brother and sister and doing volunteer work in the community. Bruce says his mother "set the agenda" for the family, while his father made sure the money was available to pay for it. Having a maid to cook and clean, his mother came to all his soccer games, served as an American Red Cross block warden during the war, helped with the ladies' auxiliary of the children's hospital, and did church work. Like her father, who had taught Sunday school for many years at the Presbyterian church he attended, she taught and served as primary superintendent in the Sunday school, supported the women's association, participated in the altar guild, and made sure the children regularly attended Sunday school, church, and youth group. Bruce thinks of her spiritual life almost totally in terms of her church activities, which were part of a family tradition that dated at least to the 1700s, when her Scotch-Irish ancestors came to America.

Bruce's father also supported the church, serving periodically on the deacon board, but sometimes he listened to a sermon on the radio instead of attending services in person. The Presbyterian church they attended consisted of nearly sixteen hundred members (approximately three times as many as now), the majority of whom lived in upper-middle-class neighborhoods within a few blocks of the church. His parents felt it was important to be loyal to the church rather than shop around to find other churches that might suit them better. In fact, they didn't think much about whether they liked it or not; they simply knew it was a good church with good programs and a well-respected pastor.

Bruce thinks you can divide people's religious lives into three phases: in phase one, they attend church but may or may not be Christians; in phase two, they accept Christ into their lives and become Christians; and in phase three, they work at making the Holy Spirit an important part of their lives. He associates the first phase with his childhood, adolescence, and early to middle adulthood; the second, with an event that happened about a decade ago; and the third, with his current spiritual life.

An important part of growing up Presbyterian, he says, was to be self-disciplined, which meant learning not only to work hard but also to keep one's emotions and impulses under control. Bruce never saw his parents argue about anything and from his mother learned to be emotionally reserved.[9] He was taught implicitly to be honest, and this message was sufficiently powerful that he has no memories of ever telling a lie; nor can he remember doing anything blatantly disobedient or having to be overtly rebuked by his parents. He learned mainly by observing how his parents lived, and although he loved them dearly and lived close to them until they died in their nineties, he admits that he lacked a warm relationship with either parent while he was growing up.

As a child, it was thus out of the question for him to talk with his parents about their views of God or to quiz them about their beliefs. He merely observed their behavior and inferred from it that they believed in God. In retrospect, he figures his mother believed that God had a plan for her life and that an important part of that plan was for her to be a servant in the church. He is sure his parents prayed, because he saw them kneeling together at night, but he doesn't know what they prayed about, because they prayed in the privacy of their bedroom.

His own sense of religion in these years inevitably focused more on church than on God. His clearest memory of Sunday morning services, in fact, is that the sermons were "way above my head" and that even the adults claimed not to understand them but they were delivered by a man with a doctorate who was moderator of the presbytery and, therefore, must be worthwhile. Because he attended Sunday school from the time he was three, he nevertheless had close friends at church and enjoyed being there on Sundays. He especially enjoyed the Bible stories he learned in Sunday school, including the ones about Jesus' birth and the Good Samaritan. His favorite was about Paul's conversion on the road to Damascus: the picture in the Bible storybook of Paul being blinded by a bright light is still vivid in his mind.

Besides the regular services, Bruce remembers the religious holidays with special clarity. Palm Sunday stands out because every child was given a palm frond to take home and keep for the year; then there would be a little ceremony at which the fronds from the previous year would be gathered and burned. Easter was special, too, because of the chocolate bunnies and jelly beans. Before church, Bruce's mother always planned an Easter egg hunt in the front yard, and afterward the family (including one grandmother and an aunt) gathered in the dining room for leg of lamb.

When Bruce was twelve, he joined the church, along with the rest of his age mates. They attended a communicants class taught by one of the church's elders, learning about the church's traditions and memorizing the catechism. Joining was expected, just as it was expected that young people would participate in other community organizations. Bruce became a junior member of his father's cricket club and devoted much of his spare time to scouting, working up from cub to eagle. During high school, his favorite activity was the church youth group that met every Sunday evening.

It provided food, entertainment, and for those like Bruce who attended all-male prep schools, a rare opportunity to mix with girls. Although the church frowned on having social dances in the building, the assistant pastor secured permission to have some well-chaperoned parties in the church basement, including periodic dances. The youth group worked long hours on Saturdays preparing for these parties. Like Jess Hartley did, Bruce also participated in church activities that drew young people from other churches and several times during high school traveled as a delegate to a national convention for church youth.

But Bruce's religion was not entirely social. He was a sensitive boy who tried hard to live up to his parents' expectations and who worried about failing them. His image of God reflected these fears: God was a stern old man with a gray beard who would punish him if he told a lie or stole something. Bruce said a prayer every night with his mother and brother, but he said it from memory and did not think much about what he was doing.

Most of the time, Bruce was able to keep his fears of God at bay by avoiding doing "antisocial" things. As a teenager, he didn't think often about dying, and when he did, he simply assumed that his soul would go to be with God. On a daily basis, he thus felt that he was growing up as a deeply religious person but that religious principles and proper, respectable living were the same thing. Being a reliable, reasonably good student who obeyed his parents and went to church was not only the recipe for a godly life, it was the key to a life that ran smoothly. Looking back on it, he says, "Religious principles and social principles sort of blend together; I was taught to be honest, to be responsible, and to love my family."

These principles were so deeply embedded in Bruce's way of life that he continued participating actively in church fellowship while he was in college and then settled into the Presbyterian church again after he returned home from the Navy. Because his wife's religious background was virtually identical to his, they found it easy to attend church every Sunday and to send their children to Sunday school. Bruce regularly served as an usher at church and became a member of the deacon board.

As the children grew, they too became involved in the church youth group. One of them recalls, "We all participated in youth group, we prayed before we went to bed, and we said grace at meals; it was just standard procedure." She also credits her parents' "solid religious upbringing" with strengthening their marriage and with bolstering their commitment to raising a family together; she's sure they wanted her to grow up sharing their religious values.

During most of his adult life, Bruce continued to think of God as a strict disciplinarian who expected him to live properly. But Bruce was also becoming an alcoholic, and eventually his children confronted him with the problem and saw to it that he entered a detox program. In the recovery process, Bruce became involved in Alcoholics Anonymous and discovered a different way of relating to God.

"I came to believe that God was a forgiving and gracious God and Jesus Christ was indeed evidence of that," he explains. "I came to see that it was all right for me to have fallen, to have, in effect, not lived up to the principles that my parents had taught me. As a consequence, I think there was a complete reversal in my mind as to what religion was about. It wasn't just living your life correctly and according to whatever group of laws you can find or that happened to be laid out before you, but at the same time coming to realize that people do fail and they fail to live up to what they've been taught. That's made a big difference ever since as far as my feeling about myself and about religion. My spiritual being was really bolstered by the experience, as I say, of having hit a low point in my life. I feel that my prayers were answered, that I did get out of the hole that I was in; it made a big difference in my life."

Although Bruce says his experience with AA has transformed his view of religion, he believes firmly that his religious upbringing was of enormous value to him. Without it, he would not have understood as readily why AA emphasizes the need for a relationship with God. He also believes, now more than ever, that "I have a responsibility to give back to my church, to the community, to support the things that I believe in, my church, my college, some charities that I'm involved in, in that respect to be responsible with my time and money." The biggest difference in his thinking is that he now believes God will forgive him even if he fails.

"I don't understand the Trinity or even the resurrection from a logical point of view," he admits, "but I believe in the mystery of the resurrection and of the relationship between God, Jesus Christ, and the Holy Spirit working in the community today, and working through me, many times not perfectly, but at times working through me. I think you just continue to work, grow, and try to improve, but I don't think there're any final answers."

The Significance of the Past

Growing up religious has a profound influence on many people's lives. It is the source of fond memories for some and of painful experiences for others. When people meet others who have stories to tell about the congregations in which they grew up, the verses they memorized, and the special holidays they celebrated, there is an instant bond. People who have been raised in the same tradition feel the connection acutely, but religious upbringings also bridge traditions, creating a subculture of common understanding.

For many people, remembering and telling their stories is a way of making sense of their lives and of their continuing quest for the sacred. Childhood religiosity is not simply the experience of children but of adults as well.[10] Memories ripen with age, especially as they are refined in an ongoing dialogue with one's experiences.

My aim is to recapture what it has meant for a significant proportion of the American public to have grown up religious. I am interested in how people conceive of their religious upbringing, and in understanding what seems memorable and significant to them, more than I am in abstract theories of religious socialization. My methodology has been to ask ordinary people to talk at length about their experiences and memories and to encourage them to tell the stories they use to make sense of their spiritual journeys.[11]

Effective religious socialization comes about through embedded practices; that is, through specific, deliberate religious activities that are firmly intertwined with the daily habits of family routines, of eating and sleeping, of having conversations, of adorning the spaces in which people live, of celebrating the holidays, and of being part of a community.[12] Compared with these practices, the formal teachings of religious leaders often pale in significance. Yet when such practices are present, formal teachings also become more important.

The past is not static. It is a remembered past and thus one that people are continually revising, making sense of, and reinterpreting. Many people of course have little in their childhood to remember about religion. But those who grew up in a religious household continue to have a very substantial impact on the character of American religion. They are far more likely than other people to be active members of a congregation as adults and to want their own children to receive religious training. Many of them sense that society is declining as a result of forgetting its religious heritage. Yet they are often painfully aware of the need for change, having undergone much change themselves. Understanding how they have changed is a way of gaining a clearer sense of how America itself is changing.

I have listened closely to the stories of people drawn from many different segments of American life. Some of them were raised in families that revolved entirely around religious convictions. Others provide valuable points of comparison because their religious upbringing was less intense.

Other scholars have conducted surveys to see whether religious training within families and congregations is significant in later life, and I draw on these surveys (including some of my own) whenever possible.[13] I am, nevertheless, concerned especially to understand how ordinary people interpret their own experiences of growing up religious.[14] It is through stories that they render these interpretations.

Journey as Genre

Stories like those of Hal Meyerson, Mary Shannon, Jess Hartley, and Bruce Gallahue clearly are more than accounts of some facts about a person's childhood. They are part of the life story that we tell and retell, both to ourselves and to others, often in bits and pieces, revising it as we grow older.[15] The accounts that make up our life story help us understand who we are by giving some coherence to our experiences and by providing us with narratives of continuity and change. When people talk about their spiritual journey, as has now become common, they are telling that portion of their life story that makes sense of their religious upbringing, the experiences that shaped their thinking about God, and their continuing quest for the sacred.

In psychological terms, the language of journeys is a form of attribution, a way of accounting for who we are and why we feel and behave as we do. In addition to helping people understand themselves, journey language helps us make sense of other people as well. Instead of saying that other people are who they are because of racial characteristics or genetic predisposition (or just because they chose to be that way), it becomes possible for us to say that they are on a unique journey—conditioned by the past but also doing the best they can to move ahead. Although stories of spiritual journeys are intensely personal, they are thus social as well, drawing on familiar conventions of speech and communicating something of our common experience.

It is in this sense that the language of spiritual journeys has become a kind of genre. To speak of one's journey is to emphasize changing conceptions and experiences of faith rather than a once-for-all-time grasp of religious truth. Journeys unfold, leading variously into the wilderness or to the promised land. But all journeys have a starting point, and most stories about journeys include as prehistory a time of dwelling and of preparation. For those who have experienced it, growing up religious is the inevitable moment of preparation that must be described.[16]

Journey language is thus an important part of what it means to live in a pluralistic culture. By recognizing that religious upbringing is an influential aspect of many people's journeys, Americans are able to identify with a subculture composed of such people, seeing an affinity among their various journeys. The fluid language of journeys, nevertheless, adds a dynamic element, so that it becomes possible to understand that some people may have moved in other directions and that people also had many different starting points.

Portals and Peepholes

I want to confront a possible misconception from the start. In considering accounts of being raised religious, we must be careful not to regard this material as a portal through which we can view the past as it actually happened or as a peephole into the inner consciousness of those giving the accounts. Both approaches are tempting.

The portal approach draws on oral histories as a way of gaining information about the events and experiences of the past. Such evidence can be of value when used to supplement information from newspapers, public records, letters, and diaries. For example, interviews are often conducted with veterans in order to pin down more accurately the position and movement of troops during a campaign rather than relying only on official records.

The peephole approach uses interview material to access the inner, psychological processes of an individual. By asking people to talk about their attitudes and feelings, the interviewer is able to elicit information that generally remains hidden, sometimes even to the conscious mind of the person giving this information. From such evidence, inferences can then be drawn about the cognitive or emotional development of a person. For example, many of Freud's observations about psychological development were derived from interviews in which people talked about their past.

As we consider what people say about growing up religious, some insights of both these kinds are evident. Some of the people we interviewed, for example, grew up in the 1920s or 1930s and are thus able to give a picture of what it was like to live in, say, an Italian Catholic or a Slovakian Lutheran community during those years. From many of the interviews, insights also emerge about the subjective thoughts and feelings that people experienced when they were children, especially when they discuss how they felt about their mothers and fathers or God or death.

What must be remembered, however, is that these accounts are filtered through the experiences that people have had as adults. The problem is not that memories may have faded or even that children's perceptions of the world may have been skewed in certain ways. The difficulty lies in failing to recognize what is actually of value about such accounts.

To provide an account of some aspect of one's past is necessarily to engage in a moral evaluation of oneself. Such evaluations can be given hypothetically by imagining what one would be like if one engaged in certain future activities. The truest evaluations, however, can only be given by reflecting on one's behavior in the past. In a real sense, then, accounts of childhood can only be given by people who are no longer children.

Accounts of growing up religious are, as I have suggested, ways in which people make sense of themselves in reference to their quest for the sacred. They are motivated in an immediate sense by the presence of an interviewer asking questions but in a larger sense by how people choose to conceive of themselves. They are as much about the present as the past.

Conversations with the Past

Understood this way, reflections on what it has meant to grow up religious take on new significance. Living as we do in a throwaway society that teaches us to discard everything from candy wrappers and milk containers to neighborhoods and spouses, the past has become a little understood or appreciated subject. Advertising encourages us to think about present gratification, and everyday life is generally too hectic for anything but the here and now.[17]

Our theories of human behavior also point more to the present than to the past. The peer group is allegedly the wellspring of our values, more so than generations past. We live in cohorts, sociologists tell us, that are exposed to common experiences, oriented toward their own members, and fundamentally concerned with the challenges that no other cohort has ever experienced. Especially when our cohorts are large, we find it easy to forget about any time other than our own. Thus, the generation that came of age after World War II was, as Frances FitzGerald has written, "so large [that] it seemed to have no parents and no memory."[18] And lacking both parents and memory, the "baby boomers" came, as many observers have suggested, to have their own distinct style of spirituality—a faith guided chiefly by the immediate needs and gratifications of the moment.[19]

Although we live in the present, our understanding of the present is nevertheless conceived in relation to the past. We compare ourselves with the past in order to see how we are doing. We differentiate ourselves from the past in order to convince ourselves that we are doing something distinct and important. And we connect ourselves to the past in order to ground ourselves in something more enduring than our own lives.

The first lesson to be learned from people's accounts of their religious upbringing is thus that particular events and experiences were significant enough to be memorable. These of course varied from person to person; indeed, it was their particularity that helped define each person's individuality. The common feature of these events and experiences, nevertheless, is the fact that they consisted of embedded practices.

Both the practical and the embedded aspects of embedded practices are significant. A practice is a cluster of activities that is pursued deliberately. It takes time and energy and it requires one's attention, meaning that the pursuit of any particular practice is accomplished only at the sacrifice of other possible activities. Growing up religious was a memorable part of people's childhood because it included such activities as praying, memorizing Bible verses, polishing one's shoes in preparation for Sunday services, sitting on hard benches, opening presents, and going to picnics. These were discrete, separable activities that took time away from other interests, but they were also embedded in social relationships. People did them with their mothers and fathers, their grandparents, their siblings, and their friends and fellow congregants.

Embedded practices are influential in religious development because they spin out webs of significance that richly connect people with the world around them. To speak of practices as being social or as being linked to social networks or even as being located within communities does not adequately characterize the way in which they are embedded. Eating fried chicken has been a deeply meaningful dimension of growing up religious for millions of Americans. Some of the people we talked to were moved to tears by the memory of their mother's fried chicken. It was the smell and the taste that remained vivid in their memory, and it was the fact that their mother served it after the Sunday church service—and the hands serving it were the same ones that patted them as they said their bedtime prayers—that transformed it into a spiritual substance.

The fact that embedded practices figure so importantly in recollections of religious upbringing challenges much of what has been written about the theological socialization of children over the past half century. Influenced by the legacy of catechetical instruction, scholars have continued to assume that children are first and foremost mental machines. Incessantly curious, children presumably start asking questions about the nature of the universe at an early age, and if they are supplied with simple answers at the right moment, then they will progress through various stages of cognitive development until they achieve the sophistication of an adult understanding of faith.

We found little evidence to support this view among the people we interviewed. Few of them remembered being especially curious about metaphysical questions as children and few of them recalled significant teachings that provided answers to these questions. They assimilated religion more by osmosis than by instruction. The act of praying was more important than the content of their petitions. Being in Sunday school was more memorable than anything they may have been taught. Fried chicken or seders or statues of Mary provided the texture of their spiritual understanding.

The implication of these memories for religious education is not to abandon catechetical instruction or other methods of passing on the content of religious traditions. Such content was important, even if people did not remember it or understand it very clearly, because it provided the rationale for everything else that was more immediately memorable. They came to believe that somewhere there were answers to the questions they someday might want to ask and that in the meantime it was possible to live as if those answers might matter.

But spirituality also came to be understood as a way of life, and it did so because people grew up living it. The parents, teachers, and clergy who understood this best were the ones who created an environment in which spirituality was fully and deeply embedded. They honored the spirituality of chicken dinners, of gefilte fish, of family Bibles, and of stained-glass windows.

Anamnesis

The second lesson to be learned as we listen to people talk about their religious upbringing is that it is part of the continuing experience of adults rather than an event occurring only in childhood. The conversations people carry on with their past transform growing up religious into a living memory; their reflections are an act of anamnesis, an antidote to amnesia, to forgetting.[20] Those who had reflected most deeply on their religious upbringing felt they were able to live a more fully integrated life as a result.

As we shall see, most people do not engage in abstract reflections about theological or denominational traditions, nor do they care very much about religious history or about sociological theories of cultural change. They may well have strong feelings about the decline of their particular religious communities or about the ways in which spirituality is being revitalized. But these perceptions are rooted chiefly in the contexts that are closest at hand. Conversations with the past are in fact implicit conversations carried on with one's mother and father or grandparents. People compare themselves with the behavior of their parents, and they wonder if they are as devout or as encapsulated within a religious community or more sophisticated in their views of spirituality.

People also carry on implicit conversations with the children and adolescents and young adults they once were. As they move into new stages of their lives, they recycle their memories of previous experiences, drawing as much insight as they can. Virtually everyone moves away from their childhood religious training, even if they continue living in the same community and attending the same congregation. They do so by taking advantage of the various points of departure that may be available to them, such as graduation from confirmation class, bar or bat mitzvah, participation in the high school youth group, the death of a parent or grandparent, going away to college, or getting married. These are not simply breaking points in the seamless web of their social relationships. They are pivotal occasions around which one's story can be reorganized.

Anamnesis is facilitated by family gatherings, such as holiday celebrations, when people sit for long hours with parents and siblings and with members of their congregations, retelling and reinterpreting the stories of their past. Such occasions are themselves memorable, serving as crucibles in which to reconsider the stories told by previous generations. When they are absent, they are missed; as one of our older respondents says in talking about her parents: "I should have forced them to tell me their stories!" These occasions are also becoming fragile because people are being geographically dispersed and living in the interstices among multiple communities.

Apart from the lessons about personal spirituality, growing up religious also teaches an important lesson about how to live in an increasingly diverse society. Those who have been raised in intensely religious families often recognize an affinity with one another, and this affinity frequently includes people whose particular traditions have been quite different from their own. They know what it was like to make long preparations for a religious service, even though the services were different, for example. They may also regard one another as kindred spirits because of having been taught a certain appreciation of God or of particular moral values. Because of their loyalty to their own tradition and their awareness of other traditions, they often have an appreciation of what it means to live in a pluralistic society.

Living in a multicultural society requires an ability to forge connections with people who are similar in some respects and different in others. Jews and Christians, Catholics and Protestants, European Americans and African Americans who were able to craft such links with one another through some understanding of their common religious experiences have much to tell us about the possibilities of cultural harmony. The pluralistic character of American religion, encouraging loyalty to particular communities of faith and yet elevating certain unifying ethical standards, also has much to teach about these possibilities.

But the four examples with which I began illustrate how little is known about religious upbringing. In the popular media, growing up religious is often trivialized and depicted as ineffective, providing irony in stories about people who lead sordid lives despite a righteous past. For example, a recent account of a middle-aged drug dealer notes that "despite a strict religious upbringing, she started smoking marijuana as a teenager."[21] In other accounts, religious upbringing provides the occasion for later misdeeds and misfortune, as in a popular play about a young woman driven to violence because of an oppressive religious upbringing or a recent book about a psychotic who claims his rigid religious upbringing magnified his problems. Other stories highlight an apparent tendency for people to reject their religious upbringing, featuring people with devout pasts who now regard Christianity or Judaism as primitive superstition.

Surveys that ask only whether one attended church or synagogue as a child scarcely do justice to the richness of some people's childhood experiences. Casual participation at worship services or in Sunday school is virtually universal, and yet people like the four we have just considered have experienced much more. They are typical of perhaps only a quarter to a third of the American public. For them, spiritual practices were woven into the very fiber of their being. Total immersion is a fitting image. Someone like Jess Hartley would know instinctively the religious roots of this image. Mary Shannon, Bruce Gallahue, and even Hal Meyerson would understand that immersion means more than simply being preoccupied with one's work.[22]

Through stories such as theirs, we can come to understand better the profound importance of growing up religious in the lives of many Americans. Theirs was an experience of particular intensity. The daily household routine was marked by rituals of prayer, by conversations about God, and by sacred objects. Holidays provided special occasions for experiencing the warmth of family, friends, and fellow congregants. And going to services became the focal point of arduous preparations and of one's public identity within the assembly of God's people.

To say simply that such people were raised in pious households, however, does not capture what they experienced. Most would have said their experiences seemed natural. Being religious was a way of life. Indeed, to the extent that they form a distinct subculture, it is their religious upbringing that forges this identity. Otherwise, they are nearly as diverse as the American public itself, including men and women, those who have attained high levels of education and those who have not, and people of all races and from all regions of the country.

Many of the people we shall meet in the following chapters experienced religion less intensely as children and they are sometimes unable to speak of their experiences as eloquently as the four people we have considered in this introduction. The variety of their experiences, nevertheless, helps us sort out the elements of religious upbringing and understand better the varied meanings of these elements. If growing up religious is, indeed, declining, and if fewer parents are training their children in the same ways they were trained, this evidence may well capture a dimension of American culture that is being lost.

PART I

The Sacred at Home

-+->-<-+-

CHAPTER 1

Family Rituals

At a recent gathering of internationally prominent theologians, the discussion turned briefly to children. In a proposal for broadening the debate about abortion, a Catholic ethicist suggested a number of related issues that the church should be addressing, ranging from the responsibilities of fathers to day-care needs to parish involvement in the support of unwed mothers to better teachings on the nature of childhood. At the conclusion of his talk, a woman at the far end of the room raised her hand and asked, "Did I hear correctly when you said there is no systematic Catholic understanding of children?" He nodded affirmatively, prompting her to continue. "Why is that so surprising? What other denomination has a helpful understanding of children? Can any of you think of a single denomination that does?" Nobody responded.

The woman had a point. Not only has childhood been a neglected topic among theologians in recent years, it has also been distorted in much of the current literature on the religious beliefs and practices of children.[1] In popular treatments, childhood faith is largely romanticized as a kind of innocent quest to know God: Children are more or less religious by nature, spontaneously raising questions about life and death, about God, and about beauty and truth. They are the teachers of adults, the source of tender, candid, and often humorous insights into the mystery of being.

The romanticized conception of childhood faith is a reaction to the much sterner view that prevailed throughout much of American history.

In this view, children needed to be guided rigorously in the development of their faith and in a divine struggle for their mortal souls.[2] Besides taking children to church, parents needed to teach them to pray, pray with them and for them, instruct them in the doctrines of their faith, and read to them from sacred texts and other sources of moral wisdom. The good home was a daily reminder of the congregation in miniature, with obedient children drinking in the spiritual teachings of their parents.

Listening to adults talking about the religious dimension of their upbringing, we gain a rather different picture of what it meant to have grown up religious. Their innate curiosity about God was often considerably less acute than theologians have supposed. Stern instruction in formal articles of the faith stands out in the memories of relatively few adults. The tapestry of real life was woven from disparate threads into a far more complex pattern of understanding. Its complexity reveals that there was often *less* than meets the eye. Indeed, it is striking that even people who perceived their parents to be exceptionally devout so often learned little from them about how to pray or about how to understand God. Yet it is important that they did pray and that they did develop an abiding awareness of God. It is evident, too, that there was often *more* happening than people realized. In retrospect, they can identify the small ways in which religion came to be embedded in the daily experiences of family life, including its routines and especially the material objects that spoke to them of God.[3] The following story is a good way of beginning to understand this embeddedness.

An Accident of Birth

In 1918, Tony Martelli's father emigrated from a small mountain village in southern Italy, where he had been a traveling wine salesman and an apprentice tailor, to the bustling Italian section of South Philadelphia. A year later, he returned to Italy for a brief visit, married a young woman he'd met in one of the coastal villages, and then resumed his work as a tailor in the United States. He worked hard, saved his money, made periodic visits to Italy to see his wife, and in 1929 was able to bring her and their seven children with him to Philadelphia. Tony, their ninth child, was born three years later.

"Their timing was great," Tony chuckles. "No sooner did they get here than the Depression hits." His father was unable to find work anywhere, so his mother supported the family. As a girl, she had learned how to weave her own linens from flax and to do embroidery, knitting, and crocheting. Jobbers came to the house every few weeks and bought sweaters and dresses from her to be marketed in New York. By the time the Depression ended, Tony's father had managed to start a small dry cleaning business and, with the help of his children, made home pickups and deliveries. They were self-sufficient people who never borrowed money or took charity and taught their children to work hard and encouraged them to learn English and do well in school.

As a child, Tony knew there were two kinds of people: those who spoke the same language his parents did, and the Jews in the neighborhood, who spoke something else. Tony assumed it must be English and managed to learn quite a bit of it from his friends. Only when he started school did he discover that he was speaking Yiddish. It was in this way that he became aware of ethnic and religious differences. Otherwise, he was reared—at home and after second grade, when he switched from public to parochial school, during the rest of the day as well—in an exclusively Catholic environment that reflected his parents' upbringing in Italy. After all, he observes, "religion is an accident of birth."

If it was accidental, religion was nevertheless a way of life to a much greater extent than it was a mere set of abstract beliefs. Tony's mother was a devout Catholic who went to mass every morning. "She had very, very full days," Tony says. "Her day started early. Her first thing was a walk to the church. Six o'clock mass. She'd come home. My father would have breakfast for her. He'd go off to work. She'd start her day at home. In the evenings, when she did have some time, she would always read her prayer book, say her rosaries."

She always half mumbled her prayers out loud, Tony remembers, so he was very aware that she had a close relationship with God. "She never cursed, she never took God's name in vain, and you dare not do it in her house, either," he recalls. "She was very religious and very, very firm in her convictions." Tony remembers that she had a little book with the "daily office" in it, which she read every day. He also remembers that she always fasted on Wednesdays and never ate meat on Fridays.

The family's customs, Tony says, were all "centered around the church, religious holidays, preparation for the various feasts, Easter, and Christmas." They devoted special attention to Saint Anthony, Saint Cosmos,

Saint Damian, and the little statues of other saints that occupied the house. Tony's mother especially enjoyed inviting people for meals on Sundays and holidays. "She was very witty, and she had a saying for everything, and so people would come over and sit and chat for hours. As a kid growing up, it was fun, because you sat around and you listened to all these tales and these stories." It was also fun because of the meals themselves. Chicken cutlets were Tony's favorite. His mother always purchased a live chicken, fed it for three or four days, slaughtered it herself, and then cooked it in a *minestra* of vegetables grown in her own garden.

Holiday meals were the main occasion for passing on tips about how to lead a proper life. Tony's older siblings came with their friends and children. "It was nothing on a holiday to sit around the table for six, seven hours and just talk and eat, and do more talking and more eating. The discussions around those tables, of course, were always very intense. They would get into what's good for you and what's bad for you, types of food you should eat, types of food you shouldn't eat. How you prepare this, how you prepare that." Looking back on it, he says "the main form of entertainment in those days was dialogue."

In comparison with his mother, Tony's father was less demonstrative about his faith, but Tony regarded him as a man with a deep religious "sensitivity." Like most of the men in the neighborhood, he did not attend religious services very often or talk publicly about his religious views. He nevertheless managed to convey his respect for God to his children by the way he lived. "He was a very kind person," Tony explains. "A very gentle person. Very loving person. I don't think you can be that way if you don't believe in God." Tony learned from him that your praying should be done privately, but that it is important to turn to God when you need help. "Let's face it, we live in a world, and it's a journey through it, and nobody gave you a blueprint to get through it. So when you're up against the wall, and you don't know what to do, who do you go to? You go to something or somebody that you think put it all together, if you believe in God. Some people don't, but that's their problem. It's nice to have somebody to lean on."

The Daily Practices

Tony Martelli's upbringing reflected the religious sensibilities of his parents, but he refers mostly to the daily practices that shaped his character rather than to particular ideas. "Principles are complex," he says. "It's hard to describe a principle and how you got it." Religious principles were woven into his parents' life and were observed best in how they behaved. "They leaned on their faith, got solace from it." So he thinks it was only natural for them to pass on this faith to their children.

One of the daily practices he remembers most vividly was his mother's lighting a vigil candle to the Virgin Mary. It was a small round candle that she kept burning in the kitchen as an offering to the Virgin. Another was gathering around the radio to listen to *Lives of the Saints*. Tony's favorite, of course, was the life of Saint Anthony. Sometimes he also traveled with his mother by streetcar to visit the shrine of Saint Anthony. He remembers with some displeasure the observances of Wednesdays and Fridays. Although he was not expected to fast like his mother, the children were permitted only to eat plain foods those days.

Sunday mass also conjures up mixed emotions. Tony remembers some days when he went to early mass with his mother, stayed for the nine o'clock children's mass, and then sang with the children's choir at the eleven o'clock service. Those were long mornings. But he also got to see his friends at church, and sometimes they found ways of their own to make the time pass more quickly — like the time they stole some of the communion wine and drank it. Or the time they set one of the altar boys' cassocks on fire.

Although Tony absorbed many of the church's teachings at Sunday services and in parochial school, his clearest memories are of the religious imagery that surrounded him at home. Besides the little grotto to the Virgin Mary and the statues of the saints, he especially remembers how his mother adorned the walls of their home with religious pictures. One was of Jesus standing at the door knocking — the door symbolized his heart, his mother told him. Another was of the sacred heart. His favorite was a picture of a boy crossing a bridge with a guardian angel watching him. Tony says that picture has stayed in his mind all his life, reminding him that he has a guardian angel to protect and comfort him.

Over the years, Tony has remained devoted to the religious world in which he was raised. After high school, he worked for two years as a delivery man before he was drafted and served two years in the army during the Korean War. He married soon after his discharge, and he and his wife raised six children. Tony worked up the middle-management ladder at one firm, transferred to another, and eventually started a company of his own distributing electronic goods to manufacturers. During some of these years he was too busy to be very interested in religion, but he seldom missed Sunday mass. Now in his early sixties, he muses, "I think you need time for religion." And he is making more time in his schedule to think about his past and to reflect on his spiritual journey. "You're not the same person you were yesterday. You keep changing. I guess I've sort of mellowed. I'm not as sure about things as I used to be. But I've also become more keenly aware that there is a God and I have a sense of the hereafter."

The various strands that shaped Tony Martelli's religious outlook as a child are not so different from those evident in the way Hal Meyerson, Mary Shannon, Jess Hartley, and Bruce Gallahue talk about their upbringing. Participating in the formal activities of a congregation is an important enough aspect that we will consider these activities in a later chapter. It is evident, however, that religion, like charity, begins at home. The daily round of family activities must somehow be brought into the presence of God. Parents praying, families eating together, conversations focusing on what is proper and improper, and sacred artifacts are all important ways in which family space is sacralized. They come together, forming an almost imperceptible mirage of experience. Yet they can also be separated in order to examine them more closely.

Praying at Home

Being taught to pray is virtually universal among people who have grown up in religious homes. They do not remember elaborate prayers or theological teachings about the nature of prayer or even, with a few notable exceptions, praying fervently for good grades, the well-being of their pets, or the other amusing petitions that have been featured so much in the literature on childhood spirituality. What they remember are the short, simple, rote prayers they learned by heart and repeated almost automatically every night before they went to sleep. Most typical is the standard "Now I lay me down to sleep, I pray the Lord my soul to keep."[4]

Jess Hartley is one of the exceptions who learned to pray in some detail about his needs, yet it is the repetition that hovers nearest the surface of his memory. "I always said the Lord's Prayer first, and after that would follow up, which is the same way I taught my daughter, with 'O Lord, thank you for this day. Thank you for Mommy, for Daddy,' go through the relatives and family. 'O Lord, keep us covered with your blood,' which is asking for protection and watching over us. 'Take us over the busy, dangerous roadways safe and sound. Help us in school,' help us in the things that we were doing. Those type of things we would ask for and then, 'Amen,' when we were done."

For most of the people we talked with, saying prayers at night is also most notable because it was habitual. Another African American man puts it well when he says, "Yes, we prayed every night. It was like saying the multiplication tables."[5] Ben Spilerman, a Jewish man in his sixties, can still say the prayer he said as a boy because it was always the same: "Praise be to thee, O Lord, our God, creator of the universe, who protects all thy children once they close their eyes. Be with me this night that I lie down in peace and rise again in health and strength. Forgive my sins and lead to what is right. Guard my parents and my brother from all danger and harm." Mary Shannon's experience of her mother's praying with her at night is much the same. "It was rote prayers, prayers that you memorized, the Our Father, the Hail Mary, Glory Be, my mom would always end by thanking the Lord for watching over us during the day and to have a home to live in, and for the food that he provided."[6]

Virtually all the people we talked with who had been reared in religious homes also remember that their families said grace at meals; indeed, table grace was said in homes where few other religious practices were observed, yet it communicated clearly to children that religion was valued by their parents.[7] Most people admit that there were times when meals were eaten without being prayed over first. But grace was a regular and expected feature of daily life. What exactly was said is not something that most people can remember. They know simply that the prayer was short and that it involved giving thanks to God for their food. A few, however, can still recite the prayer their family said. More than thirty years later, for instance, Vern Gordon can still quote the prayer his grandparents always said before meals: "Precious Lord, bless us for the food we are about to receive, for the nourishments of our bodies, for Christ, our Redeemer's sake, amen." An elderly woman still remembers the prayer her family said before every meal: "Come, Lord Jesus, be our guest and let these gifts to us be blessed."

Another man remembers his childhood prayer: "For health and strength and daily food and all the blessings of thy hand, we praise thy name, O Lord." Still another man remembers saying, "Bless us, O Lord, and these thy gifts which we are about to receive from thy bounty, through Christ, our Lord. Amen." He also recalls variations: "If I had done something incredibly stupid like knocked over a table of crystal and broken a lot of glasses, [my father] would say something like, 'Bless us as a family. Bless this food, and please bless Steve with a degree more coordination than he appears to have,' or something like that."[8]

In Jewish families, prayers and meals were also closely linked. Hal Meyerson's memories are typical. The Friday evening seder began with his father's pronouncing the kiddush, or sanctification prayer, over a cup of wine, commemorating God's blessings and the emancipation of the Jews from Egypt. Sometimes traditional songs (zmirot) were also sung during and after the meal. As another man describes it, the event had a mesmerizing influence because it was always done the same way. "My mother would first of all prepare the house scrupulously clean. I remember Friday night she'd wash the floors and put newspapers down so we didn't get the floor dirty before my dad got home. Candles were lit. The challah, the white bread, was on the table, covered, and we prepared for Sabbath. My father, in the early days, used to say the prayer over the wine before we would start to eat. The prayer over the wine was to thank God for providing the grapes for the wine. The bread was to thank God for providing bread, sustenance for us to eat. It was very much like grace over a meal, thanking God for the food."[9]

Although as children many people prayed with their parents and said table grace, few remember anything called family devotions or family worship; indeed, many say they hadn't heard these terms before.[10] Nevertheless, for some Protestants, daily devotions were at the center of their family's practices. One woman whose parents had practiced family worship while she was growing up describes it this way: "Family worship happened every day. I remember it varied as far as time of day based on how old we were, but it included reading from the Bible. I remember as a young child it included reading around. This is how I learned how to read. We would read a verse around, and we would sing [a hymn], and we would pray. So it was like eight to ten minutes long."

Her memory of how long family worship lasted stems from many days of anxiously watching the clock! Other people admit their memories of family worship are rosier than their actual experiences of it. If nothing else, children who took turns reading the daily scriptures learned to read *fast*. As one woman explains, "My brother or sister would be tapping their foot and rolling their eyes, because I was stuttering and taking too long, and Bible reading needs to be over. Let's go. Let's go."

People who remember liking family devotions usually found something in it for themselves, even as children. For example, a woman now in her forties recalls, "Mom would read and then there'd be a few paragraphs explaining the passage and apply it for our everyday living and end it with a prayer. You could ask questions or if something would come up during the day, too, if you're having trouble with something. If I was in grade school and if you had trouble with one of the other kids in school or whatever and just talk, say, 'Well, this happened today,' and just talk about it."

Curiously, especially in light of the fact that home Bible study groups have been flourishing in recent years, scarcely any of the people we talked with remember that their parents ever had prayer meetings in their home to which neighbors, relatives, or fellow congregants were invited. Prayer, in this sense, was certainly private, rather than an occasion for friends and neighbors to join in common supplications. In the rare instance that prayer was more communal, it had a memorable impact on children.

Jess Hartley is one such case. He remembers, "I believe it was every Friday. There would be others from the church, my mom's sisters and some of the other church ladies. They would come over. They would have a little bit of a Bible study and then it would be going into prayer, thanking God for his blessings, praying for protection. They would say, 'Lord, cover them with your blood. Be a shield around them, protect them. Allow your angel of mercy to encamp about them and protect them.'" It made a difference to him, knowing that all the church ladies were there praying for his protection. He remembers on more than one occasion during high school starting to sneak out of the house to do "something wild" and then not doing it because of how the church ladies had been praying for him.

In other families, children often saw their parents reading the Bible, even though there may not have been a special time set aside for family devotions. Statistical studies suggest in fact that parents' Bible reading is one of the most powerful ways in which children come to think of themselves as being raised in a religious environment. For instance, in one national study of adults, the best predictor of saying that religion was "very important" in one's family while one was growing up is remembering that one's parents read the Bible at home. And the second-best predictor is having had family devotions in one's home as a child. The study also points to the importance of children's seeing their parents engaged in these activities themselves rather than doing them only for the sake of the children. Thus, having had the Bible read to them as children is not nearly as good a predictor of feeling that one's family took religion seriously as having seen parents reading the Bible themselves.[11]

With the exception of a few people we talked with who had been raised by clergy, most people say their parents read the Bible for inspiration or advice rather than to try to gain a systematic view of theology from it. An older Jewish woman, who says God was her mother's adviser, gives a typical response when she says her mother "used the Bible like a dictionary, to get a specific answer to a problem, rather than trying to get a comprehensive understanding of the entire Bible." Another woman explains that her mother read the Bible "because it's what she grew up with, and she believed what she read, and I think it gave her strength and comfort at times."

Other than family devotions and the rote prayers children said with their parents at bedtime and at meals, prayers are regarded as deeply personal, almost like going to the bathroom. Virtually everyone we talked with insists that their parents—or at least their mother—prayed earnestly and consistently. Yet they claim to have had little idea about the nature or content of these prayers.[12] They assume, for example, that their parents prayed for their children's health and well-being. They assume that their parents sometimes prayed about illnesses and financial concerns. They infer this, however, less from direct statements made by their parents and more from the fact that they themselves believed God was there to help, and since their parents were worried, their parents must have prayed.

An example that illustrates this kind of inference comes from a man who remembers going into his mother's bedroom on occasion and finding her kneeling beside her bed. He says she was "private" and "never discussed" what she prayed about. "It's speculation," he asserts, "because she never really talked about it. But she probably would pray that she would get her children raised and that God would carry them, because she would verbalize this during the day."

If prayer is understood to be private, the possibility of its being accomplished in virtual secrecy is nevertheless a function of the privacy that most American homes provided. As houses became larger, the possibility of prayer's being private increased in proportion to other kinds of personal privacy. An older woman who says, "We were poor, and I mean really poor," illustrates how space made a difference. When she was little, she and her two sisters slept in the same bed in the corner of the kitchen. It was the family's only room, other than her parents' bedroom. She remembers taking baths on Saturday evenings in a big tub in the middle of the kitchen floor (the toilet was an outhouse). She also recalls how public it was to pray.

She and her sisters knelt with their mother and said their prayers aloud. Except when she was at school, all her time was spent in the same room with her mother and father. She knew they prayed and believed in God mostly from overhearing their conversations. She can still repeat some of these conversations. Being around them so much, she can also repeat some of her parents' favorite adages, many of which had a ring of godliness. For instance, her mother always told her, "If you sew on Sunday, you'll sew your nose to whatever it is you're going to do." So she never sewed buttons on Sunday. Living in a house with more rooms as an adult, this woman's prayers have become much more private than they were as a child.

Many people claim to have developed a more private, individualistic, or idiosyncratic view of spirituality as adults, compared with the religious outlook of their youth. But for most people there is still an underlying continuity between this view of spirituality and how they came to understand prayer from their parents. If prayer is the most important way of relating to God, then most children learned that spirituality is a kind of secret, something best not talked about because it is too close to the heart. Spirituality, like prayer, is something you have to work out on your own, drawing on your own feelings and expressing your own needs. To be sure, much of what one thinks about God is rooted in congregational teachings and experiences; nevertheless, when questions start to arise about the validity of religious institutions, it is the memory of personal prayer at home that provides the spark for a continuing search for spirituality.

Furthermore, prayers of this kind are seldom invalidated by God's failure to respond. One of the few adults who remembers anything miraculous ever happening as a result of praying is a Protestant woman who tells this story: "I remember being on a family trip, and we had stopped to go to the bathroom, get a drink, get back in the car. And it was no more than five minutes down the road, I had to go to the bathroom again, really bad. I remember praying, 'Dear God, please, *please* just let us stop. I have to go to the bathroom *so* bad, but I'm not going to ask my dad; he'll throw a fit because we just stopped.' And something happened to the car, and we pulled over [she snaps her fingers] just like that."

But this woman also explains how she came early to understand that petitions for special favors would seldom be answered. "I remember praying for miraculous things, like 'Could you please just have my room be clean by the time I get down the stairs?' I don't think I would say I ever saw that prayer answered! I [learned to] look at that as being my responsibility, not something God could change. Also I figured that if I did things that displeased my parents, it wasn't God's fault because he didn't answer my prayer. It was my own fault for doing all these bad things."

Moral Instruction

In religious families, another important part of family life is moral instruction. Such training takes on special significance because doing right and avoiding wrong are more than just good manners: they are divinely inspired, a part of God's plan for humankind. In many instances, parents added gravity to their moral injunctions by telling children that God will punish them if they disobey. Other parents made it clear to their offspring that God is a kind of silent sentinel, watching them even when nobody else is around.[13] In other cases, parents tried hard not to be heavy handed about what is right and wrong, but what they said carries weight because their children understood that they loved God and tried to do what was right.

Mary Shannon provides a good example of how her family served as a source of moral training. "They did teach us that there was right and wrong," she explains, "and we got punished in our household if we did things wrong. If we told a lie, or if we were really unkind to our brothers, or my brothers to me, or if we were disrespectful to my parents. We never

really were disrespectful to the priests or to the Sisters. We were not problems. I was strong-willed, but I wasn't a problem in school. Nor were my
brothers, really, until they got a little older, until they got into high school,
and I think that's a normal process to go through. We did get punished, but
we always knew that when my parents punished us that they still loved us
and that they forgave us for what we did. I don't ever remember my parents
holding a grudge, you know, like with you doing something wrong."

What comes through most clearly is the fact that parents were the voice
of God's expectations. "I think my father expected me to try my best," one
woman asserts, adding: "I heard from God the same things I heard from
my parents, to do my best and to discern right from wrong, to ask for forgiveness when we did wrong, to forgive others when they did wrong."[14]

With parents' words acquiring the authority of God, it is difficult for
children to escape the counsel of these words. Jess Hartley knew his parents would hear about it if he used curse words and they'd punish him. At
an early age, he could hear his mother's words inside his head, even when
his mother wasn't there, and it made him feel guilty if he did anything
wrong. For instance, he still remembers dealing with a stray cat. "I'd pick
the cat up and throw it in the street. Not in front of a car, but just 'get off
of my sidewalk!' and throw it over there, and the cat just kept coming back
to me and I'd throw it. Evidently one time I threw it, and it didn't land on
its paws like they said they always do, and it must have scratched its nose
or eyes, and I saw a little bit of blood there. I was so upset that I hurt this
cat. I went into the house and told my mama everything."

What tempered the strong voice of authority as Jess grew older was that
his parents often sat with him at meals, just discussing issues of the day as
well as personal decisions. These discussions often included references to
God, and thus carried moral valence, but they were occasions on which
Jess could raise hypothetical points about the conduct of others and thus
receive assurance that his parents understood what he was doing.

A Jewish woman provides a similar example. She remembers the seders
and her mother's lighting candles, but what she focuses on more clearly
are the conversations the family had at meals. "They used to talk about
God a lot. If I would say, 'Who cares about this?' my mother would say,
'Well, God is watching you, you have to.' It was like morals. 'You can't hurt
people. You have to be kind to people. You have to be good to [people].

You have to be thinking of people, because God is there. Don't think that you're getting away with something because you're really not.' It was a lot of that."

Jimmy Padres's Bicycle

Through conversations and from hearing their parents make casual remarks about God, children learned that God is watching them and protecting them. Generally, this image is a comforting thought, but another part of growing up religious is to have fears—fears of evil and of evil forces—and to express these fears in religious terms. The adults we interviewed are generally more reluctant to talk about these fears than they are to talk about the positive experiences they remember about their religious upbringing. But enough people refer to such experiences that we must pay some attention to them.

Vivid childhood experiences of evil emerge in our interviews as almost random events having to do with moments of danger or with being around friends who had graphic imaginations. These experiences, however, always occur within a frame of reference, and in many cases they have continued to be a significant part of the individual's spiritual biography. The frame of reference generally grows out of the religious instruction that children received from their parents. Children had vivid experiences with evil because adults taught them to believe in evil forces. And these experiences then become a significant part of the individual's spiritual biography because people felt compelled, as they grew older, to come to terms with these strange and frightening events—often by reinterpreting them, but often retaining some belief in evil as well.

These patterns are evident in some of the things Raman Wilkins—a blue-collar Protestant in his fifties, who is an African American—says about his upbringing. As he talks about how bad things have become for him financially in the past two years, Raman breaks off at one point and then resumes with the following admission: "If things get really, really bad, I'll find the easy way, maybe I can just get rid of myself, so I wouldn't be a burden on anybody. That is not an obsession of mine. No. There's certain little tiny things, say 'Well, I can be like the CIA. If worst come to worst, I can always take that pill, and pop it in my mouth.' I don't know an easy way of doing it. I'm always afraid what's on the other side. That gets back to God."

Then he explains, "When I was a kid I believed in hell. There was a fire down there, and the devil. We even knew what the devil looked like, 'cuz my friend Jimmy Padres had him on his bicycle. He stuck his hands up his nose and he had these pointed ears on the side. I remember his bicycle. We used to think the devil was like that."

Raman remembers the picture on Jimmy Padres's bicycle because teachings about evil were very much a part of Raman's life. He knows his father talked a lot to him as a child about how evil would befall him if he did certain things that were wrong. As he grew older, some of these specific memories have remained vivid. For instance, when he was seven or eight and delivering newspapers on his bicycle, older boys and men in his neighborhood would give him a nickel to carry hypodermic needles and packets of drugs because they knew the police wouldn't suspect him. Raman did it, but felt like he was dealing with the devil. When he was older, a musician talked Raman into smoking marijuana one day and Raman remembers saying, "This stuff belonged to the devil. I felt my heart beating and everything. I remember that clearly. I told my cousin, Junie, 'There are evils in this world you don't know about.' I got so wise."

Raman is no longer as sure there is literally a devil and he laughs when he thinks about the picture on Jimmy Padres's bicycle, but he remains convinced that there are forces of evil in the world and that doing bad deeds is a way of bringing these forces down on your head. He remembers vividly the lecture his father gave him about evil the time he got a girl pregnant and came asking for $150 to get her an abortion. He worries about people who don't believe in God because he fears they are a source of evil in the world. And the thought of taking his own life brings him up short because he worries about what may lie on "the other side." So the early teachings about evil that he received as a child have remained an important part of his spiritual biography.

As I have suggested, growing up religious places people in a distinct subculture and—for good or ill—sets them apart from other people. Few things do this more clearly than the experiences children have with evil. These experiences draw lines between "us" and "them," especially when "they" are the embodiments or carriers of evil. Part of Raman Wilkins's mental map, for example, is a continuing sense that the black church and its members are an embattled minority trying to be good in a world of drug dealers, criminals, and immoral people who are the representatives of evil. And, in many ways, his view of the world may be correct.

But there is another way in which childhood experiences of evil draw boundaries between the religious world and the outside world. These experiences help define those within the religious world as believers. People on the outside are skeptics, doubters, while those on the inside are more attuned to the hidden — but powerful — realities of the universe.

Raman Wilkins also provides an example of this kind of boundary. He remembers as a child that he and his brother Floyd used to talk a lot about ghosts. Raman knew ghosts existed and hated it when kids stayed up at night telling stories about ghosts or listening to *Inner Sanctum* on the radio. Floyd, in contrast, was "more scientific." He kept a large knife under his pillow at night, not to protect himself from ghosts but in hopes of catching one. Floyd had it figured out that if a ghost could open the door, then a ghost had to have substance, in which case he could stab the ghost with his knife.

In retrospect, Raman says he was never as "rational" as Floyd. Raman, in fact, thought Floyd was *too rational*. "Oh man, you crazy," he used to say to Floyd. For Raman, it just made more sense to accept the fact that there were unseen realities that one could not understand. And Raman is also pleased that in recent years Floyd has come to think more the way he does. "He would be one that wouldn't believe in God," Raman says, "because if you couldn't put it in scientific terms and absolutely prove it, it didn't exist for him. But he's turned. Life has softened him very, very much."

Sacred Objects

This exchange between Raman and Floyd is a perfect illustration of the last point I wish to make in this chapter. Most of the people we interviewed are more like Raman than Floyd: they do not believe in the immediate, physical presence of God, the devil, or ghosts (angels are sometimes an exception), but they are (again like Raman) deeply influenced by the pictures and other representations of the sacred that were in their immediate environment. Had it not been for these objects, the sacred would likely have been little understood or appreciated.[15] Especially when prayer is considered a secret, and religious doctrines are not part of the family culture, sacred objects become the principle connection between the divine and the lived experience of ordinary family life.[16]

We have already seen a number of examples of such objects. Tony Martelli talks of the statues of Saint Anthony, Saint Cosmos, Saint Damian, and the Virgin Mary. Bruce Gallahue remembers the pictures in his Bible storybook. Jess Hartley says his favorite Bible stories were the ones about David and Goliath and Daniel in the lion's den; he says he can still see the pictures that went along with those stories "as if they were standing right here." The young Hal Meyerson put on tefillin and tallis while he said his prayers. Other sacred objects in his house included a menorah kept in a breakfront with glass doors where everyone could see it, brass candleholders for Friday evening dinners, yartzeit candles that were lit for the dead on the anniversary of their death, and a picture of his great grandfather in rabbinical garb. There was also a mezuzzah on every external door in the house. Hal says these objects were all terribly important: "They were part of my life; they were always there."

Some of the people we talked with had few objects with which to associate their religious upbringing; yet there is still an important material dimension to their religious memories. The objects that hold religious significance were not necessarily sacred or religious in themselves, but they came to be associated with religious practices. The practices made the objects special and the objects, in turn, helped concretize the practice and to heighten its significance. Raman Wilkins, for instance, says that other than the Bible that always sat on his father's dresser there were no religious objects in their house. In talking about Christmas and Easter, however, he says that these were very special times because the family used different dishes. Most of the time, he says, they drank from old jelly glasses, but on Christmas and Easter they got to use real glasses. He says it was "like a religious experience."

For many of the Protestants we talked with, sacred objects seem more a Catholic or Jewish custom, and yet their own personalized Bibles functioned in the same way, serving as tangible evidence that they were on good terms with God because they had a copy of his autobiography. Indeed, some of the more devout people we interviewed acknowledge that they had only a vague idea of who God was, let alone an understanding of angels, the devil, or of Trinitarian theology, but they did cherish their Bible, taking it with them to church, underlining it in Sunday school class, and penciling notes in the margins. Like many college students I have known, a shiny textbook and a binder filled with lecture notes gave them confidence that they were learning something.

One woman, who still has the Bible her parents gave her when she was in fourth grade, tells us: "It was the size of a small school book and it had pictures in it. I know I carried it because my mother and dad . . . we all carried Bibles to church. You just did. You took that as well as your purse, you just always took your Bible to church. It was black, because all Bibles had black covers. It was small, four by six. I marked things with a red pencil that were important to me. I still have that Bible. I don't use it, but I kept it, because it was significant to me then. It's interesting just to look back and see what was important, what stuck out in my mind or struck me as being very important at that time."

As this example suggests, Bibles were an important way of linking home life and church life because they could be physically transported from one place to the other. Symbolically, carrying one's Bible to church meant that a person was personally devoted to the faith; having one at home indicated that the church's teachings were respected there. As Jess Hartley observes, "We had a large Bible, almost like a pulpit Bible, big, thick, giant-letter Bible. It mostly sat on the coffee table in the living room. We learned to respect it. We didn't sit on it or knock it on the floor."

Another woman recalls that her parents told Bible stories when she was a child, but the Bible itself was so special that they did not read it. "We had a big family Bible with all the names and dates in it for births and deaths. It was on top of a chest of drawers where my father had his shirts and things. In those days, there were just certain things that you were curious about, but you never dared touch them." Or as a Catholic woman notes, "The Bible was the word of God. Even the way my mother handled the book, you just knew that it was something holy and sacred, and that all that was important about God was in that book." Bibles of course were significant too because they were generally acquired as gifts and thus associated with special people or special occasions.

In many homes, the family Bible was important as a way of keeping records. One man, for instance, says it was common among African Americans living in the rural South to record births in the family Bible because the county did not keep accurate records and because many people were born at home: "It was like an official record of all the births. So the Bible had a lot of meaning." He also remembers getting his first Bible. It was covered with white leather and had a zipper. He says it was especially meaningful to him because everyone else in his family had a Bible and put so much emphasis on it.

Bibles were also a way of marking the home as a sacred space. Family members did not simply read their Bibles in private (they may not have read them at all); rather, they left Bibles laying around the house, often in public places, so that their very presence became a reminder that religion was important to the family. One of the women we talked with recalls vividly how her parents' Bibles were displayed: "My mom and dad, their Bibles were on an end table in the living room. My dad had his chair, my mother had her chair, and between them was an end table with all their reading things and the Bibles and a floor lamp was there also. That's where the Bibles were."

Jewelry that people received as a gift and treasured over the years is also sometimes a tangible reminder of their early religious identity. Many people mention crosses, of course, and some had medallions of favorite saints. One man, an Italian Catholic, is amused that he still wears two pieces of jewelry he received as a boy. One is a medallion imprinted with an image of Christ. It had been blessed by a pope and was a gift from his parents after they had visited the Vatican. The other is an Italian horn that, in his words, "kind of looks like an Italian pepper." It had been a gift from his sister. "You've seen them around. There were big jokes about Italians wearing them. A lot of times Italians wear gold ones. It's very, very clearly a phallic symbol. It's a fertility symbol. Obviously, it's an old tradition, but Italians wear them as symbols." He deliberately mixes his Catholic and his Italian traditions by wearing the two on the same chain. "I've often thought maybe this is a bit secular to mix these two, to put these two things together on the same chain, but I somehow don't think it's sacrilegious, so that's okay. In fact, it's very common. Italians commonly do that."

Pictures and statues in the home often hold special significance as well. A Catholic woman remembers a little statue that had particular meaning to her as a child. "As a little girl, a gentleman who owned a religious store near where my brother worked, I used to go in and drool over the things in the shop. He had an Infant of Prague statue that had a crack in it and he gave that to me. And I can truthfully say that I thought of the infant Jesus as a child as I was, understanding as a child with a child's mind. So that formed a very strong devotion to the infant child Jesus."

A Lutheran woman says there was a picture of the head of Christ in the living room, a picture of Christ on the cross in the dining room, and a cross in the hallway. Having them on the wall, she explains, "just communicated an atmosphere that Christ is part of our family and part of our house." Mary Shannon expresses a similar idea when she says that the statues in her childhood home "sanctified it." But then she backtracks, explaining, "I don't think I would have said that as a child. We just felt they were to bless the home and to keep the home safe."

For Protestants, plaques or embroidered pictures of verses are more common than statues. "'Bless this house, O Lord, we pray, keep it safe by night and day,'" one man remembered. Another was, "May the road rise to meet you, may the wind be always at your back." Pointing to the verse on her own wall, one woman says it had been in her parents' house while she was growing up. "Lord, I continue to pray daily," she read, "because I know that you bend down and listen to me."[17]

A different example of the importance of pictures comes from Archie North, a man who does *not* feel he was reared with any special emphasis on religion but who claims that his family history was filled with religious figures and that his parents were deeply religious even though they said little to him about it. One of the most tangible manifestations of this familial religiosity is a picture. "There was a picture in our hallway of an old man in a suit and tie," Archie remembers. "His name was Uncle Phil. I never met him. But he was always referred to with deep reverence by both my father and my mother. He was sort of like an icon. It turns out that he had married my parents and had been dean of St. John's Cathedral. I had the feeling that he was sort of the holder of the higher sense of values."

Pictures sometimes conjure up negative memories as well, because they were tangible reminders to children that God was watching them and might punish them or even cause them to die. One woman recalls how a picture of Jesus in the Garden of Gethsemane, which hung in the guest room at her grandmother's house, had this effect on her. "I was always afraid that I was going to be surprised by God and God was kind of like a ghost. Or Jesus was like a ghost that would come and grab me in the night." She still isn't sure why the picture made her feel this way, but thinks it was probably because she knew that Jesus' life was near its end and that he was in anguish in the Garden of Gethsemane. It made her feel that something might happen to her as well—"just this impending sense of doom would come over me," she explains.[18]

The people who remember religious or sacred objects in their childhood homes sometimes do not recall valuing these objects as children. The objects were just there and were either taken for granted or seemed strange. As people reflect on their memories of these objects, however, the objects often take on special significance as *links to parents and grandparents*.[19] That is, the object itself may not have been important, but it shows that a parent or grandparent was devoutly religious. Sometimes this was because the owner of the object kept her religious convictions to herself.

One woman, for example, remembers that her mother's Bible was *worn*. This is important because it shows that her mother read the Bible, even though the daughter generally did not see her mother reading it. In other cases, religious objects linked children to the past because these objects were the possessions of or gifts from grandparents or other relatives with whom they had little contact.

Karen Stacy provides an illustration of the importance of religious gifts from grandparents. She did not know her maternal grandmother well, but knew from occasional visits that her grandmother attended church. She also remembers a gift that did not mean much at the time, but that has stayed in her memory as evidence of her grandmother's interest in religion. "I remember her giving me a gift one time—I don't remember this very clearly—but it was shaped like a crayon box and it had like a hundred little-bitty scrolls of paper in there. And there would be the name of a Bible verse at the top, and you had to look it up in your Bible and you had to write it in there. Well, you can imagine how far I got with that. But, yeah, she would give us religious gifts, and so we perceived her as very religious."[20]

Creative Expression

Most of the pictures and other sacred objects that people mention are meaningful just because they were a familiar feature of the domestic landscape. They were sometimes ignored or taken for granted for the same reason. It helped when children knew that an object, such as the grotto in Tony Martelli's house, was special to one of their parents. What is interesting is how seldom an object was actually a creative expression of a parent's spirituality.

The one illustration of such an object that surfaces in our interviews is provided by a woman who remembers coming home from school one day when she was twelve and seeing a new piece of art on the kitchen wall. Her mother was a businesswoman but occasionally painted pictures as a way of expressing herself. The painting was of a dove and an airplane flying over a sea engulfed in flames. When the girl asked what it meant, her mother explained that she (the mother) was in the plane and that she was trying to reach God (the dove) but that her life seemed in danger of crashing into an inferno of conflict and despair. A decade later, the daughter cherishes this painting. She knows her mother was troubled about something, and the painting has become a window into her mother's spiritual longing. (As we shall see later, this painting is also pivotal in the daughter's own journey.)

CHAPTER 2

Home for the Holidays

HOLIDAYS SEEM TO MANY PEOPLE to have lost their religious meaning. They have allegedly been subverted by department store chains, toy companies, and the greeting card industry. If people are to learn much about religion while they are growing up, the argument goes, they will have to do it on some other occasion besides the holidays.

Historians and sociologists are finding that there is considerable truth to these laments about the secularity of American holidays. For at least a century, commercialization has been changing the way in which special days are commemorated.[1] Yet for many people, especially older Americans, the holidays were once a time of deep religious significance. The special preparations that may have contributed to the sacredness of weekly worship services were intensified and extended. The household was filled with people and objects that were understood in the light of religious traditions. Indeed, the regularity of how the holidays were celebrated was one of their most memorable features.

To be sure, not everything about the holidays was rosy. For children growing up in disrupted and dysfunctional families, the holidays were often a time of anguish. Not being able to participate in the loving warmth that was supposed to be present, people found it harder during the holidays to believe in the religious traditions of their families than at any other time.

Still, the holidays were sometimes the occasion for special moments of grace. "Human beings can carry the divine only sometimes," one writer has observed, and during the holidays this carrying capacity was often noticeably increased.[2] On such occasions, families were tied together and reminded of their common heritage, even though the richness of each family's heritage lay in the particularity of its unique experiences.[3]

Jesus Was Everywhere

When Harriet Sims was born, her mother, grandmother, and great grandmother all lived in the same house. Her great grandmother—Granny, as she was called—had been a slave, and many of the family traditions had been shaped by this experience. In fact, Harriet's name was chosen by Granny, who wanted her to be named after Harriet Tubman. A few years later, Granny died and the family moved from Mississippi to Chicago. Harriet still lives in Chicago, and at sixty, she recalls with great clarity how slavery influenced the way her mother raised her, especially in preparing for the holidays.

"The biggest time of year for the slaves was always Christmas," Harriet explains. Preparing for Christmas "started very early with the meager things they had, putting them away, and canning stuff and getting ready for that Christmas dinner. Putting the yams in the cold cellar to keep the yams ready after the harvest. . . . Everything was put away for the holiday and at Christmas time, I mean the feast, no matter how poor you were, the feast was magnificent, because there'd be hams, there'd be turkey, there'd be all kinds of things. People would go from house to house, eating, and they'd be praying, and the minister would come from house to house. It was that kind of southern tradition that came with us.[4] We always made the Christmas tree decorations. We strung the cranberries and the popcorn. We also made the gifts, because we didn't have much money. We would make our own stockings and sew them. My mother bought the felt material and we would sew the stockings. The only thing we'd get in it would be fruit and candy."

Although it came only once a year, Christmas became a kind of symbol for Harriet of what it meant to be religious as an African American. It meant, foremost, that everyone pitched in with what little they had, sharing it with others. Later in life, she read about an African saying, "If my village is ill, I am ill." She says it means that "everyone is responsible to keep the wellness of the village together." This attitude, expressed so clearly in the sharing of food and of handmade gifts at Christmas, is in her view what kept the slaves going and what allowed her people to survive during the Jim Crow period and after they moved north. "There were just things in the black community that we did and understood, things that seemed to transcend the white people in the neighborhood."

The white people who worked in the neighborhood generally lived elsewhere, she observes, and so the black people felt more responsibility for one another. "There was a sharing. If someone didn't have something, the adults would get together and somehow take something to that person or do something for that person. Black elderly people never disappeared from the community. White elderly people disappeared. We didn't know that they were placed in nursing homes. It never happened among black people." She also remembers how her mother took in the children of a woman who was hospitalized and how they all slept in the same bed. "She'd share what she had, and her friends would share with us some-times. So I felt that there were vestiges of our African ethos, so to speak, that survived, and that helped us survive."

Besides sharing, Christmas also symbolized self-sufficiency, especially in making meager gifts and in making do with these gifts. A favorite saying in Harriet's family was that they were "from good stock and had good char-acter." Character meant the kind of pride that comes from knowing who you are. It meant emulating Harriet Tubman, Booker T. Washington, Frederick Douglas, and George Washington Carver. For Harriet Sims, it meant learning to sew and iron because, as her mother said, "if you can't do anything else, you can make a living sewing and ironing." It also meant working instead of complaining—"if you have lemons, make lemonade" was another of her mother's favorite sayings. Harriet's mother taught her to pray for God's strength and protection but never to ask God for selfish things. "She taught us to be modest," Harriet says, "always try to achieve, but never think more of ourselves than necessary."

And Christmas symbolized the presence of Jesus, not in any mysterious sense of the incarnation, but simply as a friend whose name was con-stantly on her mother's lips. "My mother prayed all the time, and she sang religious music, and she read the Bible every day. She was a very religious person." Jesus was perhaps especially close to her because her husband was away—a man who drifted out of her life soon after the children were born and eventually died of alcoholism. Jesus was close because the family had little else to protect them. Harriet's mother thanked Jesus every day for "food and shelter," and Harriet remembers once "when we were without shelter, and my mother pulled us together and she said, 'It's going to be hard.' We went and stayed with a friend of hers, because we had been evicted from where we lived. We had to find something, she had to work, so we went and stayed with a friend of hers. She'd pull us together and we'd pray, 'Lord, give us strength to get through this.'"

But Jesus was also present because Harriet's mother had filled the house with icons and crucifixes and pictures of Jesus. Although they were Protestants, many of her mother's friends at the laundry where she worked were Catholics, and they often gave her these religious objects. Harriet's mother liked them because they helped her think about God and pray. "Jesus was everywhere," Harriet remembers.

Celebrating Christmas

Although most of the Christians we talked with (like Harriet Sims) had church services included in their celebrations while they were growing up, they generally describe Christmas as a family holiday. Insofar as it had religious significance, its meaning was thus conveyed through the warmth of family gatherings, gifts, decorations, and food. Just as the sacred objects did in so many households, these celebrations created a tangible, memorable experience of the sacred. The holidays were a practice, deliberate in their performance, but they were also embedded, richly interwoven with the place in which people lived and with the lives of those with whom one celebrated.[5]

For example, Elaine Margolis (a Protestant in her forties) paints a Norman Rockwell image of Christmas in her family. "By noon on Christmas Eve, all the presents were wrapped, everything was done. The festivities began with my grandmother and my mother's two sisters coming to our house. We would have a light meal. We would go to church together to this candlelight service that I thought was so beautiful. I remember so many times during my childhood when we had white Christmases where we'd walk to church through the snow. It was a real sense of family time, and it was a quiet kind of joy.

"We didn't open any presents until the next morning. We lived in a huge Victorian house and it had a front stairs and back stairs. We'd all gather on the front stairs, which we never used, we only used the back stairs growing up. But on Christmas we got to sit on the front stairs, and my grandmother, who was the oldest, would be first. And the youngest was my brother, who would be last, and everybody would sit on a stair all the way up to the top. When everybody was ready, we would go downstairs. When we opened the door of the family room, the entire room would be filled with presents. We had so many presents that it would take most of the day to open them all, and we would have to do it one by one. You'd go around one by one.

"Beautiful tree. Our house was beautiful at Christmas time. My mother decorated everything really nicely. And then Christmas dinner came afterwards, and it was always the same. It was turkey and stuffing, and my mother used to make sour cherries instead of cranberry sauce, sour cherry relish. We would sit around as a family and eat our Christmas dinner, and there was a lot of humor. It was a lot of fun."

This portrait is in one respect quite different from the one Harriet Sims paints. Having money meant that Christmas could be celebrated in an elaborate fashion. Still, it was the regularity, the sameness of the event, that made it a special time in both instances. Bruce Gallahue also illustrates this point; he remembers his childhood Christmases in ways that are quite similar to Elaine Margolis's memories.

"When I was a little kid on Christmas Eve," he recalls, "there was no tree up. There were no presents around. It all got done after we went to bed. So that Christmas morning, you'd come down and there was a tree all decorated and presents underneath the tree. We all had stockings which somebody made a point to hang by the chimney, and they were knit stockings so that they were expandable. And stuff could be put in there. I'm sure we went through the routine of putting milk and cookies out for Santa. Then the stockings would be at the foot of our beds Christmas morning.

"So Christmas morning there was a magical transformation, but we couldn't go down until my folks got up and said it was okay to go down, but we had our stockings to take things out of. The stockings were on our bed upstairs, but we couldn't go downstairs to open Christmas presents until everything was set up, like coffee was on and sweet rolls or whatever was going to come up for breakfast. But we could open our stockings and swap candy and whatever else seemed to work. And then Christmas was a big occasion, because I had grandparents. My grandfather Gallahue loved Christmas and made sure we kids anyway got some reasonably expensive and very desirable Christmas presents. And so Christmas Day I guess really was spent either riding the newest bicycle or trying out a sled or whatever. And Christmas dinner, we'd go down to get Nanny, bring her up to enjoy all this stuff."[6]

Here again, it is evident that there were clear rules to be followed in celebrating Christmas. Even though these rules were never written down (or perhaps not even verbalized), children knew them by heart. The rules showed that there was some authority greater than the child, probably even greater than the parents. It was simply the tradition to do things a certain way. Insofar as a church service, prayer, or reading of the Christmas story was part of this tradition, it demonstrated that religion was important, even if it was not the whole show.

A few of the people we talked with in fact mention specific religious rituals their families developed as part of their holiday celebrations. Karen Stacy, for example, says her parents "concocted" a family service each Christmas Eve. "It had scripture readings," she recalls, "but the best part from my point of view was that there were candles all over the place. I thought that was very nifty.

"I don't think we sang, although that's surprising because we usually could have, because there were several people around who could've played the piano for us to sing. I think it was mainly sort of readings and prayers—it was like it was on a one-page ditto sheet which my dad did up in multiple colors, in the days of ditto machines. It was a little Hollywoody. Someone had drawn on it. And I remember my mother correcting me one Christmas Eve when I got too excited and was running around, you know, shouting something unseemly—she said, 'This is a religious service, so go and behave yourself.'"

If Christmas was a time of joy, it was also an occasion, therefore, for demonstrating that one knew the family's rules and was loyal to them. As is always true of rituals, firm expectations were evident in most families about what to do, when to do it, and the appropriate demeanor in which to do it. An aura of authority cloaked these rules, transforming the holiday into a time when God's bounty was evident for all who willingly obeyed the rules. Opening presents by birth order, inviting the grandparents, making pilgrimages to visit aunts and uncles, saying special prayers, all demonstrated that there was some higher, beneficent code to which individual family members owed allegiance.

Years later, most people remember these rules with clarity, and many still practice them. A Protestant woman from the Midwest is yet another who describes Christmas in terms of its rules: "I remember most Christmases as being basically the same. We got up. We opened one present Christmas Eve. We could get up at any time Christmas Day and dump out our stocking, but we were not allowed to touch the Christmas gifts. We would sit down as a family and go around the circle, and each person would open a gift, and provide the proper acknowledgment and thanks. Then the next person would open a gift. Then the next person. So we'd just go around the circle, and open gifts when it was our turn." Christmas was clearly about following the rules.

Christmas was even more importantly about showing solidarity with one's family. People from less affluent backgrounds remember that Christmas was a special time, even though the gifts were not abundant, and they also remember that the familiarity of it helped make Christmas a special occasion. A man from a family that was quite poor when he was a child has fond memories of Christmas. He says, "The night before Christmas, we would go out to the field nearby and look for a tree to chop down. That would be our Christmas tree. When we got older and we could drive, we borrowed a car and we would drive into town and we'd go to the fire company where they sold trees, and any tree that was left after midnight, you could have for free.[7]

"There was usually two or three trees left, and they always knew we were coming. I don't know if they made sure [some trees] were left, they might have. But there was usually two or three families that went out. We'd get our tree, we'd bring it home, and decorating it was a family event. Before the tree was decorated, we would go to the evening Christmas service. We always went. My mother would make arrangements for somebody to pick us up, and we would go to the church. We always went for Christmas Eve candlelight service."

Then, on Christmas Day, his family followed the same routine every year. "We'd get up early in the morning. We'd come down and see what package was there. There was always just one. I can remember just about every gift I got as a child, because they were so special and there was just one. Then later in the day we would wait for my one aunt to come. She'd always bring us a gift. It was always a shirt, and we always knew it was going to be a flannel shirt.

"Later in the day my other aunt would come, and she would bring a gift. That also was always a shirt. Then we had a third aunt that would come, and she usually would bring a little box of candy or fruit. We knew before they came what it was going to be, but we didn't complain, because that was our only new shirts for the year. It was our only candy or fruit. It was special.

"Then later, four o'clock, it was always at four, my oldest brothers and sisters who were married, they would come, bring their kids, bring baskets of gifts for their kids, and they would share and exchange presents, and we'd sit and watch them. There was never anything there for us, because they didn't have the money to do that. We were always told, 'Don't expect any gifts. There won't be any for you. This is for the kids.'"

In such stories, recollections of the holidays are more than simply a stroll down memory lane; they are also occasions for moral lessons about who one was and the kind of values one learned. For many, how they had celebrated Christmas was an indication of what kind of family they were. They came from good stock, from people who enjoyed the simple pleasures of giving, and from a family that was loyal. As one woman insists, "We'd always have dinner together, like on Christmas, exchange our gifts together. We were a strong-knit family. I mean, we had our share of problems, but every family does. But we were a strong family."

The Ethnic Factor

From these examples, it is evident that Christmases celebrated during the 1940s, 1950s, and 1960s often followed a highly standardized format. Opening presents had become the center attraction, as indicated both by the timing of the event and by the strict rules surrounding it. Church services had either been minimized in importance or moved to Christmas Eve so as not to interfere with the festivities at home the next day. In most cases, Christmas trees and decorations were purchased, rather than cut by hand or made at home. Members of extended families still lived close enough to one another to gather on Christmas, and public or private transportation made it possible to do so.

Yet there were also vestiges of ethnic traditions, and for many people, these helped to distinguish how Christmas was celebrated. A German Lutheran in Wisconsin tells us she and her cousins always got together at an aunt's house on Christmas Eve for oyster stew. A man whose parents were from Eastern Europe says their Christmas Eve tradition was mushroom soup, made by boiling a soup bone of some kind with "dark, woodsy, dried mushrooms."

A more detailed description comes from another German American, who describes her family celebrations in the 1950s this way: "Christmas morning we'd open up our presents. And then we'd go to church, come home, and Mom always had a big duck dinner fixed. We never had turkey or chicken, we always had duck, because Dad raised ducks. So that was a nice smell to wake up to, and she always got up real early and got the duck going and all the dressing and everything. I wish as a child I would have paid much more attention to what she was doing in cooking, because she can't remember now, but she was really a good cook. Christmas, then, we'd usually spend the rest of the day, I think, with relatives after that, because everybody lived in the same area, which was really nice." Like so many other people, she says going to church was far less important than what happened at home.

Even in cases where the pattern was not very distinct, people sometimes describe it as peculiar to their own tradition. For example, a Norwegian woman observes, "The Norwegians start early. They start baking, trimming the home, and getting everything ready. Christmas Eve is the big day. In our house nobody was allowed to see the tree. My father closed the living room. There were glass doors and he would hang sheets up and surprise us with the tree on Christmas Eve. We came in and saw it. That was the big meal, too. That was a big festival. You usually had company, and we got our presents on Christmas Eve. Christmas Day then was more holy, celebrated just that way, quiet and nice. But Christmas Eve was the big dinner and all."

For older children and teenagers, caroling was another important part of the Christmas festivities, and it often reflected ethnic customs as well. "After the evening service," one man recalls, "we would go out Christmas caroling, and we would go up to the top of the hill, walking from house to house. We would stay out until all hours of the night, caroling, because the other families would be celebrating in the same fashion. Usually the families gave us a dollar to be used for projects at the church. For the older boys, they would also give them a shot of whiskey, and they would serve kiffles and cakes."

A man who grew up in a Russian Orthodox church has similar memories. "One of the highlights of the year was when we went caroling to different houses. As you know, the Russian and Ukrainian people are more or less drinkers. We don't hide our drinking. Every house we went to they would give us a drink. It seems that as we went through the evening, things got merrier and merrier. We had a really great time."

In most cases, food was a distinguishing feature of how Christmas was celebrated, and this seemed especially true of some of the African Americans who recall their family gatherings. For Jess Hartley, the best thing about Christmas was definitely the food. "It's easier to say what we *didn't* have," he jokes. "There'd be turkey, maybe two or three other meats, and lots of vegetables. Like corn, string beans, some sort of rice. They'd make a succotash, and I'd be the main one eating it. Macaroni and cheese, salad, just a huge bowl of tossed salad.

"My goodness, lima beans with rice. My dad's from Georgia so we did things like putting lima beans on top of the rice. And a fruit salad. [My mother] sweetens it up, puts a little apple sauce in it so it's nice and heavy. Very good. Her other special dessert is called a caramel cake. It is delicious to the point where all of the kids are like, 'Hey, Mom, make sure you make me an extra layer, okay. I'll take it home.' So it's like, 'You better get this before your cousins get over here.' And then another thing is sweet potato pie. She makes it out of this world. I hate to make that comparison, but nobody's made it like my mom."

In some families, the holidays were also a time to redress some of the imbalance between mothers and fathers. Children who seldom saw their fathers had occasion to view them performing religious rituals. Even though the holiday feast was prepared by the women, men could thus be seen in roles that reassured the family of their faith and devotion. An older woman of East European origin, for example, remembers that her father seldom went to church with the rest of the family because he worked double shifts at a meat packing plant. Either he was working, or he was too tired to attend. But Christmas, she says, was his "day of glory."

She says the whole family centered its attention on Father, asking him, "Dad, do this" and "Dad, do that." She recalls, "I think he wanted to make this very special for us, and he did. It was a very special prayer that he prepared for Christmas. Then we'd have the wafer, it's an unleavened bread, and then my mother would take honey. First of all, she'd make a cross of honey on our forehead, 'Have sweet thoughts, sweet words.' And then my father would take the wafer and with a spoon he would make a cross on this wafer, which was about this big, about a six-inch oval, and then he'd read from the Bible, 'Glory to God in the highest and peace on earth.'" She also remembers fondly how all the men would go to church with their families on Christmas.

The Variety of Holidays

For Christians at least, no other holiday rivals Christmas in importance. Thanksgiving pales in comparison and generally does not have the deep religious significance of Christmas. Easter is important, but it was more centrally connected with church, whereas Christmas was clearly centered in the home. Advent, Pentecost, and Reformation Sunday, as well as the occasional Fourth of July picnic, were other occasions on which people gathered at church. Nobody mentions Valentine's Day as having had any particular religious significance. But a few people mention other holidays that occasionally focused special attention on the family.

In Catholic families, Saint Patrick's Day was generally a day to be celebrated and remembered in this way. Growing up as she did in Saint Patrick's parish, Mary Shannon is able to provide a vivid glimpse of what it was like to revel in this most Irish of days. "Saint Patrick's Day in our home and in our neighborhood and in our school, when I was younger, was always a big, big celebration. I wore a lot of green growing up. I had dark, jet black hair when I was growing up, and wore a lot of green and wore a lot of green ribbons in my hair. My father wanted that. I guess my aunts, my dad's sisters, were all dressed that way as they grew up.

"Our neighborhood would block off the streets and we'd have like a community Irish festival. It was all the Irish songs and just a happy, happy time. The stories about Saint Patrick, and there was just a pride in being Irish. As I said, I didn't know there was anybody besides Irish until we moved. There were things that we looked forward to. Irish soda bread was a real treat. Beer and whiskey was also just a part of the celebrations. My father drank at those, but my father couldn't hold his liquor very well, and he would either get real quiet or get real silly. It's the only times I remember him dancing.

"We had several records that my father played a lot that were all Irish songs. Especially as we neared Saint Patty's day, he would play those like probably the whole month of March. So I used to know all the Irish songs and all the words.

"For us the celebration was always very family oriented, and my dad always said that was just a part of what he grew up with. So my relatives, although they didn't often come to our home, because we had a little home and there were a lot of people, would come for the holidays. Like for Easter, and Christmas, and Saint Patty's Day, my Nanny and Neeny, my aunts on my dad's side, would come to our home. We always had some kind of a big meal.

"But again it wasn't, like what I know today, it wasn't an Irish meal, but it was always potatoes. Potatoes was the staple. There was always wine at our meals, not beer, when it was a celebration. When it was Christmas, Thanksgiving, Saint Patty's Day, Easter, and all of us, from the little ones on up, had the wine. My dad had all these little glasses, and if there were thirty people there, everybody would have some. I always thought port wine was Irish wine, because that happened to be the wine that they drank in our neighborhood and at the family celebrations. To me, that was the tradition—just sitting together for a long time, and telling stories and jokes, and singing songs."

People raised in Jewish families of course remember different customs, such as fasting on Yom Kippur, having three-cornered cakes on Purim, celebrating the Feast of Weeks, preparing booths for the Feast of Tabernacles, and having potato pancakes on Hanukkah. To an even greater extent than among Protestants and Catholics, these events were woven into the fabric of family life.

An older Jewish woman describes how the family she grew up in commemorated Passover. "The family was big, twenty, thirty people at a seder. And we used to start the seders at sundown and we never finished before midnight. We never missed a mark in the Hagaddah, the prayer book used for the Passover seder. We sang every one of the songs. My grandfather, in addition to being a good rabbi, was a passable cantor, and he taught us the rote for each song. He used to make us rehearse the thing. We didn't go into a seder and just read the Hagaddah!"

She also remembers what she did on Yom Kippur. It was especially meaningful to her because she had been taught to be optimistic, to believe in miracles, and to have faith that God would work everything out. Yom Kippur was different, a time of despair, when people ritually focused on their sins, and then found release. "You took a kosher chicken, and flung it around your head three times while you said specific prayers asking God to forgive your sins. In essence, the chicken is now receiving all your sins. Then you get rid of the chicken or give it to a non-Jew. This is not to say that the non-Jew is getting your sins, but religiously you may not eat the chicken because it has your sins on it. It is a perfectly good chicken."

Hal Meyerson's fondest memories of Jewish holidays stem from the fact that special attention was devoted to the children. He says the Jewish community in which he was raised did an especially good job of this because they valued children so highly. "Among WASPs," he muses, "children are an extension of the family; among Jews, they are the reason for the family." And this attitude influenced the rituals. At Passover, for instance, the seder cannot end until everyone has had a piece of dessert, the afikomen. Hal recalls that the leader of the service would hide the afikomen and the children would try to find it. Whoever found it got fifty cents or some other small reward.

Another event that drew the children in was making the hamantachen for Purim. This is a triangular cookie, usually with a fruit-type filling, either prune or apricot, shaped in the shape of Haman's hat. Some children enjoy filling them with peanut butter. Hal says, "Oh, it was always with my grandmother and my mother. We always made them. Roll out the dough and form them and cook them. That was always part of it." These activities, along with the Friday evening seders and praying with his father in the temple, are among the most important reasons that Hal Meyerson feels it is so important to carry on the Jewish traditions.

The Celebration of Crying

The warm Currier and Ives view of family holidays lives on in popular imagination at least in part because families worked hard to ensure that everything went just right on these special occasions. When it was not possible to meet these high expectations, people remember the holidays with quite different feelings. Indeed, the strong connection between warm, loving families and positive childhood experiences of religion is perhaps best understood by considering a contrasting case.

Effie Cairn, a woman in her early seventies, is able to laugh now as she looks back on the holidays of her youth, but they still conjure up memories of strained family relationships and of religious training that she now considers badly skewed. She is a lifelong Catholic, the daughter of Irish immigrants. Her mother came to the United States by herself at age eighteen, settling within a few miles of Ellis Island, and a year later married a driver on the newly constructed IRT subway. They had a daughter a year later, and the following year the man was badly injured in a subway crash. He died a few months later, in an insane asylum. After struggling to earn a living by running a boarding house, Effie's mother eventually married one of the boarders, a truck driver, and Effie, a sister, and a younger brother were born to this marriage.

Unlike many of the people we talked with, Effie's childhood memories do not focus on a single house, because her parents moved every two or three months from the time she was three until she was thirteen. They were victims of the Depression, and moving this often was a way of benefiting from rent concessions. She also remembers tensions between her parents, caused, she thinks, by the fact that it was a marriage born of economic necessity more than of love. Of her father she says, "He was a man who never should have married. His happiest time was in the Army in World War I. He liked being with other men. He never understood what children wanted from him. My mother ran everything. Sometimes now, from this point, I feel a little sorry for him, because my mother was formidable." He did not get along well with Effie's half sister, nor did she. She recalls, "For years we lived in a house where nobody spoke. My half sister and my father did not speak. There's a book by Edwin O'Connor about an Irish family that uses silence as a punishment, and that was my family."

Still, it was a devoutly religious family. Effie's mother walked to mass at sunrise each weekday and made sure the whole family attended on Sundays. Her father was a charitable man who sent donations regularly to Catholic causes in Ireland and in the United States, served as an usher at church, kept a big drawer full of Catholic reading material, and listened to Father Coughlin on the radio. Both parents believed firmly in the biblical virtue of children's honoring and respecting their parents, and they vowed their children would receive a proper education and do well in school. Effie received moral and religious instruction every day at parochial school.

The atmosphere of their home was reproduced almost identically in their relationships with the church. Effie's mother was no less apt to let the priests push her around than she was her husband. The only time Effie remembers her mother's speaking about the old country was to tell (again and again) how the young people in her village all used to gather in an old barn with a lovely wooden floor for dances until one night the local priest broke in and destroyed the floor with an ax. "She was never one to suck up to the priests," Effie asserts. Her mother's relationship with God was not entirely congenial either. "I think he was a vengeful God, someone who kept score," Effie says. "I don't think my mother found a lot of solace in the idea of God as a comforter, that his eye is on the sparrow, and all of that. I don't think she thought that." And of her father, she says, "He was trying to buy his way into heaven. We didn't have very much. He was always sending money away to the missions or to various religious orders. If my mother saw a letter coming in from a religious organization, she tried to throw it out."

Despite the intensity of their commitment to the church, the family was sufficiently unsettled not to put in place the minor religious rituals that so many other families practiced. Each member prayed and said the novenas as he or she saw fit. As simple a ritual as table grace demanded more cooperation than could be mustered. "Nobody spoke at dinner," Effie explains. "Dinner was terrible. There was no point in sitting down and praying for the blessings of the Lord when you're eating in an atmosphere of intense tension. After a while even that stopped, and my father ate by himself and then we ate. So there was nothing, no tradition."

The holidays thus became a special symbol of her turbulent religious upbringing, just as they did of love and warmth for other people. "They were just terrible," she admits. "We mostly celebrated by doing a lot of crying." Laughing, she says it was not exactly Irish to celebrate them this way. She thinks they were terrible because of the strains in her family. "When things aren't going right all year, and then the holidays point out all this loving family stuff, it's got to be a very tense time of the year." She remembers vividly herself as an eight-year-old, having an idealized view of what Christmas should be like and trying to force her parents to buy a tree and give presents. But it did not happen that way. "I think they just made a conscious decision about it. Since they were unhappy, they saw no point in having holidays. It just wasn't a festive home." Eventually, as the family pulled itself up economically, the holidays did become a more regular habit. Yet what Effie remembers most is that "usually there was some terrible fight and the whole thing went down the drain."

In retrospect, it is surprising that Effie Cairn did not abandon religion entirely when she grew up (her sister did). The reason she did not is that she became a frequent visitor as a teenager in other people's homes. Meals in her family, she muses, took about seven minutes at most, and so she was amazed to visit in homes where the meals took much longer. "To go to an Italian person's home and see them all eating together and talking and laughing was incredible! I couldn't believe that! And to stay at the table. They would sit there for an hour, two hours. Incredible! Or to go to a Jewish wedding. The first Jewish wedding I went to was in a storefront over in the Bronx someplace. It was a very simple ceremony. But the whole attitude towards getting married seemed to be so much more open than it would be if it were a Catholic who were about to do this."

These encounters forced her to think harder about what it meant to be Catholic. "Moving with different people and meeting people who seemed to lead very productive and ethical lives and yet who had different beliefs or no religious beliefs at all made me think that perhaps I had been very narrow in my thinking." Gradually, she shifted from thinking of God in "legalistic" terms, as a chairman of the board who was keeping track of everything she did, to a God who could be worshipped thankfully. "I began to think of God when I was happy, not when I was sad." Increasingly, she says, "I have moments when I'm just floating along, feeling at peace with the universe and with God. It's almost scary!"

Moments of Grace

Such moments are memorable, even scary, because they happen so rarely. We did not find, contrary to a popular impression in some writings on this subject, that memories of childhood religiosity center around dramatic and mysterious "peak experiences," such as encounters with angels or special revelations from God. Indeed, one reason why holidays were significant is that they were often the rare occasion on which people remember feeling the special joy of being lifted out of everyday life into something more ethereal and sacred.

People may not have experienced miracles, but they knew God was closer during the holidays than on most other occasions. For example, one man has cherished a special moment that happened on Christmas Eve many years ago. "I've actually thought a lot about this as the years have gone by," he begins. "I can isolate this moment as the moment in my life when I felt the most absolute, total peace, that everything was perfect.

"We were living out in the country, and it was Christmas Eve. We decided that we needed another string of lights for our tree. And because we were in the country, we had to go into town to get them. We drove into town and we were coming home and it must have been about twilight. The route we were on was Route 313. I know the exact spot in the road. It was just my father and me on Christmas Eve, in the car. It must have been about five o'clock, because I know exactly what the light was like in the sky. And I knew then that things were perfect, right at that particular spot in the road."

But not everyone's moments of grace are this positive. Indeed, it is more common for people to remember times of grief, tragedy, or illness as having had particular religious significance. Sometimes children themselves feel close to or protected by God on such occasions; in other instances, the feeling is more of bewilderment or fear, but the actions of adults show them that an appropriate response is to turn to God. These experiences are like the holidays in that a crack in the reality of everyday life opens up, permitting the sacred to burst through; only these cracks are neither planned nor joyous.

For example, one woman describes how she felt as a child when her grandmother had a stroke. She remembers her dad's breaking into tears when he came home and found out about it, and when he quit crying, he went into the next room and started praying. "So this is what I remember about prayer," the woman recalls, "this absolute dilemma about what's the best thing for grandmother and having to leave that up to God because you could do nothing about it." She learned that "prayer was very much associated with being powerless."

Harriet Sims's moment of grace did not happen at Christmas, either, but during a stressful time when she was five years old. Her Aunt Velda, who had been as close to her as a second mother, took ill and within a few weeks was dead. "I don't think this was a dream," Harriet begins. "But when my Aunt Velda died, I was in the room in the bed by myself and there seemed to be something like this that came in that room." She makes a swirling motion with her hands. "And it touched me. I know it was her. And I just felt her spirit and I can't—even now, thinking about it—I just—this woman's spirit. I think this woman has looked after me. I think her spirit has been with me ever since I've been a child, and my life has not been the same since then. So it never leaves me, never ever leaves me. I'm a spiritual person. I guess I always will be."

So often, these special moments have meaning because they are embedded in family relationships—and their significance continues because of later stories, interpretations, and memories passed along by the family. Another revealing example comes from a woman who tells about her grandmother's death. "When she died, we were living out of the country. I know my mother had gotten some kind of a phone call late at night, and the next morning, we got up to go to school, and she was still in bed.

"So we knew something was wrong, and she was just crying. I think she was just partly sad that she couldn't even go to the funeral, because we couldn't afford it. And she just always thought the world of her mother, and had the highest respect for her, so she was sorry that she was going to be gone. I never heard her ever criticize anything her mother had done or anything. Both of her parents she just thought the world of, I know, and she tried to follow their example in their spiritual lives because they were just such dedicated Christians. They just dedicated their whole lives to serving God. And she wanted to do the same. I know she's talked about that."

Clearly, the moment itself is important, but it continues to have meaning for this woman because it has come to symbolize her mother's deep respect for her grandmother and her mother's commitment to the same faith. Like the holidays, illness and death break the ordinary cycle of family life, drawing people closer together but also opening a crevice through which light from the Beyond can shine.

For people who have found it harder to relate to God as adults, these experiences sometimes continue to have special significance. An older Jewish man, for example, says he has only felt close to God once in his life, but he remembers it vividly. "I was eight years old and we were vacationing in the Catskills. One day I went off alone to wander through the hills and pick berries. I just had this feeling of a presence. It was a feeling of not being alone, like I was being protected. And it made me feel very good. To this day, I can't explain it."

CHAPTER 3

->-<-

Generations in the Spirit

As many of their comments suggest, people who celebrated religious holidays often did so by going to their grandparents' house or by inviting grandparents to theirs. When these people were children, grandparents were one of the most important links with the past, including the family's ethnic and religious traditions. In some families, this link was strengthened by the fact that grandparents lived with their children and grandchildren—or close enough to be a regular part of the family routine. Prior to the 1960s, when nursing homes and retirement communities became popular, many grandparents depended on being close enough to children to share meals or transportation and to receive physical care.

The role of generations is so fundamental to the perpetuation of religious traditions that it is often taken for granted. The Hebrew scriptures are full of genealogies and of stories about the impact of ancestors on their descendants. In recent years, so much attention has been devoted to the nuclear family that the significant influence of grandparents in religious training has almost been forgotten. People may not live in the same house with their grandparents as commonly as they once did, but the fact that people live longer than in the past suggests a need to rediscover the possibility that grandparents may continue to be an important part of growing up religious.[1]

There are three important aspects of generational continuity in being raised religiously. The first is the direct influence that grandparents have had in households where several generations lived under the same roof or where children were exposed to the teachings of their grandparents. The second is the way in which memories about grandparents (or about parents)—specifically a special piety on the part of even one parent or grandparent—shape people's views of their own spirituality. Finally, gender differences are particularly relevant in this context, for it is mothers and grandmothers who so often play the decisive part in childhood religious experiences.

Grandpa and Grandma Upstairs

Ezra Feldman, a man now in his early fifties, illustrates the deep impact that living near one's grandparents sometimes had. "We called them Grandpa and Grandma Upstairs," he chuckles, "and even later, when they no longer lived there, we called them that, just to distinguish them from my maternal grandparents."

Until he was six, Ezra and his family lived in a first-floor apartment, and his paternal grandparents lived in the same building on the second floor. Ezra was very fond of his grandfather and remained close to him even after the family moved a few blocks away. Sitting with his grandfather in a big blue wing-backed chair, Ezra learned to say the Hebrew letters his grandfather pointed out in his Hebrew newspaper and quietly assimilated the religious values embedded in the stories his grandfather read to him.

As a young man, Grandpa Upstairs had studied in Lithuania to become a rabbi, was forced to emigrate for economic reasons when his father died, and came to the United States, where he finished his education. After graduation, he married a woman whose father was instrumental in helping the young couple establish themselves as chicken farmers in California as part of the Jewish agricultural movement.[2] A few years later, he left the chicken business to become the rabbi at a nearby congregation. By the time Ezra was born, his grandfather had retired but was still active in the synagogue, often being asked to read the Torah.

From observing his grandparents, Ezra soon learned what it meant to be Jewish. "I knew very early on that there were a bunch of things my grandparents did that were different from the rest of the world and those had to do with being Jewish. My grandfather wouldn't go around without a head covering during the daytime, my grandmother wore a wig, had her hair cut short and kind of pulled back. They kept a strictly kosher home. They didn't turn lights on and off on the Sabbath. It was real obvious that they didn't live the way most people did." After the family moved, Ezra and his parents generally went to synagogue and then spent their Saturdays with the grandparents.

In retrospect, Ezra thinks his grandfather was somewhat uncomfortable around people and thus offered "to do a lesson" as a way of relating to his grandson. Often these Hebrew lessons were less intriguing to Ezra than being outside playing ball. But they were also better than going to Hebrew school. After a few years of the latter, Ezra refused to attend any longer, preferring instead to learn what he could from his grandfather.

Grandpa Upstairs was also the source of Ezra's understanding of the holy days. When he was little, all the family (including aunts and uncles and cousins) would crowd into his grandparents' apartment for the annual Passover seder. Ezra remembers the bustle of activity surrounding preparations for the seder. Special dishes and utensils were brought out and special foods were prepared, all of which made it a "big day" of the year. His grandparents' apartment was also where he came to realize that Judaism is a scholarly religion involving the use of many books. "There were all these books that were very important. I remember at even a very young age being impressed by them. About the time I first could read Hebrew, I remember asking my grandmother, pointing to a Talmud up there and saying, 'When will I be able to read that?' and she said something like, 'Well, it will be a long time.' I still remember that. I guess I grew up thinking of those books as holy objects."

But mostly Ezra credits his grandfather with shaping his beliefs. "I think my view of God was very much influenced by his. It was a very rational view, very interesting. I remember, for instance, when I was growing up, hearing all the stuff about heaven and hell from my non-Jewish associates. I remember asking him one day, 'Grandpa, what do we think happens when you die?' He said, 'We don't know. Nobody's been there and come back to tell us about it.' And this was marvelous. Even at that young age I was thinking, 'What a great idea, you know, you come out of this tradition where people have that kind of a view of things.'" Ezra also appreciated the fact that his grandfather, while strict, was nevertheless able to bend the rules once in a while to suit his grandson. For instance, he re-members playing checkers with his grandfather on the Sabbath and re-calls that his grandfather was more forgiving of him than his grandmother: "Sometimes I'd forget and turn on the lights on the Sabbath, and he'd say, 'That's okay, just don't tell your grandmother.'" Ezra thinks maybe God is forgiving, too.

Praying on Our Knees

Vern Gordon actually lived with his grandparents, so he is also able to pro-vide a more detailed account of what they did religiously and how they in-fluenced him than most people can. An African American in his early for-ties, Vern works as a production scheduler in the materials department at a plant that manufactures light industrial goods. His father worked as an orderly and died when Vern was a child. His mother held a clerical job at a government office and Vern was raised by his grandparents.[3]

He describes them as "very much believing in a higher source—a very religious family." Every Sunday morning and every Sunday evening his grandparents held a prayer meeting for the family. Vern describes it: "We started out each Sunday morning before breakfast or before any other type of activity. We would have prayer meetings, which were pretty much headed by my grandfather and grandmother. We would have prayer ses-sions and we would, of course, be on our knees. They would thank God for the blessings they had and for all the things, even though we were not a rich family or even middle class by any means.

"We were always thankful for what we did have. Probably with the prayer sessions we had and the Bible readings and what have you, it would last maybe an hour, hour and a half or so in the morning, and then we would repeat that right before dinner in the evening." Most of the time in between, he says, was spent in church—a Baptist church about fifteen miles away. There, the custom was to have an extended revival meeting one Sunday of every month. On that day, people did stay the whole day, attending long services in the morning and afternoon, with a luscious pot-luck dinner in between.

Vern's most vivid memories of religion as a child are not the church ser-vices but those long times spent on his knees in the living room with his grandparents. "My grandfather would be on his knees and he would be thanking God for all the gifts that God had given him: his health and strength, and for his family. He'd be very vocal and thankful and go down the line of things he was thankful for. He was, I thought, very long winded in what he was saying. And also, after he was finished, my grandmother would go and say her little things, and Bible verses were read."

Vern sighs, "At the time, I thought a lot of it could have been shortened and that we didn't need to be as strict and disciplined about going through all this before eating or being able to watch our favorite cartoons on television. I thought it was a little much, because my grandfather did most of his praying on his knees—and when he was on his knees, we were all expected to be on our knees also."

In retrospect, Vern says he believed it was right to be giving thanks and felt guilty about his impatience with his grandfather's prayers. He also thought his grandfather was "overly strict" in how he expected the family to behave—no card playing, no dancing, no alcohol, and no profanity.

Otherwise, Vern felt comfortable with what he heard his grandfather and other people at church say about religion. "They would preach from the Bible and just tell you pretty much that if you were good and you followed what was thought to be the straight and narrow path, that good things would happen to you. And if you did unto others as you want them to do unto you, the Golden Rule, that you were doing what God wants." Vern says, "There was basically nothing within their preaching which went against anything that I believed."

He also describes his grandparents as "disciplinarians." They insisted that he and a cousin who also lived with them do chores, avoid using profanity, steer clear of such vices as card playing and dancing, and not stay out late. In retrospect, Vern thinks they drew a clear line between good, church-going people like themselves and the rest of the world. "They knew there were a lot of bad things out there, and certainly they had confidence, I'm sure, in us, but they were trying to protect us," he says.

Another manifestation of his grandparents' faith was that they "would constantly have the Bible around, and [they] would constantly read from the Bible." The Bible was, to them, *the book*, Vern says. It contained the answers for life, and Vern recalls clearly that his grandfather used to quote to him frequently from the Bible, "especially if he thought what I was doing was wrong or that I might be led astray." Vern also knows that his grandparents prayed, not just on Sunday, but each day of the week. Talking about his grandmother, for instance, he says, "It was evident physically by her being on her knees in a praying position on the side of the bed in the morning when she got up and the evening before she went to bed."[4]

The Ancestral Legacy

When Vern Gordon was twelve, he moved to another state to live with his mother. She was not as strict as Vern's grandfather, but she also attended a Baptist church. The only significant difference, Vern says, is that the church his grandparents attended was all black, whereas the one his mother attended was mostly black but included a few whites and Asian Americans. Vern says he continued to believe pretty much in the same things his grandparents had taught him. He was glad not to have the long prayer sessions on his knees and to have shorter church services but felt that he was still leading a good Christian life. In fact, he says he still believes what he was taught as a child and considers Christian faith as the best route to living a good life.

The reason his faith has remained strong, he says, is that he has continued to receive a lot of support from his family. His mother died when Vern was in his early twenties, but he is still close to his aunts and uncles and cousins. "They all pretty much have the same beliefs," he volunteers. "They're all Christian people. Some maybe would spend more time in church or go on a more regular basis than others, but they are all, I believe, good practicing Christians."

He says that his mind and his feelings were molded by this strong family environment in which everyone shares common religious beliefs. "I'm a strong believer in the family unit," he adds. "My family does show that they are Christian in their belief and their actions. It prompts me to continue in that same line. I know I would be an outcast from the family unit if I did have beliefs or actions that were contrary to what they believe."

When asked to describe his spiritual journey, Vern says there are no dramatic events or turning points. "Some people say they have had visions or that the Virgin Mary has come and spoken to them personally," he says, "but nothing like that has happened to me." For him, spirituality is a much more ordinary feature of daily life. He explains, "I see it through people and their actions. The people I respect and think are positive people, the way they carry themselves and the things they do and the things they say—I look at that as being the characteristics of people who are God-fearing.

"So I look at the actions of others and I see the way the world is and my belief just becomes strengthened, because I know I could not be in a situation where I didn't believe that there was a higher source. It would be such a depressing situation that it wouldn't be worth living. When you see all the negative things out there, and there seem to be more and more negative things happening, I don't see how anyone can stay in this society, in this world, without thinking that there's a better place for them to go and there's somebody that is more caring and who does not have negative feelings toward you or somebody who is completely honest and open and somebody who does not discriminate. It's just a feeling that I have, but I have not had any visions, per se. I have not had that. But I don't think that's really necessary. It's just something that you believe inwardly."

At present, Vern summarizes his religious convictions by asserting, "I'm a very God-fearing person. I do believe in a higher being. I feel that there's a purpose for all of us being here and that we do have some control over our destiny. It's up to us to do what is God's will, and if we do the things that we should, then we'll be rewarded in some way. I don't know what will happen once we die, but the only thing that can keep me going is to think that if I do the right thing and treat people the way that Christianity says to treat people, that I will be rewarded. But here again, what that reward would be, what's on the other side, I don't know. I do think that we're here for a reason and that we do have some control over our destiny."

By his own account, then, Vern Gordon is a person of deep faith. His religious convictions sustain him and give him the courage to have a positive outlook on life, even when so many bad things seem to be happening in the world. He asserts that his "basic beliefs and spirituality" have not changed over the years. They are simply part of the core of his existence. "There's been no big crises in my life which have made me question whether God exists," he explains. But he also thinks that having faith means not having to ask for all the answers.

"I think those who do believe in a higher source find times when you sit back and you see some of the negative things that happen in society and ask how, in a supposedly Christian nation, people can do some of the things they do. I think we all question that at times. But it's just a question that is raised; it doesn't deter us or make us feel that there isn't a higher being. It's just questions we ask ourself, and we just can't answer. A lot of things there's no answer for, at least nothing that we can understand."

As he talks about his faith, Vern offers two explanations for why it is so strong. One is the teaching he received from his grandparents and from the church they attended. He says he became a Christian at the time he was baptized—age eight or nine—and that he became spiritually oriented from the time he first learned about a higher being by hearing the Bible. The other explanation is that his faith has made it possible for him to lead a good life.

"I've always felt that there's a guiding light somewhere," he explains. "If I thought there was nobody and that we had complete control over what we do and there is no higher being, then I just can't personally see how anyone can go through life feeling that way. It just seems like such a big void. During the time I suffered through a depression, I'd always look and say, hey, there's going to be a better day and God is going to get us out of this situation, both personally and overall. Because I think that if there is not somebody spiritually involved with us, it would be just so depressing."

Grandparents in Religious Memory

The role of grandparents has been virtually ignored in recent theories of religious development.[5] Presumably, this is because their influence is thought to be mediated by parents. Yet there is often a direct influence as well, and the memory of that influence may be as important as the actual relationship between children and their grandparents.[6] Generally, these memories are from early childhood and thus subject to a great deal of re-interpretation. In many cases, direct memories have also been filtered through family albums, reunions, and the retelling of family histories. Although the memories are as different as people themselves, three characteristics occur repeatedly in our interviews.

First, one grandparent (if not several) is remembered as having been especially devout, dutiful, perhaps even rigid in his or her religious practice.

In comparison, people describe themselves as more flexible or tolerant and their beliefs as less certain or as more subjective. Whether or not they see one style of spirituality as being preferable to the other, they do use their grandparents as a point of reference. Indeed, many people attribute these differences to broader shifts in culture. If grandparents were strict and stern, it was because life was not as complex then, because communities were more tightly knit, or because religious authorities imposed stronger controls on their members. Part of the difference is consistent with my argument about the formation of a wider subculture among people who have grown up religious. Grandparents are thought to have lived in more localized and distinct religious enclaves; in comparison, people see themselves as being more open to diversity and less bound to specific sets of rules.

It is also interesting parenthetically, given what I have just suggested, that many people do *not* think their own faith is more private than that of their grandparents. Personal, idiosyncratic, subjective, yes, but not private. They say their grandparents were more private than they, meaning that their grandparents did not talk about their feelings, show emotion easily, or pray about personal concerns in the presence of others. In comparison, they themselves are more likely to emphasize feelings, to talk about them, and to disclose their inner thoughts about spirituality to others.

Second, despite the negative connotation that dutiful, rigid religious practice in grandparents often carries, people nevertheless respect their grandparents' religious commitment and worry that something valuable is in danger of being lost. Indeed, what social scientists have called "secularization"—the declining influence of religion—is often evident in the way people remember their grandparents. The one or more grandparents who were devout symbolize a golden age, a time when people took religion more seriously, and in comparison people's own generation, and their children's, seem to have slid into secularity.

This perception is all the more interesting because most people acknowledge that several of their grandparents were *not* very religious. And others, upon questioning, suggest that their grandparents may well have been more religious in later life than they had been when they were younger. But what impressed them as children was the religious devotion of at least one of their grandparents. Perhaps it was because they them-selves were searching for a secure image of God at this age that a grandpar-ent's faith was especially memorable.

And third, because of the age differences separating them from their grandparents, and because most people knew their grandparents only when they themselves were children, there is a lingering sense of mystery about their grandparents' faith—one that is often strong enough to moti-vate people to search for something that might provide them with clues about the nature of the sacred. Often their grandparents did not talk openly enough about their personal beliefs for people to know what they thought; they were, in this sense, inscrutable. But it was obvious enough from stories of hardship or from watching grandparents become ill and die that they had some deep reservoir of spiritual strength. Especially when people admired their grandparents or implicitly modeled their view of God after a grandparent, they are likely to have embarked sometime later in life on a quest to recover this sense of the divine.

These themes are all especially evident among people, like Ezra Feld-man and Vern Gordon, who actually knew and interacted with their grandparents, but they are sometimes evident among people who did not personally know their grandparents as well. One of the more interesting examples of this is Elaine Margolis. "My maternal grandfather died when I was two," she recalls, "and he was a Renaissance person. He was an artist and he was a photographer and he was a lot of things that I later became very interested in myself. When I would visit my maternal grandmother's house, I would go up to her bedroom, where I wasn't allowed, and talk to his picture because I desired so much to know him. So when I thought about death as a child, I thought about meeting him and I really wanted to do that."

Elaine Margolis also perceives religious change in generational terms. Her maternal grandmother was, in Elaine's words, "extremely rigid" in her religious views. Elaine remembers a huge fight between her mother and grandmother over the story of Jonah, in which her mother explained that the story had been told to make a point, while her grandmother in-sisted that Jonah really had been swallowed by the whale. Elaine's mother left the house crying, shaken terribly by her mother's accusation that she no longer believed the Bible and thus had lost her faith. Elaine believes there has been a moderating influence in religion, and points to the differences between herself, her mother, and her grandmother as evidence.

People who did not know their grandparents were sometimes told stories that helped not only carry on family traditions but also remind the listeners of the value of remembering the past. A Jewish woman who never knew her grandfather has a vivid image of him nevertheless. "He had this, they call it in German, open table. People were always coming, because there were a lot of hungry people in those days. And they always knew that this was a place where they could go to eat. They always had groups of people. And he'd feed people, and he'd take care of people. There were people that were gentiles working for him, and when it was time for them to get married, when they had to plan a wedding and they couldn't do it, he would do it for them. He always taught them that you have to think about other people and treat them as you would want to be treated, regardless of whatever their religion is."

The reason she has such a vivid memory is that her grandfather died in the Holocaust, and the family had vowed to remember him. She has seen notebooks prepared by survivors from his village, and they tell how religious her grandfather was and how much he cared for other people. "He did so," she understands, "for the same reason all people did, because it was a commandment from God."

Other people remember grandparents as particularly religious because of their grandparents' profession. As in Ezra Feldman's case, it is not uncommon for people to remember at least one grandparent (or great uncle or aunt) who had been a preacher, rabbi, or missionary.[7] Sometimes these are the illustrious ancestors about whom stories were told, perhaps because they were better educated than average or because they held positions of leadership. Typically, these were male ancestors, but occasionally they stand out because they were women.

One woman in her thirties tells how her mother talked often about how her parents had served as missionaries in China. "My grandfather died when he was sixty. Heart problems. So my grandmother became a Bible teacher. I forget what she did, but she traveled around to different schools as a Bible teacher in Oklahoma, and so she was sort of a missionary, too. I know from what my mother tells me that she always prayed daily and had her devotions and she was active in her church even after she was older and couldn't carry on any kind of mission work of her own." This woman also knows there were stories about her grandparents' fleeing from the Chinese communists and of her grandmother's giving birth with the assistance of a Chinese midwife.

Besides ancestors who stand out in family history as saints and heroes, there are also the ones (more common, in fact) who gave an explicit sense of generational continuity to people's religious practices. For example, a Presbyterian woman in her thirties remarks, "My mother taught me to come to church regularly," and attributes her mother's behavior to a longer family tradition. "She taught me that we should have faith in God and that we should attend church regularly. I know that when I was growing up she'd bring me to Sunday school every single Sunday. This is very important, my grandparents were very good Christians and they did a lot for the church."

Another telling example of generational continuity comes from a Catholic woman whose mother was quite religious. "I think it came from her grandmother," the woman explains. "My mother always said she got her devotion to Mary from her grandmother, who always said the rosary." Mary Shannon also perceives such continuity through her father and her paternal grandmother. "My dad would say that it was through my Nanny that he had gained his faith," she says, "because my Nanny had been through a lot and had always believed and never turned against God, even though she had such a hard life."

A Jewish woman, who describes her grandfather as deeply religious, also paints an eloquent picture that helps her understand why she is so interested in spirituality herself. "He would pray every morning. He would lay the tefillin every morning. He would go to temple religiously. Go to synagogue religiously, Friday night, Saturday morning, all the holidays. I think he felt that the practice of religion was a matter of life and death. Among those Jews, this was something that you just did without question. It had to be important, otherwise not only would your life come apart, but probably the whole society would come apart if you didn't do this. Everyone felt that it was your responsibility to be observant for the good of humanity, to save society. This is what I think propelled him. The alternative was just unthinkable."

Repeatedly, though, we also hear about grandparents who were indifferent toward religion. A woman in her eighties, whose grandparents had been young shortly after the Civil War, knows that they had seldom attended church, because it was too far away, and that there had been no Sunday schools in their community. A woman raised in the 1950s tells us her father did not start attending church regularly until his mother, who had always ridiculed the idea of church, died. When asked about their grandparents, others say simply that one or more of them had no interest in religion at all. Thus, it bears caution whenever people argue that American society was simply a great deal more oriented toward religion in the days of their grandparents than it is today. They may think so, especially if one grandparent was especially devout, and yet they may also be overlooking other ancestors for whom religion was unimportant.

The Role of Women

Plenty of examples in our interviews suggest that fathers and grandfathers were sometimes the significant influence in people's religious upbringing, and yet any consideration of family as a source of childhood spirituality must also acknowledge that family life was more often centered around the activities of women than of men. In this respect, the closeness of Ezra Feldman and Vern Gordon to their grandfathers is atypical, although it is equally evident in both cases that relatively little is said about their fathers. Indeed, from what we have observed, it is not difficult to understand why women were generally more involved in children's religious activities than men were. As Barbara Kingsolver has so eloquently put it: "My mother's job was me."[8]

Mothers assumed responsibility for child rearing to a greater extent than men; if religious training was to be given, it was done by mothers more than by fathers.[9] In the process, mothers' own religious commitment was often reinforced. They were on the front line in dealing with illnesses, death, and emotionally difficult subjects, such as courtship, marriage, and childbirth. Many of them prayed for strength to handle these situations. Mothers also prepared the feasts for religious holidays, decorated the house, and made sure children were bathed and dressed properly for religious services. One man, an evangelical Christian, expresses the difference when he quotes the words he had heard the minister say many times while he was growing up: "More men come to the saving grace of faith through a pious mother and her example than the strong words of a father directing." A woman takes this idea a step further, re-marking "I think [my father] believed through my mother. I think he had his doubts, but if anybody could take anybody's word for it, he was going to take hers."

Gender differences also perpetuated themselves in the expectations to which girls and boys were exposed. To guard their chastity, girls were sub-jected to biblical teachings about the sanctity of marriage (to a greater extent than boys), and to find a suitable marriage partner, they were en-couraged to participate faithfully in congregational gatherings. Girls also saw their mothers praying and heard them talking about God more than they did their fathers (whom many describe as not very demonstrative), and girls assumed such behavior was appropriate for women. Boys saw the same behavior, but assumed they should behave more like their fa-thers.

In contrast to the *Ozzie and Harriet* image of family, where the father seems not to have had enough work to do to keep him away from the fam-ily for any length of time, many of the people we interviewed (especially older ones) note that their fathers were simply absent so much of the time that they were not important people in their children's daily lives. An older woman whose father worked twelve-hour rotating shifts in a mine, for example, says she has few memories of him. The one memory that stands out is hearing him say, "How terrible for children to lose their mother. Better that a father is lost than a mother because a mother can be both father and mother, where a man cannot be a mother. He can only be a father."

Perhaps because mothers were emotionally invested in their children's lives to a greater extent than many fathers were, women turned more fre-quently to God to help them through the emotional crises that invariably arose in the course of their children's upbringing. One of the women who tells us she had never been close to her father makes this comment about her mother: "God was an important being in her life. When she would be emotionally upset, she always would say, 'God, why is this happening to me now?' Especially during the war, when all three of my brothers were in the service and I lost my middle brother (he was killed in Italy), she turned more to the church than before." She adds that her brother's death did not have the same effect on her father.

A man whose father was actually a preacher also notices an interesting difference between his parents in spirituality. Of his father he says, "As far as religious things at home, in retrospect, I always kind of found it a little surprising. He was less the mover in religious instruction at home than Mother was. Mother usually was the instigator of our family get-togethers, worship, and prayer. He was involved, but it seemed like she was usually more of the mover of it."

Despite the fact that it was their mother who read Bible stories to them, most people (male and female alike) say their favorite stories were of Moses, Abraham, Isaac, Jacob, King David, Daniel in the lion's den, and Jesus—in short, stories about men. For the women, these stories were interesting and adventuresome but removed from real life, just as stories of Paul Bunyan and the Blue Ox were removed. What women remember was their mother's touch, her prayers, and her singing; these became the marks of women's spirituality. It is thus notable when women remember biblical stories of women in leadership positions. In fact, the story of Queen Esther is one of the few that women regard fondly. And in nearly every case, the woman remembering is herself a professional in a position of authority.

Another gendered custom was the practice in many congregations that a woman was not permitted to leave her house after giving birth until the baby had been baptized. Thus, the first public outing was the mother's coming to church to have the baby baptized and to receive special prayers for her health and for the well-being of her baby. One woman remembers, "I broke that tradition. With my daughter, when she was born, we were living with my mother at the time, and I wanted to go out, but [my mother] said, 'You cannot go out until that baby is baptized.' I went out anyhow. Matter of fact, she always used to talk about that, oh how terrible, how sinful that was that we went out. You know, that the first place a woman should go after having the baby is to church to pray that the baby was well and we came through it all."

Yet another reason women were more likely to have been involved was that for years churches offered little else on Sundays (other than the worship service) to attract people; thus, teaching children's Sunday school classes was one of the few responsibilities that ensured people would be there each week. Women, of course, were (correctly) assumed to know more about children, more likely to have taught Sunday school in the past, and more likely to be elementary school teachers, and so they were expected to be at church, whereas men were not.

The Absent Father

It is difficult to overestimate the significance of these gender differences in people's recollections of their mothers, fathers, and grandparents. Although fathers were forcefully present in the religious upbringing of some children, they are notably absent in the accounts of many. Because they worked long hours outside the home, they were physically absent on many occasions when prayers were said at meals or at bedtime or when casual conversations emerged about God and morality.

"The missing father," James Hillman has written, "is not your or my personal father. He is the absent father of our culture, the viable senex who provides not daily bread but spirit through meaning and order. The missing father is the dead God who offered a focus for spiritual things. Without this focus, we turn to dreams and oracles, rather than to prayer, code, tradition, and ritual. When mother replaces father, magic substitutes for logos, and son-priests contaminate the purer spirit."[10]

The pain of such absence has been expressed well by one poet, who has written, "I love my Daddy like he loves his Dollar."[11] Fathers' lack of expressiveness also means that they are often perceived as being emotionally absent even when they were physically present. Despite the leadership positions in congregations that were often reserved for men, fathers and grandfathers were also less likely than mothers and grandmothers to have attended services or devoted their time to helping with congregational activities.

With fathers who were less demonstrative and less involved in family religious rituals, it was easy for sons to grow up with a different attitude toward religion than daughters. For instance, one woman remembers how she always prayed before going to bed, but that her brothers were always "too embarrassed" to pray, even though their mother wanted them to. Another woman explains how she learned Bible stories: "I always hung around my mother as a child, and she used to tell me different things from the Bible that she'd heard as a young girl, and I was always interested in that." By implication, she would have learned more from her father and would have perhaps been less interested in her mother's teachings had she been a boy. A Protestant woman from the Midwest remarks, "It was always Mom leading the prayers and Mom reading the devotion, and Dad kind of sitting there grumbling because he didn't want to sit there."

Karen Stacy offers insight into the added responsibilities that women often shouldered as a result of fathers' being absent. Karen is a woman in her early forties who attends a mainline Protestant church and is still trying to figure out what she really thinks about spirituality. She grew up in the South, and her parents were both well-educated, middle-class professionals. Like many families in the 1950s and early 1960s, Karen's parents divided up the work of raising the children. Her father worked full time (and then some) and her mother stayed at home, did the cleaning and cooking, and tended to the needs of Karen and her three siblings.

When asked about the values she learned as a child, Karen explains that she associates these values with her mother much more so than with her father. "My father seemed to me like a very jolly guy. He was virtually never around. He was always off at work. And what I see now is that he was probably avoiding the chaos at home. My mother was very definitely the central figure in our household. She was the discipline figure; she was at home, so she was always there after school." As she elaborates, Karen remarks, "I'll just leave my dad out of it because he was sort of tangential in a way to the family."

What Karen and many of the other people we talked with remember about their mothers was a strong sense of *order*. If their fathers stayed at work to escape the chaos, their mothers tried to impose order on the inevitable chaos involved in raising their children. And religious sayings and activities were an important part of this order. It was a major effort to keep religion in the picture, but the result was a set of habits that people look back on as an essential part of the routine of growing up. One thing they could count on, for example, was attending religious services. Or they could count on their mother's saying prayers with them or doling out punishments with religious adages attached to them. Karen says that the central value she associates with her mother is obedience. "And part of that I think was because she was a really good manager, and she had a big operation to manage with us four kids on not very much money. And we were very disciplined kids. I recall always doing what she told me."

As far as church going was concerned, the following comment, from a Protestant woman of Scandinavian descent about her father, is not uncommon: "He just wasn't practicing it as much as far as going to church. I mean, he was a very good man and a man that would treat people fairly, but he just wasn't a real good church goer." Another woman says pointedly, "My father, he's the type that only goes to church maybe three times a year. My mother was the one that came to church every single Sunday." Her father was a blue-collar worker; her mother, a housewife. She was not as close to her father as to her mother: "I'm very close to my mother, I always have been. But as a little girl as I was growing up I never had the love of my father as much as I wanted. No I did not. He was always working and my father was the type where he doesn't show his love the way I needed his love."

Of course fathers were not absent from the religious activities of all households. Mary Shannon, for instance, regards her mother as the more devout of her parents, but she knows her father was religious, too. "My father prayed, but not from the Bible like my mother. He would say his prayers. We had a quiet time in the day, and we knew that was his time for saying prayers. It usually was in the evening after supper, after homework. After we did our homework, we were allowed to have time, like we would get washed for the night and in our pj's, and we were allowed to come down and be together. We went to bed when I was little like at eight. My older brothers went at nine. But my dad, we always had sort of like an easy chair, and he would sit in his chair. His music, although it was classical and not religious per se, he always said he felt closest to God through his music. So he listened to his music a lot. His music was his way of, I think, being in touch with God."

In Mary's case, it has been easy to feel close to God, rather than viewing God as a distant or judgmental being, because she felt close to her father, regarding him as a gentle person who cared about her and who was also close to God. She recognizes this connection herself: "My dad was God in human form." Choking back tears as she remembers her father, she continues, "He didn't say, 'I love you, Mary,' but I knew he did. I think that's why I have the strong relationship that I have with God, because I had such a good relationship with my father, and to me God is male. I don't mean that for everybody that he's male, but he is for me. I think that that's a gift that my dad gave to me. He was kind and gentle, accepting, caring."

A contrasting example helps put this comment in perspective. When fathers were absent or emotionally distant, people did not adopt a maternal image of God; religious teachings that associated God with maleness were too prominent for that to happen. Instead, a wrathful, distant view of God emerged, sometimes closely resembling that of the absent father. Or, more interesting, the absent father actually created a kind of psychological space in which a more loving God-father came to dwell.

A Catholic woman, Lynette Supinsky, draws this connection as she talks about her childhood with a father who worked at two jobs and was seldom at home. "I think I really needed a father because my father wasn't there for us. And I think when I heard of God the father, most people are afraid of God the father, but I saw him as daddy. I went to him as daddy and started my faith journey with my heavenly father."

Now age fifty and a grandmother herself, a woman who has worked as a secretary for three decades, she has become more reflective about her views of God. She realizes how God became the "man" in her life. For example, when she was a teenager she prayed earnestly to God every day, hoping to feel his presence tangibly in her body. "I wanted him to be the spouse of my life and started to pursue that need through praying most of the time," she recalls.

For a time, she seriously considered becoming a nun, literally becoming the spouse of God, and as she prayed, she imagined herself sitting on God's lap. The reason she did not become a nun is that the priest who was counseling her realized her longing to be married and encouraged her to find a husband. She is glad she did. Yet she says her greatest longing is still "to be in-dwelled by my God."

Manly Spirituality?

The idea that God should be a loving spouse, a mother, or an emotionally intimate father has perhaps become so familiar that any other notion (except perhaps for the wrathful, distant God) is difficult to imagine. The term *manly spirituality* is an oxymoron. Yet the earlier prominence of so-called muscular Christianity in American culture, and more recent efforts to recapture a sense of manly spirituality, such as the quasi-secular men's movement that emerged around Robert Bly's spiritual retreats or the evangelical Promise Keepers movement, suggest that a more masculine image of God remains appealing, if difficult to express adequately.

It is thus interesting to conclude with an example rich in this alternative imagery. One person who talks at length about his father is Raman Wilkins, the man who also tells the story about Jimmy Padres's bicycle. Raman is the grandson of slaves. His paternal grandfather was freed at the age of sixteen, and Raman suspects his grandmother gained her freedom about the same age. Raman is the second youngest of nine children. When he was four, his mother died, and Raman was raised entirely by his father.

Raman's father, Garrett Wilkins, had a third-grade education. He worked in construction and did haircuts for people in the neighborhood at thirty-five cents apiece to earn extra money. Garrett Wilkins was a deeply religious man. Three years ago, at age ninety-four, he died. Raman still misses him terribly. Our interview gives Raman a chance to talk about his father and as he does he often pauses to choke back the tears. On several occasions he cries openly.

Raman himself is not a particularly religious person. He does not attend church and, although he believes in God and has tried to live morally, he has had run-ins with the police, lived with a number of different women, and done things that have distanced him from his church-going neighbors. So the story he tells about his father is not a story of dutiful devotion to the merits of a pious life. The story has some hard edges. But it also reveals important insights into the manly nature of fathers' spirituality.

I say *manly* because that is a word Raman uses repeatedly to describe his father. "There was something that was a *man* about my father," he says. "To this day I still can't think of myself as being the man that my father was. There is something about men like my father—they don't make 'em like that anymore." Raman says he was always impressed by his father's muscles. He liked to watch his father eat because of the way the muscles in his jaw worked. And he liked to look at his father's hands while he was working.

Being manly, though, also meant taking responsibility. Raman remembers his father's walking home in the evening, tired from working all day, only to find that one of the children had broken one of the neighbor's windows with a ball. His father always went over and fixed the window. A couple of times the family received welfare checks, and the welfare officer was dumbfounded when Raman's father came in a few months later and repaid the money.

Raman insists that his father was a very religious man. "He used to go to church every day," Raman says. "My father believed in God and he used to quote the Bible a lot." His father, Raman elaborates, was not a religious zealot, but had "a strong, *strong* belief in God. If one of us did something, he would tell us that the consequences of our act is already ordained through the teachings of the Lord. That there are certain things you just don't do, or else God would punish you for it."

Raman says his father prayed a lot about doing the right thing and talked to his children about what was right. "My father," Raman says, "talked a lot about God out loud, not to prove the existence of God, but to show God working in the affairs of man." Sometimes his father's manliness came through in standing up for what was right. For instance, one of Raman's sisters was raped one time, and Raman's father paid a visit to the boys who did it. "He carried a gun to their house and set down the law to them," Raman recalls. "That's why I say he was a man's man."

A word like *strength* can be used to talk about mothers as well as fathers, of course. But it is evident in Raman's case that his father's style of spirituality is one that Raman can admire because there is nothing wimpy about it. There is firmness in his father's convictions, just as there is in his muscles. When asked about his father's principles, for instance, Raman asserts, "My father just knew right from wrong, according to the Bible. He knew. There was no question about what was right and what was wrong in God's eye. And I think he would find it very difficult if he thought he strayed away from the teaching of the Bible, that part of the Bible that he learned that guided his life. I think everything he did, he did with the hope for God's blessing."

Robert Bly has captured the imaginations of a largely male, educated, middle-class audience by telling—and interpreting—the mythic tale of Iron John.[12] Bly encourages his readers (and those who attend his retreats and who watch his films) to rediscover the manly nature of masculinity and to reconsider how manliness can contribute to their spirituality. That same sense of masculine spirituality can also be captured in the more readily accessible figures of men like Garrett Wilkins and perhaps in the memories that many other people cherish of their own father and grandfathers. Garrett Wilkins does not radiate the tenderness of the Virgin Mary or the introspectiveness of Teresa of Avila. He is a practical man and his faith is fully integrated into the practice of his daily life. He carries what he knows of the Bible around in his head and, like Tevya in *Fiddler on the Roof*, he carries on an active conversation with God. His conversations with the Bible and with God tell him what is right and what is wrong. And when he remains uncertain or worried, his spirituality gives him the confidence to proceed anyway.

PART II

Going to Services

CHAPTER 4

➤➤◄◄

Houses of Worship

THUS FAR, I have suggested that the most memorable aspects of growing up religious occur within families, especially through the daily routines and sacred objects, the holidays, and the intimate relationships of which families are composed. Now that the value of the family is being rediscovered, as it were, this argument should be sweet music to the ears of family advocates. Yet it is equally clear that religious socialization seldom takes place only within families. Clergy and other religious leaders would certainly feel that something important was missing if due attention were not paid to congregations.

Protestants, Catholics, and Jews of all varieties have always insisted that children learn from an early age to be faithful members of a particular congregation. In theological lore, the stated reason for sending children to religious services is to train them better to understand, and thus worship, their Creator.[1] For most of the people we talked with, however, going to services is vividly associated with the sights and sounds and smells of a human creation: the house of worship.

Bells and Windows

Alan Threadwell, a sixty-year-old lifelong Lutheran who grew up in an ethnically diverse town of steel workers, says his earliest childhood memory is of the church bells tolling on Sunday mornings near his home. He remembers vividly the church he attended: "It was a two-story affair with a parish hall–Sunday school room in the bottom. It had a sanctuary on the upper floor. It was a stereotype church, except that it was in stone. It had a sloped roof with a steeple. It had a balcony up there where an old pipe organ was located. The church was built in 1930, so it was relatively new when I was a youngster. It was remarkably plain on the inside, painted an off-white. It had pews, a red carpet runner down over hardwood floors. It had an altar, a high altar, freestanding from the rear wall of the chancel, with a picture. At that time it had a picture of the ascending Christ. It was a horrible painting. I always thought it was lousy even as a kid. We eventually painted it over in 1951. It had a high pulpit, a pulpit in which the pastor stood over the floor by about three, four feet. The pulpit was on the left side, the lectern on the right side, kind of an ornate communion rail around it. People would go up for communion and then go behind the altar to drop an offering."

This description is not atypical. People who have grown up in churches and synagogues can often describe them in as much detail as they can their own homes. Just as the populace did in the Middle Ages, when cathedrals were built to provide object lessons that even the illiterate could understand, children absorbed a significant part of their religious heritage by staring at the altar, the paintings, and the stained glass windows week after week.

The windows are often particularly memorable. Alan Threadwell continues his narrative: "On the west side [of the sanctuary] you had the pictures of events in Christ's life. You had him in Gethsemane, the Crucifixion, the appearance after the Resurrection. Gorgeous center panels! You had a picture of the Ten Commandments, of the two tablets. One marvelous picture was a profile of Jesus holding the children, a little lamb. It was the famous painting, that was put into glass. That particular picture was in the left side of the church, just about middle. And when I was a youngster I sat there. And when you're not paying too much attention to the sermon, you're looking at that picture. And the bright light came in from the southwest at that time of the morning, and the picture just became ablaze with color."

Other people have equally vivid memories. A man who moved away from the church of his childhood at the age of twelve says that many nights he still dreams of that church, even though more than thirty years have passed. "I actually dream at night about it," he explains, and he thinks the reason is that he had such a deep, material relation with it as a child. "I knew it in interesting physical ways. It was built so that, as a child, I could actually climb up the walls. I'd come out of service and I'd climb the walls. It was a particular stone material where it had little garnets embedded in it, and I'd chip out those little red stones and keep them. It was just a tremendous sort of hands-on relationship with this church. I knew every nook and cranny on the inside."

People remember that the buildings were homey but also hallowed. Another man expresses sentiments almost exactly like Alan Threadwell's in telling how the stained glass windows depicting the life of Christ made him feel. "I absolutely loved those pictures. And the one that I loved the most was the one of Christ in the Garden of Gethsemane. My eyes would always be attracted to it. I always felt when I walked into that church, even as a child, I always felt I was in the presence of God, in the presence of Christ, that he was there, that he lived there, that this was his place, and I wouldn't dare do anything in that sanctuary. And everybody, I think, felt that way. You just respected it. If we wanted to do anything that was not of a reverent, worshipful nature, we would go down into the basement."

Similarly, for Mary Shannon going to mass was always special because, as she says, there was a feeling of "sanctity" just from being in the church. The altar and windows were important to her, too, but one of the most memorable aspects of Saint Patrick's was the candles. She recalls, "When we would go into church, we always lit the candles. My father, even though we didn't have a lot of money, he would always have a coin for us to put in so we could light the candles and pray for a special intention, and it was always whatever we felt was the special intention. Like they didn't try to tell us. I've seen parents who will say, 'Now, pray for your Aunt Susie.' It was, 'Here is your coin. Light your candle and pray for what you want to pray for.' That was within ourselves."[2]

Making Space Meaningful

Religious leaders have of course been aware of the importance of sacred space, rediscovering the role of architecture and imagery as a result of living in a television era. Having been so greatly influenced by her church as a child, Elaine Margolis, a New England Protestant, has tried as a Sunday school teacher herself to make children more aware of the material culture of their faith. "I designed an activity sheet for kids using a stained glass window in the church as a learning device," she says. "It's very important to me that children be connected with the architecture of a church and know it as a way of understanding what is going on in a church." Speaking from her own experience, she adds: "The symbol itself is really important. When I see a cross, I don't automatically jump to what the cross means, but there's something about the cross itself and focusing on that image that helps my mind to travel to places that connect me to something that I couldn't understand in any other way."

Another reason these material artifacts were so meaningful is that they were often homemade. Men got together to construct the new church building; children knew their fathers or grandfathers had done this. The names at the bottom of the stained glass windows were evidence of ancestors' importance to the congregation. The building itself was a source of community pride, a symbol of commitment. As one older woman remarks, "Oh yes, we had a fine brick building; most of the others in town were wooden."

And if fathers built and repaired the building, mothers made it home. Church dinners were one of the best ways of filling an empty building with homey, welcoming smells and tastes. "Coffee parties were always the best," observes a Protestant woman. "They were always a lot of work, always the best, in other words, fancy. The sandwiches were just so, and everything had to be fixed just so." She says her mother took great pride in helping with these parties.

Singing was another way of expressing ownership of one's congregation. Many people speak warmly of the fact that their father or mother sang in the choir or that they sang in the children's choir or simply that they loved to sing during the worship services. In some churches, art served a similar function. For example, one of the people we talked with describes a painting that was special both for its beauty and because a local congregant had painted it. "Upstairs there was a big, big painting. One of the boys in the church painted that, an artist, and that was of the twelve disciples, the Last Supper." The same woman remembers how wonderful the altar and the pulpit furniture were; they had been handcarved by one of the men in the church.

Jess Hartley also took pride in his church because of its connection with his own history. His grandmother and a woman pastor founded it. "My grandmother started to worship with Mother Tompkins," he recalls. "This was all in homes at the time, this wasn't done in churches. Then they got a little storefront church, with a potbelly stove in the middle of it. And that is where they built the church where we are now; however, that church was taken down and then a bigger church was built from that one. So as far as the founding, I think it was because they started to fellowship together, worship together, trying to form something in that area because there wasn't, again to my knowledge, much happening in that area from the standpoint of building churches and things."

Preparations

Attending services was special because people went to a building that had been consecrated but even more so because they consecrated themselves. The weekly service was more than an hour or two spent sitting in a sacred building. For those who grew up in intensely religious homes, the weekly service required elaborate preparations, often beginning a full day in advance.

For Alan Threadwell, the Sunday service was embedded in preparations that generally began on Saturday morning and that culminated well after the preaching was over. Typically, his family ate chicken soup on Saturday evening, so throughout the day the aroma of boiling chicken and spices filled the house. After dinner, shoe polishing was the next act in the family ritual. "It took forever to do our shoes, because there was always a dialogue between my mother and the boys. There's that talking that parents do. Then we had to do our father's shoes. So you were gearing up for all of the worship and for Sunday school. I can remember also when I was a kid, if it snowed, my mother would send me out [to] make an opening in the snow so we could get to church."

On Sunday morning, before leaving for church, Alan's mother generally put a pot roast in the oven to slow-cook, and when the services were over, everyone returned hungrily to take part in the family feast. Sometimes they turned on the radio to hear J. Fulton Sheen on *The Catholic Hour*. And without fail, at two o'clock everything stopped so the family could listen to *The Lutheran Hour*. Alan remembers how the program always began "with the herald of trumpets, and it would say, 'The Lutheran Hour, bringing Christ to the nations.'"

Elaine Margolis offers a similar description of how her weekends were spent as a child. On Saturdays, all the children were expected to help their mother with housecleaning or their father with yard work. She remembers that there was a frenzy of activity because none of this work could be done on Sunday. Toward evening on Saturdays, everyone took a bath, did their hair, and laid out their clothes for church. Then they were allowed to watch *Perry Mason* on television. Getting dressed for church the next morning was "mechanical" and "very organized." After church, the family generally ate a light meal rather than a traditional Sunday feast because Elaine's mother felt Sunday should be a day of rest. Then they usually went for a family drive in the afternoon. Elaine observes, "Sundays were good. I looked forward to them. It was really the only time set aside just to be a family without working."

Clothing was also a significant part of the preparations that made religious services special. People did not attend services in the same clothes they wore to school or for doing housework or for farming or working at the steel mill. Especially for children, religious services were a time to dress up, to look handsome or pretty. The clothes were sometimes uncomfortable, but they clearly demarcated sacred space from the profane world of everyday life.

Elaine Margolis, true to her New England upbringing, provides a clear example. When asked what she wore to church as a child, she exclaims, "Starched. I was starched from head to toe. My socks were starched. Absolutely, we always had our Sunday outfits. And when we traveled [to another church], we'd have to travel in our underwear in the car because this was before permanent press. My dress would be hanging, and I would have my slip on, and when we'd get to the place we were going, we'd put on our Sunday best and go. I wore a hat and gloves to church. In the fifties that's what you did. I liked it, I loved it."

Although the clothes people wore may seem superfluous to what really went on at religious services, it is wrong to draw too sharp a distinction between the two. Special clothes symbolized a separation between the sacred and the profane, and thus came to be associated with the content of the sacred itself, sometimes to such an extent that memories years later are interwoven with texts and dress.[3]

A vivid example of this connection is given by Elaine Margolis as she talks about her confirmation: "I remember I had a powder blue wool suit with a pleated skirt. It was a short jacket and it was very, very stylish. The minister stood in the front and we had to kneel in front of him, one by one. And when I went up he laid his hands on me and he did this verse from Romans, 'I appeal to you therefore, brethren, to present your bodies as a living sacrifice before God.' See, I can remember it now. 'By the renewal of your mind to do what is acceptable to God.' That verse has stuck with me throughout my whole life and kind of been my report card for how I was doing."

The Weekly Feast

If the Sunday service often began on Saturday morning, it generally did not end until the family had gathered for the weekly feast. Mothers were thus intensely engaged in the activities surrounding the Sunday service, and children learned as much about God's nurture and bounty from the meals their mother prepared as from what they heard at church.

A Norwegian woman remembers how hard her stepmother worked to prepare the Sunday meal for their family of seven, plus almost always a visitor or two. "Sunday we usually had a big leg of lamb or roast beef or chicken, mashed potatoes, and always in the dining room. . . . [The table] was set special, and [the meal was] very special. Fancy desserts. The Norwegians, they could always make something, fancy desserts. Then later on coffee, in the afternoon, three o'clock coffee, cream cake and coffee."

A woman in her eighties who grew up in a Presbyterian family says salt mackerel was what made Sunday a special day when she was a girl. She remembers little about the church services but looked forward to the salt mackerel her mother broiled on the coal-burning range as a Sunday treat.

Mary Shannon also has positive memories of Sundays, largely because the elaborate preparations and often burdensome time at mass culminated in an exquisite feast. "There was more to have than just firsts; you could have seconds," she chuckles. Even the dishes were special. "We had Melmac for every day, but it was sort of I guess like a better grade of Melmac or something when I was younger. When I got a little older, my brothers began to buy china for my family, because my father always said he wanted to be able to hear the clink of the plate with a fork. So we had a special set of dishes, but they weren't blessed or anything. It was just that they were for special occasions. I remember we always had the linens on the table for our Sunday meals, and those were Irish linens. They were pressed and starched. We [each] had our own linen napkin."

Not surprisingly, food was an important part of Sundays for Jess Hartley, too. His Sunday dinner was usually fried chicken, eaten at church. "We'd always have chicken. Mama would usually cook two meats on Sunday. She'd have chicken and then she'd either have beef or pork, but it was almost always fried chicken. Everybody loved her fried chicken, so we'd get to church and everybody's spread would be out and we'd go wherever we wanted. We'd have our own family, we'd be sitting there with our family and we'd be getting what we wanted, but cousins, aunts, uncles, anybody, could come over and we could go over there too."

Eating went hand in hand with godliness, so much so that most congregations also encouraged their members to eat together. The people we talked with remember having fellow congregants over for Sunday dinner and sometimes eating lunch at church, like Jess Hartley's family did routinely. Their fondest memories, however, are of the church picnics.

One of the best descriptions of church picnics is given by Alan Threadwell. "The highlight of the summer," is how he describes it. It still conjures up fond memories for him. "We would go to a grove. One of our families owned a farm out there. It was not a heavy-duty farm in terms of heavy harvest, but they had orchards and did some light cultivation. They had a pond. And we would go out there on a Sunday afternoon, typically in July, and they would sell hot dogs and hamburgers and stuffed cabbage — cabbage with beef and rice inside of it.

"They would have cake, and there would be beer on tap for the men. Some who enjoyed a good amount of it would go to sleep under the trees. Kids would play games. It was a big, wide expanse. You could go swimming. And I can recall my father would give us a big roll of tickets. They were five-cent tickets, and you could buy birch beer, all the hot dogs and things you wanted. You came home and you were sunburned and tired. The church picnic was a real highlight for kids! No question about it."

Another man has vivid memories of the picnics at his church because the custom when he was growing up was to have one a week during the twelve weeks of summer. "At our church we'd have the typical races, games, three-legged races, games for the kids, softball games, horseshoes, quoits, bobbing-for-apple-type things, a lot of games, a lot of activities, the cakewalks. Everybody would bring something to eat. Then they always had concession stands with food which was very cheap. It was basically a donation. A lot of barbecues, chicken barbecue. Chicken barbecue sandwiches, which doesn't have any barbecue sauce on it. That was very big. Corn on the cob, pies, a lot of pies. Just a lot of good fun, a lot of good food, and then a band concert."

Onward, Christian Soldiers

Besides the bells and windows, the special clothes, the weekly feasts, and the picnics, most people who were raised religiously remember going to Sunday school. Doing so was often quite unpleasant, as we shall see, but for some, Sunday school was also a fond experience.[4]

What stand out most are the group activities. "Theology, knowledge?" asks Alan Threadwell rhetorically. "Naw, it was all action!" His most vivid memories are of singing and marching. "My favorite was 'Onward, Christian Soldiers' because we would all line up and march around in big circles."[5]

Elaine Margolis was not a musician, but she also enjoyed singing as a child, because the music allowed her to express herself rather than just think about God in intellectual terms. She is especially fond of the choruses she learned in the Cherub's Choir, as it was called: "Jesus loves me, this I know, for the Bible tells me so. Little ones to him belong, they are weak but he is strong." And: "Savior, like a shepherd lead us, much we need thy tender care." Those songs made her feel at home with God. And others, like "Jacob's Ladder" and "Michael, Row Your Boat Ashore," were just fun to sing.

Bible stories filled with action were also favorites. When asked which stories they liked best, most people select Noah's ark, Moses crossing the

Red Sea, and Daniel in the lion's den. In addition to the stories themselves, people remember the pictures, the flannel-graph lessons, and the
coloring books. "Typically it was a beautiful painting of a biblical scene,"
one person observes.[6]

Sunday school sparked children's imagination because it gave them an
opportunity to do what grown-ups did, only in their own way. As a child,
Mary Shannon and her three best friends learned how to celebrate the
mass. "You know the candy Necco Wafers?" she asks. "I think a lot of Catholic children used those. Those were hosts. So we used to play the mass,
and imagine the girls' being the priests, which, you know, was a no-no."

Jess Hartley remembers sitting beside his best friend, Johnnie Chumb,
whispering to each other, and passing the time eating half-melted chocolate candy they'd smuggled in when their parents weren't looking. He also
remembers the time his Sunday school class lined up at the front of the
church to show the adults what they'd been learning: when the teacher
asked, "Now who can tell me who Jeremiah was?" one of the little girls
waved her hand and said, "I know, I know, Jeremiah was a bullfrog!"

Especially for younger children, Sunday school was generally more interesting than the formal worship services. In the best cases, Sunday
school was taught by someone's mother or by the pastor's wife. Unlike the
clergy, who spoke over the children's heads, these women spent long
hours finding ways to make the lessons interesting. Delmer Schwartz, a
man in his early fifties who was raised in a rural Congregational church
in New England, reports that his favorite Sunday school teacher was the
pastor's wife, an older woman who loved children. "We really liked her,
and the parents liked her, too," he says with a hint of nostalgia in his voice.
"She did a good job of keeping the children interested. She was a tremendous Bible teacher." He also remembers that she gave the children "Sunday pics"—pictures with Bible stories printed on the back. "Most of us
didn't understand the preacher," he laughs, "so we spent most of the service looking at these stories."

The Boredom of It All

The reasons some people enjoyed Sunday school become clearer from listening to people who went but who did not enjoy being there. These

people, too, were raised religious, but their experience was quite different. One woman who was raised Catholic recalls, "I was sent to Sunday School, and that was it, because those were the rules. You had to go to Sunday School to receive the Catholic sacraments, which are baptism, first communion, confirmation, and extreme unction. To receive those, you have to go to Sunday school."

Another reason people found going to Sunday school less than fulfilling had to do with changes in the wider culture. By the 1950s, kindergartens had been established in most schools, children were being encouraged to read even before they started school, some were attending nursery schools, and public elementary schools were shifting from eight-month to nine-month calendars and becoming more academically rigorous, all of which had mixed implications for children's experiences in Sunday school. On the one hand, Sunday schools that aspired to the same standards as Monday-through-Friday schools left children feeling like they needed a break. On the other hand, Sunday schools that focused on crafts and simple activities often struck children as boring, if not "rinky dink."[7]

One woman remembers especially how boring Sunday school was. "It was very, very boring. There were these standard books that you would be given. These little workbooks, or you'd be given these sheets to color in the picture of Jesus. There was nothing really challenging about it. It was kind of like all the kids sitting around a table, waiting for the hour to be over, while the teacher went through this kind of rote exercise."

Karen Stacy, a Southern Methodist, also remembers Sunday school as sheer drudgery. "There were no breaks from this—I mean, Sunday school, all summer, all winter. We were dragged to church and to Sunday school for God knows how many years."

It is surprising that anyone with memories like this continues to attend religious services. The reason people do, it appears, is that their memories, while full of drudgery, also suggest the pride of accomplishment that comes with having survived years of practicing the piano or an ordeal in the desert. Attending religious services instilled habits and a sense that religion is not all fun and games. Children learned that going to services was part of family life and a way of participating in something that they did not yet understand but that their parents or grandparents took seriously.

Going to Sunday school was also an opportunity for some children to learn leadership skills, which I will talk more about later. On the whole, however, being sent to Sunday school was not a very powerful indication to children that they were being raised in a deeply religious family. In a national study, Bible reading and table grace emerged as activities that were strongly associated with saying that religion was very important in one's family during childhood, whereas being sent to Sunday school was neither positively nor negatively associated with this perception of one's family.[8] Other findings in this study suggest that the reason Sunday school made such little difference to one's perceptions is probably that many parents were not themselves involved in going to Sunday school. Also, many more parents sent their children to Sunday school than read the Bible at home.

Even if Sunday school was inconsequential, it nevertheless made an impression on those who became most deeply immersed in it. William Blake once wrote, "You never know what is enough unless you know what is more than enough."[9] When Sunday school was more than enough, it at least helped define what was enough.

Impressions of the Clergy

Maya Angelou has given an unforgettable image of her childhood views of the clergy. Of her pastor, Reverend Thomas, she writes, "I hated him unreservedly. He was ugly, fat, and he laughed like a hog with the colic. The fact that he never bothered to remember our names was insulting, but neither was that slight, alone, enough to make us despise him. But the crime that tipped the scale and made our hate not only just but imperative was his actions at the dinner table. He ate the biggest, brownest and best parts of the chicken at every Sunday meal."[10]

Most of the people we talked with are unable to dredge up such powerful memories. They may have loved the fried chicken or even the stained glass windows and hated going to Sunday school, but most people have virtually no compelling childhood memories of the clergy. Except in rare instances when the clergy was someone's father or uncle or a family friend, children seem to have had scarcely any meaningful encounters with the clergy. Nevertheless, they were aware of the clergy's existence, and this awareness was an important part of their upbringing. If nothing else, they viewed the clergy as a distant, high source of authority who exemplified the distance, height, and authority of God.

For some of the people we talked with, the ambiance of the church itself was also their clearest childhood indication of clergy authority. As much as what the pastor said, it was where he said it that made it special. For example, a man who attended a Methodist church as a child remembers that the front of the church was a very special place. "You had on the left the choir pews and the organist. Then next to that you had a large chair for the pastor to sit on when he's reading the Scriptures. Then there's another large chair on the right that he sat on when he's getting ready to preach the sermon. Then he had the pulpit in the middle, and there's a little baptistery in front of that. Then there was a large Bible that was on a large wooden table. That was in front of the pulpit.

"I always used to revere just the setting of the Bible and the pastor's large chair with the red velvet on it and coming to the pulpit, just that general area. I remember it vividly and always respected it." He explains why the front area seemed so special: "I just had a sense that when you were there, you were anointed of God. You didn't go up there in our church unless you were invited. We did not have altar calls. We did not have the freedom of approaching that altar. It was not the same as being off-limits. It wasn't that it was off-limits, it was just that you didn't go up there. You just respected it. That was the pastor's domain. You just felt that if somebody was up there, something special was going to happen." This man also remembers that the pastor was a young man, about thirty, who was friendly and fun to be with when he led the youth group. But when he was in the pulpit, he seemed to become a different person.

For other people, the clergy were generally distant figures, remembered far less vividly than buildings, friends, parties, and teachers. In some instances people remember actually disliking the clergy as children, perhaps because of a reprimand that offended them or their parents. Nevertheless, the memories that people do have of clergy are mainly respectful. Clergy were viewed as people who knew and understood God, who often spoke for or symbolized God, and who commanded respect by virtue of their office, skills, and personality.

"He spoke well and he was respected," notes one person. "I could see the impact that he had on people when he preached, either making them uncomfortable or the intensity with which they watched him. I didn't fully comprehend what he was saying, but then it became obvious that he had a knack for using words. He was a master of words."

In contrast to these memories of authority, knowledge, or homiletic skills, the ones that actually brim with admiration are memories of clergy who had actually done something to live out their faith. For example, the person in our interviews who had the greatest respect for her pastor is a young woman who had grown up in a Presbyterian church. The reason she respected him was that he had actually lived his faith in a dramatic way, rather than simply talking about it.

She remembers hearing the story of how he gave a ride to a hitchhiker one night. The pastor knew it was dangerous to do so but decided he should "do the Christian thing." Before they had driven more than a few blocks, the man pulled out a gun and directed the pastor to pull into an alley. The pastor thought about his wife and children, prayed silently for his own safety, and tried to make conversation with the man in order to prevent him from doing something rash. As they talked, the man revealed that he had once been a Christian, but had become involved in drugs and was now in desperate need of money in order to get his car fixed. "I'd have been so scared, I wouldn't have known what to do," the woman says. "But by the time it was over, the man took some money and left peacefully. He told the pastor nobody else had ever come out of that alley alive. I think it was just an incredible act of faith for [the pastor] to trust in God in a situation like that."

Thee and Thou

On the whole, church services were most meaningful because they were closely integrated with the religious practices of families, especially in such tangible ways as the preparations one made on Saturdays or the meals one consumed after the service. There was, nevertheless, an important dimension to the church service that was not present in most homes. Indeed, religious services complemented what children learned in their families.

The God to whom children prayed at home was often an intimate, watchful, loving God who cared about them personally, much like their parents did. The God they learned about at church or synagogue was a more formal, dignified, public being who coveted respect and who inspired awe, even fear, but who also impressed one with an all-encompassing sense of power and wonder.[11] The former could be approached in pajamas; the latter required dress clothes. The one could hear people when they were alone, huddled in their beds during a lighting storm or selfishly asking for a new toy; the other listened only if many people came together and said words that had been in use for many years.[12]

Because the stories one learned were the same in both places, and because family members were also present at formal services, the two perspectives could be recognized as addressing the same God. Yet it was important that a balance was struck between the two. When children saw only the formal God, they felt distant from and afraid of that God, but when they conceived of God only as their invisible friend, they lost sight of the divine authority of that God.[13]

A man who grew up in a Catholic parish in New Jersey during the 1950s illustrates the side of God that came through most clearly during formal services. His parents attended mass every Sunday and often went to a Friday service as well. His father often served as a lay reader, and he saw both his parents praying during the mass or during the two-hour rosary services on Fridays but never heard or saw them pray at home and did not hear them express their personal views about God. Virtually his entire understanding of God was thus governed by what he learned at church, and he admits that he was more afraid of God than anything else.

It is especially revealing to see how this man describes his childhood understanding of prayer: "I don't think you prayed *about* anything. Prayer was something that you learned and you recited. You would say the Lord's Prayer, you'd say the Hail Mary, you'd say the Apostle's Creed, you'd say the Act of Contrition. When I thought of praying, it was these prayers. Maybe my parents thought of it differently, but they never talked about it. I never thought of praying as a communication with God, where you would speak to God or talk to Him, except in these very formal ways that you were taught." He muses, "It's funny, but prayer was a very formal conversation with God, as it were. You were given the words to say in particular circumstances, and you said those words. You didn't improvise. It wasn't a free-flowing conversation. You spoke in one way and that was it. To pray for something and to ask for something, you just didn't do it." It was only later in his life that he learned how to pray informally and thus came to feel a closer and more personal bond with God.

The opposite tendency—thinking of God only in intimate terms—is most evident among younger people who attended evangelical Protestant or charismatic services. Their churches insisted on using family imagery as frequently as possible, as if to make a political statement in favor of family values, and their view of God was that of a good buddy, perhaps the intimate father they never had or the close friend they wished they had known as a child.

In these churches, people sang songs about their personal relationship with Jesus and eschewed formalized prayers in favor of spontaneous petitions so personal that they would have embarrassed people in formal settings at most times in the past. These people were often worshipful, thanking God warmly for the personal blessings they had received, much like they might thank their mothers for baking cookies, but they sometimes had little sense of God as a formal or austere being whose essence was fundamentally different from that of even an idealized parent or friend.

In contrast, when there was a mixture of formality during weekly services and informality during prayer and conversations about God at home, people grew up sensing both the transcendence and the immanence of God. In this respect, formal services functioned well by virtue of their very formality. Mary Shannon summarizes this idea well. As we have seen, she experienced the more intimate side of God because of the way she was raised at home. Church thus provided a necessary balance. "I think the value of going to mass was to worship God. That's what my mom and dad always expressed to us, that we went to worship God for what he had given us, and that the way in which we did it was to go to church." She elaborates, "As a child, mass doesn't mean a whole lot to you, but there was a religiousness, a sanctity to being in church and being a part of that mass, even though a lot of times I didn't understand what was going on."

-+->-<+-

CHAPTER 5

The Ties That Bind

IN 1936, a young housewife in the Bronx went to see the film *These Three*, produced by William Wyler and written by playwright Lillian Hellman. Pregnant with her first child, the woman was so taken by the film she decided that if the baby was a girl she would name her after the playwright. A few days later, she returned to the theater to look at the marquee and copy down the playwright's name. As she was to learn much later, the last letter of the playwright's name was hidden by another sign. Thus, her daughter came to be known as Lillia.

Lillia's People

A vivacious, petite, second-generation Italian American with short black hair and large brown eyes, Lillia Rizzo has deep roots in the Catholic church. As a child, she attended Saint Ann's church every week, went to the nearby Catholic school, and regularly visited her grandparents and the numerous aunts, uncles, and cousins who lived in the same parish. She has relatively few childhood memories of her father, because he worked two jobs—as a chef during the day and as a bartender in the evening—to support the family. But she was close to her mother and to her godmother, an aunt who lived a few doors away. They were strict with her, but she also feels they showed her a great deal of unconditional love.

Feeling loved was also the main sensation she experienced at church.

Indeed, her story is a powerful illustration that going to religious services is most meaningful and memorable when the congregation functions as a community that is more than a set of people who attend services together, when it is a neighborhood, a place to celebrate and to mourn, a cacophony of voices, and a medley of sights and sounds.

As we've seen, attending services was meaningful for people who grew up religious for reasons that generally had little to do with the content of those services, as least as homileticists and liturgists have understood them. People absorbed their understanding of the sacred from staring at stained glass windows, from realizing that the altar was elevated and on one side of the church or the other, from picking garnets out of the church walls, from singing "Onward, Christian Soldiers," and from eating fried chicken.

These activities all point to the importance of community in congregations but fail to give an adequate sense of how social relationships create that feeling of community.[1] The examples that follow help us understand more clearly that community is seldom limited to the congregation itself (at least when it is most effective), that it depends on both formal and informal activities, and that it requires occasions for celebrating and grieving.[2]

When Lillia Rizzo was a girl, going to church was a positive experience because it was interwoven so closely with her extended family. Typically, she would spend Saturday nights with an aunt and uncle who lived two blocks away, having a sleepover with three female cousins about her own age, and then going to church with them the next morning. These Saturday evenings gave her something to look forward to each week. "It was like party night," she recalls.

"My uncle would cook a big meal, and they'd buy a case of soda pop, and some of our other cousins would come over, and we'd all sit around and talk and watch *Hit Parade*." After church on Sunday, the families usually ate lunch together, then went to visit their grandfather, and from there visited several of the other aunts and uncles. Lillia remembers these visits fondly because someone usually gave her a penny so she could go to the candy store on the way home.

Lillia's parents did not go to church every Sunday. Her father's work schedule kept him from doing so, and her mother devoted many Sundays to caring for an elderly relative who was ill. But generally they made it to mass once or twice a month, and they communicated to Lillia that they went because they really wanted to be there, not because it was customary.

Of her mother Lillia says, "I really believe my mother was the type that when she went to mass, she wanted to go. She wanted to pray. She wanted to be there. I think that was one of the things she instilled [in me] is the wanting to do things in life rather than the having to." The reason Lillia thought her mother wanted to pray was that she so often heard her mother praying at home. "She might be standing at the kitchen sink, angry about something, and I'd hear her talking to God about it." Lillia came, therefore, to think of God as a confidante.

In retrospect, Lillia realizes that virtually all the people she knew growing up were ones who lived in her neighborhood and whom she met by attending the same church they did. "People were very much into their parish," she says. It was an area composed of three-story row houses on tree-lined streets, with corner grocery stores, barber shops, tailors, and restaurants mixed in with the houses. Friends' and relatives' homes, the church, and school were all within walking distance, or there was a trolley if one wished to ride. "You generally met people in church and at the church school or went to a birthday party with them or got together on Halloween."

If church was an extension of her family, it was also a way to bring the sacred visibly into the presence of her family. Lillia kept a font of holy water inside her bedroom; she'd bring the water home with her from church. She also had a small statue of Mary on her dresser, and when the church paid special attention to Mary each May, Lillia would light a votive candle or put some flowers beside the statue. May and October were months when families were also expected to gather at the church for mass each weekday before the children's school day began. Even though Lillia's father had to work, most religious holidays were also special occasions. For instance, on Christmas he always put up a large tree and surrounded it with a toy village he'd made by hand, and on Easter he cooked huge plates of ravioli with leg of lamb and Lillia's mother baked special cookies.

For as long as she can remember, Lillia was steeped in Italian traditions, including religious observances, food, and the language her parents and grandparents still spoke, but she was also aware of cultural diversity and was able to embrace it. At the Catholic school, there were African American Protestants, Polish and Irish Catholics, and some Asian Americans. After school, the children played together: "We never questioned the differences; it was just children playing together." Lillia credits her mother with giving her a broader appreciation of cultural diversity. Although the family was intensely Italian and Catholic, the neighborhood was a mixture of Italians, African Americans, and other European Americans.

As a child, Lillia saw her mother going to church and praying the rosary, but her mother also told her that non-Catholics could be good people, too. "She would always say, 'You know, there is only one God in heaven and he's the God of all people.' And as I say, because of our living in neighborhoods where it was mixed races and also naturally mixed religions, that she would try to teach us to understand that we were all children of God. She would go beyond the traditional and say, 'Yes, it's good to go to church, it's good to say your rosary and so forth, but I want you to know that there is this wonderful universal God out there for everyone.'"

In Lillia's case it was clearly the people that made going to church meaningful. They were part of her life, not just people who happened to be at the same services on Sundays. The congregation was scarcely distinguishable from her family and neighborhood. Yet, growing up in that highly localized setting, she also learned to understand God in ways that included other people.

Men and Women with Accents

Although Jewish services were quite different from Catholic ones, what children remembered in these settings was often similar: the familiar sights, sounds, and smells of the house of worship itself, and the people. Ezra Feldman, the man whose grandparents lived upstairs while he was growing up, offers a vivid illustration of why such experiences are memorable. In his case, the sights, sounds, smells, *and* the people blended easily together. When there was richly textured interaction, he thought services were great, and when social distance held him at arm's length, he quickly became disillusioned.

One of the things Ezra liked best about his Grandpa Upstairs was that Grandpa often took him along for Saturday afternoon discussions in the back room after the service. "Most of the people I remember being there were older people, of my grandfather's generation," he says. "Men with accents and women with accents. And in the back room, people ate herring and French bread and drank whiskey. I didn't, because I was a kid. I ate herring and French bread, but somehow I never got around to drinking whiskey. There would be these great wide-ranging discussions, which usually started with a Torah portion but would end up talking about everything else. I remember always liking that, always being interested in it. There was something about that I found compelling. I really enjoyed it."

The other services Ezra enjoyed were ones he attended with his cousins, whom he describes as "Reform in spirit, but Orthodox in practice." One of the places he attended with his cousins was a rather formal synagogue with a European atmosphere. The one he liked better was "kind of a made-over store front; we used to call it Rabbi Isnik's joint." He remembers that the men and women were separate and that people sat at long tables instead of in pews. "Everybody would have several commentaries. Somebody would be reading the Torah and everybody else would be arguing commentary. Everybody would be talking at once. I really loved that kind of environment. Everybody knew what was going on and everybody was comfortable with it and they just fit in where it was good for them."

His experience is much like that of Hal Meyerson, who also speaks fondly of the heated discussions that took place in the synagogue. Hal Meyerson legitimately mourns the loss of this community because it was much more than a weekly service.

One Big Family

"Oh yes, I can tell you a few things about community," says Irene Petrowski, a German Lutheran who grew up in Milwaukee, just prior to World War I. Her parents had immigrated a few years before she was born, settling in Milwaukee to work in the brewery. They lived in a tenement building with fifteen other families. Virtually everyone they knew was German and almost all their neighbors went to the same church, which was about six blocks away. Irene's earliest memories are of falling asleep during the service.

She had good reason to fall asleep. The services typically lasted two hours. She remembers clearly that it was the custom to sing four hymns at the start of the service, each of which had twelve or thirteen verses. Then there would be a lengthy sermon. This was followed by everyone's going forward to the altar to take the bread and wine, and as people left the altar, they'd file past the offering basket and put in their nickels and dimes. Sitting there beside her mother (the men and boys sat separately), Irene knew she was not supposed to sleep. But the picture behind the altar of Jesus holding Peter's hand to keep him from drowning had a kind of hypnotic effect. Irene imagined herself floating like Peter—but on clouds instead of water—as she drifted into a haze of contentment.

In one sense, it is hard to imagine why Irene has fond memories of her religious upbringing. In addition to the two-hour service on Sunday mornings there was one equally long on Sunday evenings. Two evenings a week she attended Sunday school classes. These always lasted three hours, and as she grew older, a third evening was added. These classes consisted largely of memory work. Starting at age five, children were expected to learn Bible verses in German. Irene says she was probably fourteen before she realized that God spoke other languages besides German. She always prayed in German and repeated Bible verses to herself in German.

The children were also expected to memorize the more commonly used hymns—all twelve or thirteen verses of them—and to memorize the answers to catechism questions. When Irene was eleven, her preparation for confirmation began, culminating three years later. The reason it took so long was that each child was expected to learn the answers to all 590 questions in the catechism. "I'll never forget it," she says. "I guess there were about fifteen of us, and I was the tallest in the class. It was a long service, all in German. We sat in front of the altar on wooden chairs and the pastor would ask us questions and we would raise our hands and answer. Some of them were just recitation of Bible passages, some of them were answers to specific theological questions. I would say it was very thorough." Three quarters of a century later, she can assert: "I certainly know what my church stands for. I think like a Lutheran!"

The church also provided clear expectations of how its young people were to behave. "We were almost like the Puritans," she muses. One of the practices that seemed harsh to her even as a child was the rule that every girl had to be married in the church. Anyone who eloped, married outside the faith, had a wedding performed by a justice of the peace, or, God forbid, became pregnant out of wedlock was automatically excluded from membership. If they wished to be reinstated, they had to "stand before the congregation and beg forgiveness." When motion pictures became available, they were prohibited. Dancing was also taboo.

But Irene insists that going to church was the high point of her life. She not only followed its rules and learned her verses, but she also looked forward to being at church. One reason was that she got to dress up. With six children, the family seldom had new clothes, and their better garments were carefully reserved for special occasions. Going to church was the only time Irene was permitted to wear her best dress. She remembers her favorite. "My mother did housecleaning for people, and one day she brought home an old coat someone had given her. It had a black satin lining. My mother ripped out this lining and made me a satin dress which I thought was glorious. I had a pair of high-top shoes to go with it. I felt absolutely elegant."

The more important reason Irene liked attending church was, as she puts it, "the closeness of the people." It was "one big family," quite literally. In addition to her parents and siblings, three of Irene's aunts and uncles (with their families) attended the church. Many of the families (there were about a hundred members, including the children) were related by marriage. All of them, moreover, had come from the same three villages in Prussia.

Being a family meant eating and playing together as well as worshipping together. At least once every summer, the whole congregation got together in the park for a picnic. "We'd have fried chicken and potato salad, coleslaw, cucumber salad, and then of course all the ethnic pastries and fruits. You ate yourself sick at the picnic. It was a wonderful time and they'd start about eight o'clock in the morning and they would go until dark."[3] About once a month the church gathered for a party or fund-raiser. Typical fare included stuffed cabbage and noodles, followed by a play put on by the young people. After Sunday morning services and on holidays, people from the church ate elaborate meals together. And Irene's favorite gatherings were the ones that followed Sunday evening services. "We'd go to someone's home and there would be a pot of coffee and there would be cake and we'd sit and play cards or chess or whatever there was. The old player piano with the rolls, we'd put those in and we'd sing all these crazy songs together," she recalls.

Nothing dominated these events like the innuendo of boy-girl relationships. Knowing they were expected to date and mate among their own kind, children learned early to think of church as the wellspring of romance. Seating men and women on opposite sides did more to dramatize the dance of the sexes than it did to keep them apart. As soon as they could persuade their parents to let them, boys sat on one side balcony and girls occupied the opposite balcony. Irene remembers learning the fine art of "making eyes" across this expanse. As children grew older, the Sunday evening gatherings also took on greater significance. "That was how young people got to know each other," she explains. "It was a source of romances. People married and had stable marriages because the parents knew each other and because the couple had known each other for a long time."

As it had in German villages, the church also functioned as the geographic center of the community. All the members lived within a ten-block radius and walked to church. The church bells thus played an important role in reminding neighbors of their common identity. Irene recounts the code. Exactly one hour before the service, one bell was rung several times to let people know that it was time to start dressing for church. Then on the half hour, two bells were rung alternatively to announce that it was time to start walking to church. And a half hour later, all three bells were rung to indicate the beginning of the service. The bells warned people not to start out too early or too late. It was usually some of the men who started too early, Irene remembers. "They'd stop at the pub and you could smell whiskey on their breath."

Unlike congregations a few decades later, Irene's church was also a community in an economic sense. Members supported it financially, putting their nickels and dimes in the basket after taking communion. Irene and her friends could tell by the way the coins hit the metal bottom on the basket whether they were nickels or dimes, and they could tell when people put in paper money or nothing at all. If she knew the difference, she figures everyone else did too. In addition to these "voluntary" contributions, each family in the parish paid monthly dues. "They would come with a little book and every family's name was in this book," she recalls. "Two men would come, they would be the elders of the church and they would come every month to collect the dues, which were fifty cents for the whole family."

Congregation and Community

If people look back most fondly on their sense of community, this is also the one aspect of religious life that many feel has been lost. Congregations may still be thriving as places to worship, but community is thought to be lacking because people move around more, don't have the time or interest to spend long evenings and weekends at their places of worship, don't know people in their congregations or neighborhoods as well, and seek entertainment elsewhere. A woman who had grown up in a Welsh American congregation remembers longingly how much community there was among the women: "The women's fellowship would make these meat pies with potatoes and onions and meat, and they must have sold them for a dollar or two dollars. I used to go often with my mom when I was very little when she would help, and all the women would gather in the church and they would make these pastries all day and the smell was absolutely out of this world. There was a real sense of community there, too. I mean, church was, when I was growing up, community. I don't find that anymore."[4]

But what was it about "community," this greatly overused word, that was most important to people who grew up in congregations? Part of it, of course, was that people actually cared for one another and helped one another. People remember their mother's baking casseroles for someone in the church whose husband or wife had died, visiting those who were sick, calling on expectant mothers during their time of confinement, giving friends rides to work, helping care for a neighbor's children.

As Irene Petrowski's remarks suggest, congregations sometimes provided financial assistance to their members as well, but economic transactions were generally shrouded in the same secrecy that covered nearly all deeply personal topics. Alan Threadwell's father, however, told him enough about the economic problems of people in their congregation that he came early to have some understanding of what the churches did.

He recalls: "Lots of churches here started not because of high degrees of spirituality. They started for pragmatic considerations. Prior to the formation of many parishes, they formed what were called 'beneficial societies.' These were insurance companies, life insurance, or sickness and health. What is forgotten about early ages of capitalism is it was terribly exploitative, and labor was regarded as a disposable commodity. The steel mill is a dangerous place to work, and the management was not enlightened.

"So people formed these beneficial societies. Slovaks called them the 'Jednota.' It was a lodge where the people paid their dues and then the beneficiaries—the widows or the sick—would receive. It was an economic incentive. My father always had a saying, 'If somebody says to you, "It isn't the money, it's the principle of the thing," you can be sure it's the money.' And I suppose that this economic need even exceeded their need for spirituality!"

Apart from economic transactions, congregations also fostered a norm of equality that gave a sense of neighborliness, even though there may have been acute differences in actual wealth and social standing. For example, a retired automobile mechanic from a rural community in the South (a white man) remembers that African Americans lived on the other side of town in very humble quarters and that during World War II some German prisoners were deployed to the area to help pick fruit. He also names people who were bankers and lawyers and others who were sharecroppers and day laborers. Yet he says that his parents insisted on treating everyone the same. "My father had this very strong belief that everybody was equal and should be treated that way." The man himself has internalized that belief. He asserts that it makes him just as happy to see a neighbor get a new car as to get one himself, and realizing how such a view must sound to an outsider, he adds, "I hope that doesn't sound like I'm boasting, because I'm not. That's just the way I feel."

More important than its economic functions, the congregation was a physical gathering place, and as such it was well integrated into the surrounding neighborhoods in which people lived. Churches in rural communities typically functioned as a center of gravity for the people who lived there. An older man who grew up in a Brethren church in Virginia repeatedly uses the phrase "center of the community" to describe his church. In retrospect, he thinks people spent so much of their time at the church because there was little else to do. Few of the members had ever been more than a hundred miles from home. Their world was, quite literally, the people they knew at church, and it would have been strange not to get acquainted with someone in the community. Now he has people three houses away he's never met.

An older woman from a farming community also observes, "In those days attendance at church on Sundays was important socially. They were all out on the farms, cut off really. Not too much in the way of transportation. So it was important to them to be there on Sundays to see people."

Our interviews with other older people also confirm what historians have suggested about the relationship between churches and immigration: congregations were the place where immigrants went to socialize. A woman of Norwegian descent who was a teenager in Brooklyn in the early 1920s remembers distinctly how exciting it was to go to church, even though it was some distance from her home. Immigrants from Norway were flooding into the city, so rapidly in fact that the church was constantly engaged in new construction. At one point, the Sunday school program had about two hundred children, and only a few years later the number had grown to nine hundred! This woman met her future husband at church when she was fourteen. Three years later they were married.

If there was a seamless web connecting the congregation with the wider community, the congregation nevertheless distinguished itself, sometimes by erecting high walls between itself and other congregations, and often by making it difficult enough to join that people valued the opportunity to become members. Sometimes the distinctions could not be escaped, as we see in Hal Meyerson's case. Being the chosen people, he says, came out in numerous ways: "Whenever we would go out and somebody in a group, you know, ordered the great American cheeseburger? Jewish kids didn't order cheeseburgers. We ordered black-and-white milkshakes or tuna fish sandwiches, because all fish is kosher, not all meat is kosher. You don't have to kill a tuna fish any specific way to make it a kosher tuna fish."

Among people of all ages, becoming an official member of the congregation was sometimes an insignificant occasion that meant little in retrospect. Yet, for some, it was of extraordinary importance. It was so because joining was not easy. People had to study, pass an examination, appear before the congregation's leaders, and then commemorate their joining in a solemn ritual. A woman who had joined a Protestant church in 1922 remembers, "We had to study and know whatever lessons we were given. We really had to know everything by heart, Bible verses and all. So you were drilled into it, really." Then, on the day she joined, all the girls wore white dresses, and the boys wore suits and bow ties. "You had to meet with the elders and you had to be a Bible-believing Christian to belong to that church," she explains. "So it was serious, it wasn't just happenstance."

Making a congregation function effectively in all these ways required a lot of work. For example, the new suburban developments that sprang up during the 1950s and 1960s were often described in the media as anonymous places in which people did not know their neighbors and felt isolated, and certainly these neighborhoods did not have the old churches and established rituals of rural villages or older ethnic communities. Yet it was common for people to devote enormous energy to creating new congregations.

A woman who was a young housewife in the original Levittown, on Long Island, in the 1950s, for example, remembers how she already knew people there from a previous church she had attended, and how they set about developing a new congregation. "We knew so many people there, and it was friends," she says. "We really had lots of friends there, and we were all interested in getting a church started there. We had a lot of fellowship and good times building that church. It was all volunteer. We really all worked together."

More generally, effective congregations depended on intense organizational efforts, just as other subcultures do. People felt part of their congregation because of the warm, familial experiences generated there, but few of these experiences happened without behind-the-scenes activities. Especially for young people, having a full menu of activities available to participate in was a significant reason for staying involved.

Karen Stacy illustrates the importance of these organized activities as she talks about her experiences as a girl in the Methodist church. "I always went to church, always went to Sunday school, went to vacation Bible school, sang in the choir," she repeats. Starting in junior high, and then especially in high school, she began to find a wider set of activities. "I was an absolute regular at MYF, the Methodist Youth Fellowship. This church I went to was a huge operation. I mean, it had two separate free-standing education buildings, along with the church, and one of them was the youth building. It had a lounge; it had a big gathering area; it had a kitchen; and it had six classrooms, or something like that. And it had a gym upstairs.

"I would go there, sometimes, after school to hang out, which was seen as a safe thing to do. I played on our basketball team for a couple of years when I was in high school. And we played other little Methodist churches, and always got roundly slaughtered by them because we had no idea what we were doing. I ran for president of the MYF one year, and lost. I wrote for the newsletter. We would do retreats. We would take trips. The first time I went to New York City, actually, was with this Methodist youth group. It was called a UN seminar. We went to the UN, and somebody came up and talked to us for a couple of days."

Karen also became actively involved in church politics when she was in high school. "I became a member of the National United Methodist Council on Youth Ministry," she recalls. "This was not an election, it was an appointed thing. I went to a General Convention where we were trying to get something passed. We were fighting with some bureaucrats. So I met a bunch of employees of the national church. There were kids from all over the country. And that was really exciting for me." Looking back on it, Karen says the church was "pretty central" to her life in those years.

In contrast to a highly organized experience like this, it is interesting to consider what happened to young people who were sent to church unsu-pervised and thus were able to experiment with a side of life their parents little expected. For example, one woman recalls how shocked she was to discover at her junior high youth group that other girls were sneaking out back of the church to drink beer and smoke cigarettes.

Another woman lived in a remote, mountainous region of New Mex-ico and was sent with a male companion some distance on Sundays to at-tend church in the valley. On the way, she remembers, the two of them often stopped at an Indian village along the road where the people were smoking something that tasted like tobacco. Only later did she learn that they were smoking dried cow dung. "I have smoked quite a bit of cow dung," she admits. "That was my religious experience in the first two years of high school."

When Community Is Lacking

Although people remember the activities and the physical space in which they attended services, it is the sense of *belonging* that clearly matters most. They look back with fondness at the cousins and best friends with whom they attended services, at the fact that church or synagogue was where they saw members of their extended family, and at teachers who made them feel special. When this sense of community is lacking, people who have nevertheless attended regularly still feel in retrospect that religion was difficult to understand and was somehow removed from the rest of their life.

A man named Peter Arno speaks with particular eloquence about the consequences of not being sufficiently integrated into a religious community. He grew up in an Italian neighborhood in Chicago during the 1960s and, until college, went to mass every Sunday and celebrated all the religious holidays. Nevertheless, he did not experience a sense of community at the church his family attended. "I never really became involved as a young person in the church community," he admits. "There really wasn't much of a church community."

When asked to elaborate, he says, "It was more a kind of place where you came, where you went to church on Sundays and left. There wasn't a lot of socializing that seemed to be connected with the church. It was basically a place you went on Sunday or on holy days and you left." When he went away to college, he did find a church that gave him a better sense of community, so the church of his childhood seems all the more lacking to him in retrospect.

Catholicism thus seemed to be an external reality, rather than something to which he belonged. His choice of words is revealing: instead of saying he grew up Catholic, he says he grew up "with Catholicism." He also says it was hard for him to connect Catholicism with the rest of his life. "When I was growing up with Catholicism," he asserts, "I had a very difficult time integrating the religious aspect of my life into the everyday aspect of my life."

As he has discussed his upbringing with other people, he has decided that he is not atypical in this respect. He thinks men who were raised Catholic are especially prone to compartmentalizing their faith because they were never drawn into the religious community while they were growing up as much as girls were. As a result, they view the church as an institution, but do not integrate religion into the rest of their lives.

Celebrating New Life

A remaining aspect of congregations that must not be neglected is their role in commemorating special events. Too often, it seems, communities have come to be described by social scientists as purely instrumental exchanges of favors or as the performance of badly needed civic duties. Religious leaders have generally known better. The religious calendar has been an established way of celebrating the changing seasons and of reminding people of their common traditions. Christmas, Hanukkah, and Passover are among these rites.

For the people we talked with who had grown up in Protestant or Catholic families, Easter was the most important occasion in the annual cycle of congregational life. Most people knew, even as children, that it was to commemorate Christ's Resurrection. It was also a joyous, sunny time — an occasion for new clothes or flowers or candy.[5]

Vern Gordon remembers it this way: "The flowers and the Easter bonnets. And everybody had their Easter clothes and new spring wardrobe they were wearing. There was no special message, other than I guess Grandfather and Grandmother would talk about Christ died and how he arose on Easter Sunday. Also the Easter eggs. When I was younger, we used to paint those."

Mary Shannon also remembers that Easter was a very special time. It came, of course, at the end of Lent, a time that Mary's family observed by giving up something they would really miss (for Mary, it was often chocolates; for her mother, it was not sitting in her favorite rocker). Easter itself was a time of preparation within the household. "My mom would do the spring cleaning tied into Easter. So the house got cleaned very thoroughly, everything, walls, floors, ceilings. That was always to prepare for Easter Day, for the risen Lord.

"Special foods, too. It probably was ham and potatoes and homemade applesauce. My mom's good at baking, so it was different baked things. It also was the Easter baskets. We would get those to put out. We always did the Easter eggs. It was the only time we ever saw a lot of eggs in our house. My Nanny would always give us eggs at Easter time. She bought a chocolate coconut Easter egg for each of us. So she would come on Easter Day after we would come home from mass, and she'd have dinner with us. Easter was probably the very sacred holiday in our home, and yet happy and joyful, because we did celebrate the Easter bunny. Because there was always somebody little, there was always somebody to keep the Easter bunny alive for. So you had that joy."

Compared with Christmas, Easter was generally more associated with religious services than with family traditions. Nevertheless, what people remember most fondly about Easter was the part involving their families. Only a few remember lilies at church or going to sunrise services, but many treasure the memory of new clothes purchased to wear to church or of Easter baskets and Easter egg hunts. Most just remember that Easter was thus a positive experience, although a few realized there were religious connotations as well. For instance, Elaine Margolis remembers the new Easter outfits her mother bought her, explaining, "We always had something new during that season; it was associated with the Resurrection."

The Norwegian woman I quoted earlier offers another example of the importance of Easter. Thursday evening before Easter, the congregation gathered for communion. Then were was a Good Friday service. People were supposed to be quiet and sad on Saturday, and then Sunday was a very special day. "Sunday was all day, a real Easter. We had concerts. The choir had concerts usually on Easter that were special, and we had beautiful choirs there in that big church. We really celebrated Christ's Resurrection."

People from Russian Orthodox churches had a different tradition. As one describes it, "You have a basket with a special baked bread called paska. That's holy bread. We usually had homemade butter, and salt and kielbasa, and ham and horseradish, horseradish dug out of the ground and shaved. Sometimes it was horseradish mixed with beets, a little vinegar in it. That was separate from the shaved horseradish. Then the basket was taken to church by someone on a Saturday night and blessed. That's a tradition in our church, everybody brings their baskets and it's blessed. Also in that basket was included hard-boiled eggs. Then the next day, you'd have a big feast."

In some traditions, Easter Monday was also a special day. An older man remembers, "On Easter Monday the tradition was for the males to go out and sprinkle the females. We would recite a verse and then the parents of the girls would give us something. It was better than Christmas. In fact, a friend of mine and I, we had a good thing going. He would take me to his friends and I would take him to my friends, and we would end up with all kinds of Easter eggs, chocolates, and money, because a lot of the people were starting to get away from the old language, but we didn't. And when the parents heard us little pip-squeaks recite something in the old language, the tears would start flowing. Boy, they'd go for the wallet. We made out like bandits."

In Jess Hartley's church, Easter was also a memorable occasion. He speaks animatedly: "Easter started out as a regular Sunday from the standpoint of what we did at home. We were up and getting ready to go to church, and everybody getting dressed. However, Easter was all-new clothing. So you had an Easter suit, as we called it, or the girls would have a dress and their bonnets or hats. We'd go to church and everybody was dressed up in their new clothes. Even the excitement of getting the clothes leading up to Easter was just unbelievable. It was the highlight of the year for us. So we would go, we'd buy these clothes and we would get all dressed up and we would go to church. Everybody sort of strutted around, especially at offering time. We walked up to the table for offering. We'd put it in and look around [he laughs] and do a little strut."

He also recalls, "We had an Easter program that was always sponsored by the Sunday School, and we'd have little speeches that we called our Easter piece. For instance, my daughter just did one. Hers was, 'I just stopped by to say Jesus is alive, Happy Easter Day.' So it would be a rhyming type of thing. Depending on how old you were. The younger you were, it was two, three lines. Real little kids, one line. And then, as you grew up, they turned into poems. So by the time you were in ninth or tenth grade, you may have had a three-stanza poem that you memorized."

Other Holy Days

Relatively few Protestants and Catholics mention any holiday besides Easter and Christmas as being a memorable occasion, but one exception is a Lutheran woman whose congregation always celebrated Advent. She says, "It was a Wednesday service about four or five weeks before Christmas, and it was a way of preparing our hearts for the coming of Christ. It was really nice, too, because you got so busy in that time before Christmas, just to push all the other things out of your mind, push out the presents that you're trying to get and the decorations and the trees and just go and sit and think what this is really all about."

A Catholic woman recalls the Holy Thursday procession before Easter with equal fondness. "I used to think it was wonderful, because you got to wear the crown that was made out of the real fine fern and you carried one single calla lily, and all us little kids, if you had already received your first communion, you wore your white first communion dress. And then you stood for hours, and that incense going, I can remember that."

A few people also celebrated New Year's Eve with fellow congregants. One of the more vivid recollections comes from Jess Hartley. "On New Year's Eve we would all pack up and we'd go to the church, about eight, eight-thirty," he remembers. "We used to joke about it because we were the first to arrive and the last to leave! Service would begin about nine, and we'd start with devotions, singing, testifying, and there would be some other singing, maybe the choirs would sing.

"The order of service was that before the midnight hour we'd all approach the altar. When the altar was full, then you'd just kneel down at your pew, and we'd go into prayer. We learned early on, you thank God for what he did for you in the previous year. And also asking, if he allowed you to see the new year, for protection through the new year. That was what we'd do. Then, there wouldn't be anybody saying, 'Okay, it's over.' It would just sort of start to calm down and some would still be praying.

"Then they would eventually stop, and you would get up, and there would be an announcement that the Lord allowed us to see a new year. From there, there would be another sort of devotion. Again, thanking God for allowing us to see a new year and whatever else you wanted to say after that. And some more singing and a prayer from the pastor for protection throughout the new year, and the service would be over and we'd head back home."

Raw Grief Displayed

Being part of a congregation also meant that people one knew died and that one was expected to attend the funeral. For most of the people we interviewed, attending funerals was a vivid, if relatively infrequent, aspect of growing up religious. The funeral became an occasion for reflecting about their own death or the possibility that their parents, siblings, or close friends might die at any time. Funerals raised more questions than they answered, but young people were at least exposed to grief, perhaps seeing people they loved expressing sorrowful emotions for the first time. Although they were dark times, funerals occasioned new insights; as Theodore Roethke has written, "In a dark time, the eye begins to see."[6]

An older woman provides a typical account as she recalls the first funeral she attended. "I was about twelve, and it was the funeral of a woman in our church. I think she had died in an accident; at least it was unexpected and tragic. There was a viewing at her home in the evening and a funeral at church the next day. The church was packed. I remember the casket was right down there in front of the pulpit, and it was open.

"After the service everybody, by row, went up around and walked past the casket again. The family was last, and how terrible for them to stand in front of that entire church, grieving and viewing their mother for the last time, in front of everybody. That was raw grief publicly displayed." She remembers how sad she felt and how she thought all during the service what it would be like if her own mother died. Not much later, after a sermon that spoke frankly of the "fires of hell," this woman decided to be baptized and join the church.

Lillia Rizzo remembers with equal clarity when her grandfather died. She was nine at the time, and her grandfather had lived with the family during the last months of his life. When he died, the mortician brought his body back to their house. "He was laid out in the house for three days and three nights, and there was a lot of religious activity going on. People couldn't afford funeral parlors. So the funeral was always brought into the home.

"The grandparents were always in the coffin for two or three days or nights in the living room with the flowers, and people would be coming in and out and parish priests would come and pray. They'd have a service in the home. And then the undertaker would take him to the church and then to the cemetery. So it was interesting. There was Grandpop. He was dead. He was in his coffin. That's where he's supposed to be. The family came and you'd go up to bed and you'd say, 'Good night.'

"And you'd come down in the morning and you'd say, 'Good morning,' and life would go on for children. As a child, I never found that to be a problem. It was just sort of part of living. It was always like that. It was the custom. It was nice to be able to have your loved ones around a little longer. It didn't upset me."

In contrast, children who had been taught to fear God were much more likely to experience funerals as traumatic occasions. A woman who grew up in a mainline Protestant church thinking that God was just waiting to catch her doing something wrong remembers vividly how she felt when her Uncle Joe died suddenly at the age of fifty. "I loved him very much. I was only about ten years old. After the funeral I remember thinking to myself, 'Now does this mean that if I do something wrong that Uncle Joe's going to see it too, the same as God?'" Because it was the first death she had encountered, it also raised many unanswered questions for her. "I was very upset. I had questions like, Why, why did this happen? I had questions like, Where did he go? I remember feeling kind of a despair, like, Well, is that all there is? Wondering. I did a lot of thinking."

When things went well, deaths in the family became a time when people felt good about being part of a congregation. A woman who had been very close to her grandmother wants us to know about how her grandmother died. "The associate pastor took a tape of the church music to my grandmother's bedside. She prayed with her and she let my grandmother hear the tape. And at the end of that tape, my grandmother just closed her eyes and died, just like that, just closed her eyes and died, to the church music. When I think of that, it gives me chills. And do you know what we did at her funeral, what I did? I took that tape and I played it at her funeral."

Without needing to make a conscious transition from her grandmother to herself, or from the church to Christ, this woman continues her narrative: "She was a courageous woman. She could withstand pain and suffering like you don't know, and I'm like that too. I believe that right now in my life I feel Christ suffering in my soul. I do. I cry every single day, once a day at least, because I feel his suffering."[7]

The Feeling of Mystery

Saints and mystics have always asserted that an elemental dimension of the sacred is the sense of mystery it inspires. As people recall their childhood experiences in religious services, relatively few mention any such awareness of mystery. Indeed, it is as if the services themselves blocked out any possibility of mystery because they were so well organized, so formal, so routine. But the *mysterium tremendum* did break through occasionally, more likely than not on unusual occasions, such as the ones we have been considering, the special rituals surrounding the holidays and the grief displayed at funerals.[8]

A person we talked with who had grown up across the street from a Catholic cemetery remembers how the burial rites she would observe from a distance affected her. "I would stand outside the cemetery, looking through the bars, at the people in the flower-laden cars. On more than one occasion I saw women throw themselves on coffins, and that was very scary for me as a kid. That kind of wrenching grief that I never saw anywhere else—it had an effect on me." She especially remembers one time when the funeral was for an elderly neighbor. "He was always there, and then he was missing. It gave me such a missing feeling. It was all very much a mystery."

Community is also a mystery at some deep level. At least it seems increasingly so to many people who look back on their childhood and sense that it has been irretrievably lost. And yet, for it to be regained, it must be understood as well as appreciated. The insights that people have shared with us about the social ties that bound them to their congregations are certainly a place to start.

‑►‑◄‑

CHAPTER 6

Learning to Be a Leader

ALEXIS DE TOCQUEVILLE probably did not have children in mind when he wrote that churches and other voluntary associations were the cradle of democracy.[1] Adults coming together to hash over community issues fit more closely with his view of grassroots democracy. At the same time as Tocqueville's visit, however, the Sunday school movement was gaining steam in America, just as it had been in Great Britain, and it was this movement—especially among children—that was to contribute immensely to the shaping of American democracy.[2] As their teachers hoped, millions of children learned to sit still and listen to stories about Adam and Eve; they also gained opportunities to *lead*. Sometimes, in creative ways.

Blowing Up the Church

Sarah McElhinny went to an old-line Presbyterian church that still believed anything other than the spoken word on Sunday mornings was an abomination. No pictures, no crosses, not even a stained-glass window was there to distract her (she would have been happy for transparent panes opening out on the cemetery, but all the windows were made of a translucent, yellowish brown substance that stifled the imagination). When she was not dutifully trying to take notes on the pastor's sermon, her only relief was to count the acoustic tiles on the ceiling. But Sunday evenings were different.

To make sure the children didn't shrivel totally from boredom, the teacher let them dream up their own activities, and even the youngest were given a turn leading. It was a bit like putting on here's-what-we-do-in-school plays at home in the basement to entertain one's parents, except this was just for the children. Sarah McElhinny's best Sunday afternoons were spent preparing an activity when it was her turn to lead.

One Sunday she decided to have the children act out the story of Elijah on Mount Carmel praying for fire to come down and consume an altar that had been thoroughly drenched with water, Elijah's way of demonstrating Jehovah's power compared with the gods of his competitors. "I remember having it all made. I made it with mud. This little platform, and I had the little plastic cow there on the top, and I had the trough around the bottom for the water. I was going to tell the story of how Elijah pours the water on the animal, because all the worshipers of Baal had been cutting themselves and praying for their god to consume their offering.

"And I had practiced, too. I was going to dump gasoline onto this thing, pretending it was water, and I was going to drop this match from heaven to show how God consumed this thing that had been covered with water."

Fortunately, her father discovered her plan and vetoed the idea. "I never did get to do my gas bomb in the basement of the church," Sarah laments.

Nevertheless, her aspirations to lead were not quashed. She found that safer stories, such as Jacob's ladder or Jesus feeding the five thousand, could also be dramatized (and later, that there were nonviolent ways to depict Peter cutting off the soldier's ear and Jesus running the pigs over a cliff). "I could turn almost any of the Bible stories into a play," she recalls.

Sarah grew up and became a teacher. She credits these opportunities in Sunday school with turning her into the leader she is today.

Scared and Shaking

Walt Brubaker grew up in poverty. His maternal grandfather was a rich man who lost everything in the Great Crash of '29; his paternal grandfather worked as a blacksmith, never earning more than a meager income. Walt's father came home an invalid from fighting in World War I; for a time, he was able to earn a living, but his health gradually deteriorated and he died when Walt was eight. Walt was the youngest of eight children. After his father's death his mother took part-time jobs cleaning motel rooms, but the family mostly depended on the oldest son, only twenty-one at the time, to keep food on the table. That, and hunting and fishing. The children also picked vegetables in the neighbors' fields, wore hand-me-down clothing, and earned nickels and dimes husking corn and milking cows for nearby farmers.

The church Walt grew up in was also poor. Coming into town on County Road 19, you passed the crest of a small hill and then descended gradually past the one-room school house on the left and the gray stone church on the right. It was a Union congregation, called that because two churches, one Lutheran and one Reformed, had been forced to share the same building in order to survive the Depression.

On the first and third Sundays of each month, a Lutheran pastor came by horse and buggy from a neighboring village; on the second and fourth Sundays, a Reformed pastor preached. Some of the congregation showed up only when "their" pastor was in town; about half the members attended every Sunday. Walt's mother, increasingly withdrawn after her husband's death, seldom went at all. But she insisted on Walt's going.

"We have one God, one Christ; you go every Sunday," she told him. So she dressed Walt in the suit that someone had given him for his father's funeral and marched him out the door. As he grew older, he wore hand-me-down suits from his brothers, but he went every Sunday and, later, every Tuesday evening to youth group.

Despite its precarious economic base, the church became a platform for developing leadership skills. Walt says the worst effect of his father's dying was that he became a very shy, reclusive child. Being the youngest, he became his brothers' whipping boy. As the last to arrive, he felt he was an unwanted imposition on the family. He'd wander off to some quiet corner and try to become as invisible as possible.

Walt's self-image was ridden with guilt, because he blamed himself for his father's death. He remembers how he had heard as a child that if a bird flew against a window, it meant someone in the house was going to die. One day Walt came home from school and ran up to his father's bedroom to say hello. Just then, a bird hit the window. That night Walt's father died. Walt felt it must have been his fault. He was afraid to interact with other people for fear something would happen to them, too.

But people at the church gradually drew him out. They gave children in the church small leadership roles, and then expanded these roles when the young people entered high school. "It was called 'building up,'" Walt explains. "You would read the Scriptures. You would maybe read the announcements for the day. For me, for some reason, I remember that very vividly. I think it was important to me and to the other children involved, because it gave us self-confidence. We developed some public speaking ability even though we were scared and shaking."

He says reinforcement from adults in the congregation was especially valuable to him because of his shyness and because of his family situation. "I think we looked for the reinforcement, or at least I did. I looked for that reinforcement. I looked for the words of praise from the pastor or anybody in the congregation that we did a good job."

As the high school youth group went around with the itinerant pastors to their other churches, Walt also learned teamwork. "We didn't do it independently, we did it as a team. That team would rotate on the churches, and as I said, each year you would take on a different aspect. So from the time that you were in ninth grade till you were in twelfth grade, if you stayed with the group, which almost everybody did, you would have the experience of all the different elements of leading a service."

Walt Brubaker was drafted into the army shortly after he graduated from high school, spent three years in the service, got married, and started a family. He has worked at various odd jobs, including door-to-door sales and short-order cooking in restaurants. But he has also finished college and now holds a job as a media technician at a high school, and he devotes much of his spare time to an elected office he holds in the municipal government. He feels he has come a long way from his childhood, perhaps fulfilling some of the dreams that his father left unrealized. He credits the church with having helped him find his way. Over the years, it has always been the social support at various churches that has kept him involved.

All Good Things Must End

Seymour Nesbit, age seventy-two, is a retired nuclear physicist who believes in God. He illustrates the tension that many people in the sciences have experienced between rational thought and religious faith. How he was able to put the two together, however, is a story about playing roles in religious institutions long enough that one finally comes to believe in spirituality.

Seymour was raised in the Bronx, the son of Orthodox parents and the grandson of Polish Jewish immigrants. His father was a butcher at a kosher butcher shop and his mother was a housewife, whom he describes as "far more assertive" than his father. From an early age, he learned about Jewish dietary customs and household rituals. He remembers the great preparations his mother made for the seders, how his father described slaughtering the animals to keep the blood separate from the meat, and how the men participated in activities at the synagogue.

Judaism was a way of life more than it was a religion; indeed, Seymour realized as a young child that his mother and father prayed only on ceremonial occasions. They said they believed in God when he asked them, but he wasn't sure what they believed. So unusual was it for them to talk about God that when they did, it stood out in his memory. He still recalls the night his father tucked him into bed, saying, "If you say your prayers every night, the devil won't get you." Seymour tried it only once.

His most distinct childhood memory of Judaism is being taken when he was six years old to a room in the back of his father's butcher shop where there was a tall, older man with a long gray beard. "He opened a book called *The Beginning of Knowledge* and started teaching me phonetic Hebrew. He would sit me down, and I would recite these vowels and consonants, and we went through the whole book. I didn't know why I was doing it, but I was doing it. And of course I was being introduced to Judaism, which is the religion of my parents and their parents all the way back.

"Then from the butcher store, as I got a little older, I was able to go up to the rabbi, to his apartment, which wasn't too far away. I recall getting quite fluent in being able to read phonetic Hebrew. And then he would introduce me to the prayers, the prayer book. I would read the prayers. He would introduce me to the Torah, the Bible. I would read the Hebrew and he would translate it into Yiddish, a language I didn't understand at all. And so here we were, I was reading the Hebrew, and he was translating into Yiddish, and I really got very little out of it."

Seymour says he learned to be "a disciplined young man" from these experiences. He studied hard for his bar mitzvah. Much to the annoyance of his parents, he began rising at five-thirty in the morning to study Hebrew and to read the prayer book.

A year later war broke out in Europe, and Seymour's interest in Judaism was deflected into a Zionist organization, in which he participated actively during high school and college and through which he met his wife. He continued participating in temple services on the high holy days, and his habits of personal discipline helped him achieve an advanced degree, working nights, in mechanical engineering. During the 1950s, he found employment in the government's missile program and eventually worked his way into a senior position at one of the nation's top nuclear energy laboratories.

As he reflects on his journey, he describes his religious involvement as "just the thing to do" and says it had little connection with God. "It was part of life, and I never questioned it. I grew up in a neighborhood that was Jewish. My father was, I wouldn't call him a deeply religious man, but he was an observant Jew. We celebrated all the holidays. We had the Passover seder, we celebrated Purim. My father went to synagogue on high holidays. I came to realize, of course, that we were a Jewish family. And at the termination of my bar mitzvah, the day of my bar mitzvah, I was really inspired to continue with my Judaism. I was educated in an Orthodox environment, which means that I was taught to lay the tefillin, to pray every morning. And I attempted to do that, not so much because of deep conviction as because it was the thing to do."

The Zionist youth organization kept him involved. "I remember the first night I attended a meeting. I was absolutely overwhelmed. I was bowled over. All these kids, wonderful kids who were singing and dancing in Hebrew and having a good time, and after that we would sit down and have discussions. We had leaders who would lead discussions about Jewish history, about Israel, about other topics. We talked about social movements. It really blew my mind. On Sundays you went on hikes. We went on picnics. We lived a real integrated life in that group. So my real introduction to Judaism was through this Zionist movement. But there was no mention of God. There was no religious practice at all. It was strictly Judaism, in its secular sense and its political sense. One was Jewish because one was born Jewish and had a tradition, but not a particularly religious value."

Seymour nevertheless learned to be a leader, and soon he was teaching Hebrew classes himself. Over the years he has stayed active as a teacher in the various synagogues to which he has belonged. "What motivated me was the kids," he suggests. "They're looking up to you. They admire you. I liked that, to be very honest about it. I also enjoyed imparting knowledge to them, of course. I thought this was a positive thing I was doing, but it was an added benefit to get adulation from the students. There's a great deal of ego involved."

Gradually, he became much more involved in temple activities. "I began to like it," he says. "For some strange reason, it sort of began to grow on me." He nevertheless discovered, as he puts it, that "all good things must end." It started to bother him that people at his synagogue were bickering so much about little things, and so he and his wife left. After a few years at another synagogue, he became disillusioned again. He has stayed at other places for as long as ten years, but he never feels completely comfortable.

Yet, as a result of these experiences, he has had to think more deeply about what it means to be spiritual. "You keep reading the prayer book, and after a while you start to look at the words. I began to take them seriously and I loved it. I loved the prophets. I began to love the prayer book. It was very inspirational."

In the process, the struggles he has had with rational thought have started to diminish. He believes that God created the universe and that is sufficient to animate him spiritually. "Where did we come from? Where did it start? How come I'm here?" he asks. "My answer that satisfies me spiritually is that God is the Creator of the universe. I'm happy with that. What happens from there on I don't know.

"God doesn't always reward the downtrodden or the poor, or punish the wicked, that I know. This is a fact. He doesn't always do that. There's a lot of things that God doesn't do that he should do. But maybe that's not God's role, you see? All I know about God is that he's created the universe, and I'm content with that. That satisfies me spiritually." This realization, long in coming and yet rooted so plainly in his religious upbringing, has been a good thing that he feels will not come to an end.

Sleeping on the Couch

Ruth MacMann grew up in a Presbyterian family in Los Angeles. Her parents lived in a working-class section of the city that included large numbers of recent immigrants from Korea, China, Japan, and Malaysia. Her most vivid memories include her parents' efforts to be of service to their Asian American neighbors. Ruth's father ran a small bookstore and her mother worked part time in the store while raising three children. Both parents devoted large amounts of their time to the small Presbyterian church they attended. Her father taught an adult Sunday school class, served on the board of elders, and sometimes preached when the pastor was away. Her mother taught a Sunday school class for children and took an active part in the ladies' auxiliary, which supported evangelistic and missionary work. It was the church that taught Ruth the value of sleeping on the couch.

As a youngster, Ruth gained an understanding of how much her parents believed in helping people. She remembers her father's bringing people home from the bookstore and letting them sleep on the couch. Occasionally, these visitors would be given her room and it was she who ended up on the sofa. Often they were immigrants who had run out of money and had no place to go. Her parents would put them up for the night and then buy them a bus ticket in the morning. Once in a while, her father brought someone home who had been drinking and needed a place to sober up. Typically, her mother would cook a meal and then her parents would talk to the visitors, listening to their stories and trying to find ways to give helpful advice.

Ruth thinks her parents came by these impulses naturally. Whenever she visited her grandparents in Michigan, she noticed that her grandmother was in contact with an endless stream of neighbors. Some were Scotch-Irish, some were German, others were Scandinavian. They'd stop by the house to chat. Later, her grandmother would be baking cinnamon rolls to take to someone whose wife was sick or stopping to visit a family who had run into financial trouble. Ruth remembers her grandmother's saying she just loved to do things for other people because God had done so much for her. As she grew older, Ruth also realized that her parents and grandparents didn't drive as new an automobile as their neighbors and that the women of the family seldom wore makeup or bought new dresses.

Somehow, Ruth came to understand that helping people necessitated respecting them, rather than thinking you were better than they were. "We were never taught to look down on anybody," she says. "If somebody was a beggar on the street, we didn't think of them as an inferior being or something. We tried to respect them. You want an example? I guess it was just the way that my parents would welcome anyone into their home. And that was part of their mission in life, to connect with people, in any walk of life."

When she was in high school, Ruth's parents began drawing her into their efforts to help their neighbors. Her father was keenly aware of the language barriers many of the new immigrants faced, and so with the help of others from the church he started offering free instruction in English. People came to the door, indicating that a friend had sent them, and Ruth's father or mother would set up periodic meetings. Soon, the house was overflowing with students. Ruth and her siblings were enlisted to help.

She laughs, "We had classes meeting in the kitchen, the living room, the hallway, even in the bedrooms." It took a lot of time, but Ruth came to love helping people. She also benefited enormously from the experience. By the end of high school, she was fluent in Japanese and could speak some Korean as well.

She thinks it was this experience that sparked her interest in becoming a doctor. A good student, she felt instinctively that she wanted to enter one of the helping professions. Attending college several thousand miles away from her family was a struggle, but Ruth found support from one of the campus ministry organizations. Later, as a medical student, and then as an intern putting in long hours and spending sleepless nights on duty, she found a Christian medical society that helped maintain her commitment.

Now in her middle thirties and established in her practice, she is able to reflect on this commitment. "Basically I think most doctors go into medicine for reasons that are good," she explains. "They enjoy taking care of people and helping people. But it seems that over time, getting money and time for themselves becomes more and more important, and the patient becomes less and less important. So I work hard to try to preserve my reasons for being a doctor, which is to help people and to pass on some of what God has done for me to others by helping them.

"I think spirituality does influence the way I practice. A lot of times I could just see the patient and leave the room and go on to the next one, but if I know that they really need some attention, I will take the extra time to do that. And I think it's because of my belief in God that I don't mind taking the extra time to do things like that. I would rather get home later knowing that I did the best I could and that I really helped people."

And many nights, dozing fitfully in the on-call lounge at the hospital, her mind drifts back to those nights she spent on the couch in her parents' living room.

Associating with Adults

In each of these cases, the congregation functioned as a kind of extended family. Growing up religious was thus a way to learn roles that would be valuable later in life. For Sarah McElhinny, the church provided a platform on which she could perform, honing the talents that would make her an effective teacher. In Walt Brubaker's case, the church got him out of the house, away from his brothers, and gave him a chance to develop the self-confidence he would need to join the service and attend college. Seymour Nesbit learned to work hard and to respect ideas, staying involved with the synagogue even when he was unhappy with it and eventually feeling closer to God as a result. And for Ruth MacMann, the church complemented her parents' efforts to help new immigrants, putting her in immediate contact with people who needed her help and instilling values in her that would make her more caring as a physician.

In other cases, the congregation was a place where children could feel special because someone — an adult other than their parents — gave them affirmation or because they acquired special skills. One woman says the reason she continued going to Sunday school as an adult was that one of her Sunday school teachers in grade school always made her feel special by letting her help with the lesson, printing words on the chalkboard or assisting with the refreshments. A man admits that he had mostly taught himself to read before starting school by figuring out the words in the hymnbook while the congregation sang on Sunday mornings. For others, religious services were one of the few times they did anything with their parents. One man says he realized that his father was proud of him by the way his father talked about him to other people in the congregation.

If nothing else, children also came into regular contact with adults who were not their parents but whom they were supposed to respect. Jess Hartley illustrates how contact of this kind was sometimes quite literal.

"We learned to respect our elders no matter who it was. I, to this day, say, 'Yes, ma'am' and 'Yes, sir' to people. I could say something to my mom or dad later, but this was the time growing up in our church, whether it was aunt, uncle, and a lot of relatives went to our church, if we did something wrong, they could whack us on our behind and no talk about it. Nowadays, if the kids [are] doing something wrong, you grab their hand to keep them from writing on the back of the pew, parents are like, 'Why are you touching my kid?' Not then, it was like you got whacked there. And then, when you told that they whacked you, you got whacked again because they had to do it!"

For some people, congregational activities were also an important occasion for seeing their parents in a different light than at home. Dad might be friendlier or more businesslike, Mom might be more gregarious or authoritative. For children whose mothers did not work outside the home, seeing them doing church work was sometimes especially meaningful because it revealed a new side of their mother.

Elaine Margolis typifies a number of people when she recalls how seriously her mother worked at preparing for church dinners. "She was a very artistic person and she would always do the decorations or the favors or whatever had to be done, and she would often ask for our help in doing that sort of thing. So there was this idea that what happened in the church was very special. That's something that my mother contributed that I think was unique, because I've been in many churches since then where they just slap something on the table or the bottle of ketchup goes on the table. But my mother had made sure that at their dinners there was candlelight and that there were fresh flowers. You didn't give it your second best, you gave it your best."

Youth Groups

Although children were exposed to leadership roles in a variety of contexts, it was often the junior high or high school youth group that stood out most clearly in their memories. Walt Brubaker and Seymour Nesbit attribute special significance to their youth groups. In other cases, youth groups conjure up mixed emotions. Indeed, many of the people we talked with took the opportunity during high school to pull away from their parents' urgings about religion; others went unwillingly to youth group, feeling out of place or that the activities were beneath them. Yet enough people remember youth group as a positive turning point in their religious development that it is worth considering why.

One theme that emerges in a number of interviews is that youth group provided the opportunity to develop a more thoughtful understanding of one's religious beliefs. Especially for young people who had gone to services so regularly as children that the activity had become unthinking, it was now possible to study and reflect on what one was doing.

For example, a man raised in a Methodist church joined a Presbyterian youth group in high school mostly, he admits, because he was interested in meeting girls. But he remembers starting to read the Bible for the first time and really becoming more interested in what it had to say. Similarly, a Jewish woman recalls that Judaism had been a kind of ethnic custom within her family and a source of embarrassment at school until she became part of a youth group at her synagogue. "They started teaching us about the Sabbath and they used to pray and they used to do all these things in a fun way. So you had many, many teenagers gathered together, really for social reasons, but at the same time, they showed us how it was possible to do it in a religious way. And they used to have many lectures, and study groups, and I was always the kind of person anyhow who thought a lot."

The same woman recalls that her youth group encouraged her to be more observant but also to think more about the meaning of what she was doing. "When I joined this youth group, I began to want to [observe the Sabbath], and then for the first time I started eating kosher food, because we used to have meetings all the time and everyone did that. I began to see the purpose in it. One of the purposes, by the way, is that you should not think that everything in life is just given to you."

She gives another example: "There is a commandment that says 'You shall not boil a kid in its mother's milk.' So they got these reasons, right? The rabbis took that particular line and from that they built this whole complicated thing about there are a certain amount of hours that have to go by between when you eat meat and drink milk, because you have to think about what it is that you're eating. A person can't just be an animal and live like an animal. You have to think about everything."

The one thing that hardly any of the people we interviewed say they worried about as children is whether or not they had been "born again" or become true followers of God. Some of them had dramatic conversion experiences as adults. But all but the few who were raised in fundamentalist homes simply grew up feeling that they were members of God's kingdom. Even the ones who grew up in churches that emphasized personal faith and salvation generally felt that they were exempt from having to worry about such matters. Thus, youth group was a time when some churches tried explicitly to disturb the conscience of young people enough to encourage a more deliberate commitment to God. Confirmation classes sometimes accomplished this purpose; in other cases, revival meetings and summer camps played a similar role.

Mostly, though, youth groups were remembered favorably when they treated young people as adults, giving them greater responsibilities in the congregation and permitting them to try on roles that might be useful in later life. Youth groups that functioned best were like the wider congregations that people cherished, communities in which caring social relationships were present and places where interaction was safe but not removed from the rest of life.

Gendering the Future

Late adolescence was also the time when young people learned instinctively that women and men were supposed to play different roles in their congregation. At one level, they already knew this, of course, because they had been taken to services more often by their mothers than by their fathers, had probably been taught by women instead of men, but had most likely seen men instead of women serving as clergy. With the onset of puberty, young women now saw more clearly that only certain roles were open to them, while young men envisioned the future differently.

For one thing, women's caring for one another was centered in the congregation more than men's relationships with other men were. Men might be from the same congregation but saw each other at work or at the pub, whereas women met each other through ladies' auxiliaries or through activities in the home that were carried out under congregational auspices. For example, the women we interviewed frequently remember their mothers' getting together with other church women to make quilts or featherbeds for new brides in their congregation, to prepare potluck dinners, or to bundle up used clothing to ship to missionaries.

As the persons directly in charge of training children, mothers were also subject to closer scrutiny by leaders of the congregation. For instance, one of the older women we interviewed describes the custom in her church called "churching the bride," in which a special portion of the wedding ceremony was devoted to counseling the bride. In his sermon, the minister cautioned the bride (more than the groom) about following in God's ways, and then the bride approached the altar with her bridesmaid (while the groom sat down) and thanked God for helping her remain chaste and for giving her such a wonderful husband. Especially in cases where the bride was an outsider to the groom's church, counsel to lead a godly life was given in detail.

On some occasions, young women saw that the congregation was not only interested in supervising their behavior but also a place where they could be empowered. For instance, a young African American woman talks about how her mother had become more powerful as a result of participating in a Jehovah's Witnesses congregation. "It was the thing that kept her in the marriage and that kept her husband with her," the woman says. "She didn't want to have her children raised without two parents. At that time, she hadn't gone back to school. She immersed myself in that religion. And she was very good at it.

"She went from door to door, talking to people. She became very good at holding Bible studies. On Saturday mornings we'd go out on field service with her. Tuesday we were at prayer meeting, Thursday we were at ministry school. She went to every convention and took us children everywhere, wherever they had a convention." The woman credits these activities with giving her mother the confidence to go back to school and eventually finish college. "Time management, being able to teach, and being able to help people learn" were among the benefits.

But it was more common for young women to see their mothers in helping roles than in leadership positions. And these differences became self-perpetuating. Excluded from leadership positions, women came to be viewed as lacking in leadership skills compared with men, even when they were recognized as strong nurturers within the family.

An older man who had grown up in a Methodist church provides a revealing example. His father, a mechanic who repaired tractors for local farmers, taught Sunday school, directed the choir, and was considered quite a leader among the church people (they joked that he should wear gloves on Sundays to hide his greasy hands). His mother, in contrast, "was very quiet, not assertive at all, very gentle. She was not an outspoken leader, as such, in church." Yet, the man says, "at home she could always handle us when we gave her a fit, when the five of us ganged up on her." Then, as if to accentuate his point, he repeats, "My mother never took a leadership role in the church itself. But at home she was very much of a spiritual leader for us children."

In Jewish families, gender was an important dimension of religious practice as well. Fathers and sons learned to read the Torah; mothers and daughters prepared the food. Women played a pivotal role in household services, of course, but it was clearly a role that sons were not expected to imitate. One of the Jewish men we interviewed is particularly candid about the expectations governing his mother. "What she did in terms of religion was to prepare the house for the religious holidays."

When asked to elaborate, he says, "Well, for example, Passover is a holiday where we celebrate the exodus with a seder, which is a dinner and a prayer session combined at a table. And remember, my parents were brought up in Orthodox tradition, and they continued the tradition. The dishes have to be changed. You have to use special dishes for that holiday. Food has to be brought into the house for the whole week. The house has to be cleaned. The tablecloths have to be arranged. In other words, there are a great deal of preparations for this banquet. And my mother got very involved with that. So her role was primarily as the one to help along, prepare the services to make it successful."

If young women learned that theirs was to be a submissive role, they nevertheless saw in their mothers' activities that this role could be performed meaningfully. In contrast, young men saw that older men with rare gifts, especially ones with divine callings, became preachers, priests, rabbis, or elders and that many other men remained largely indifferent to the activities of their congregation. It was relatively easy for many of these young men to drift away.

PART III

Moving Away

＋＞＜＋

CHAPTER 7

Points of Departure

As we grow older, some of us stay within the religious subculture in which we were raised and many more of us switch to other subcultures. But the process of maturing is, for virtually everyone, a transition away from an identity that was simply taken for granted and toward an identity that is more distinctly ours and more a function of the varied experiences we undergo. We say, with Rilke, "I live my life in growing orbits, which move out over the things of the world."[1] Or perhaps more aptly, we follow the pattern identified by a more recent writer: "When humans reach a certain age, they identify precisely what it is their parents want for them and bolt in the opposite direction like lemmings for the cliff."[2]

Moving beyond the familiar, comfortable religious routines to which people have grown accustomed in their youth has always been encouraged within religious traditions. Gerald Vann writes: "Our Lord did not say 'I am come that ye may have safety, and have it more abundantly.' Some of us would indeed give anything to feel safe, about our life in this world as in the next, but we cannot have it both ways: safety or life, we must choose."[3] Similarly, Paul Tournier asserts that "there must be new flowerings, new prophets, new adventures—always new adventures—if the heart of man, albeit in fits and starts, is to go on beating."[4] The poet Steve Turner creates a vivid contrast, writing that he once thought of God "as a symphony neatly structured, full of no surprises," but that he now experiences God "as a saxophone solo blowing wildly into the night, a tongue of fire, flicking in unrepeated patterns."[5]

In this process of moving away, we negotiate our particular individual identities by bumping into different people or groups and by comparing ourselves with them. The conversation with our past continues, but we now add new conversational partners. Some of them affirm our childhood identity. Others contribute new ideas and roles.

I think we can understand the significance of public events, social movements, and well-known personalities in this way. Most of us do not participate directly in—let alone submerge ourselves in—these movements or events, but we use them as landmarks as we move along on our spiritual journeys. Even more often, it is the personal landmarks that become points of departure.

If we listen closely as people talk about their spiritual journeys, it becomes evident that most journeys unfold slowly and gradually rather than rapidly and abruptly. There is often a great deal of continuity between where people are and how they grew up. Going away to college, participating in the civil-rights movement, serving in Vietnam, getting married, or getting divorced generally did not precipitate as sudden a change as some theorists have posited. Yet it is important for us to emphasize these landmarks as we tell our stories. They permit us to divide our life narratives into chapters.

Turning Points

For many people, moving away occurs in late adolescence and takes place so completely and unconsciously that they realize only much later how deeply rooted in a religious subculture they remain. Writer Kathleen Norris, for instance, talks about an awareness she has come to in her forties about the influence of her Presbyterian grandmother during early childhood: "It is my Christian inheritance that largely defines me, but for years I didn't know that."[6] Others move away more completely.

But moving away should not be thought of simply as a developmental task. Young people move away from the faith of their parents because there are powerful institutional forces pulling in this direction. Colleges and universities pride themselves on how many states and countries their students represent, as if it is better to have a flock of migrants on their hands than students with roots. Corporations shunt executives from region to region, apparently preparing them to do Midas's bidding anywhere in the world. Government agencies show more interest in relocating workers to new places than in relocating new businesses within established communities. All this disrupts families, severing the generational ties that nurture religious commitments over long periods.[7]

For Delmer Schwartz, who grew up in a rural Congregational church, the move away from his childhood faith started when he graduated from high school and joined the Air Force. Flying combat missions in Vietnam made him realize he might not live very long. In retrospect, he wonders why he did not turn to God at that point. Yet the men in his squadron chose to cope by focusing on the pleasures of the moment. They enjoyed drinking and gambling, and on days off some of them visited prostitutes in Saigon. It was not until he returned home that Delmer realized how thoroughly he had been influenced by the daily culture of the military.

So instead, his turning point came when he was back home. Delmer's father had struggled with alcoholism most of his adult life, and one day he was driving the tractor while he was intoxicated and it tipped over. During the three hours he was pinned beneath it, his father had time to do some hard thinking about life. And during the next six months, as his father recovered, Delmer did a lot of thinking too. He decided he was on the wrong track. He could easily go the way of his father. The Sunday school and church going of his youth would not be enough. He figured he'd have to "get serious about God" or die an alcoholic.

Margaret Vanderline, a woman from a Reformed background, explains that for her, "the big split came when I went away to college. It was such a different experience for me. I was in a school with people that had parents that were much more educated than mine, had a *lot* more money than I did. I was a working-class kid. These people, their parents were professionals, and they were lawyers and doctors and different kinds of things. And I saw another society that I really didn't even know existed, to be truthful with you, or that I knew existed but didn't pay a lot of attention to, because it wasn't part of my world."

It was the ambiance of this new world, more than anything she learned in the classroom, that moved her away from her religious roots. "I became more liberal in some of my thinking about women and the way they should be. That is where my father and I differ completely, because my father is very much a male chauvinist and always was his whole life. Women really were secondary. Women existed for—they should cook, clean, and make love. That's a nice way of putting it. That's essentially what women exist for."

Just talking about it causes some of the resentment she felt growing up to emerge, forcefully. "As far as my father was concerned, a man will have sex anywhere, any time that he can, and a penis has no conscience, as far as he's concerned. This is like just the antithesis of everything I believe in, because I think that men are quite capable of controlling themselves. I obviously don't think women are valueless. But this was the way my father was. He had a love-hate relationship with women, and I think that has a lot to do with it. But I did spend a long time growing up thinking that women were secondary creatures. My mother kind of reinforced this, because she sort of gave in to my father. She waited on him hand and foot and catered to him. This is how the women were."

Marty Schott went regularly to the Presbyterian church until she was twelve, loved the music and the parables, and really felt that she was loved by Jesus, then gradually quit attending and has been shopping around ever since. She muses, "Yeah, that was a good experience there. I think then, as soon as I entered, you know, early high school and college, then of course, you know the question-and-answer period started in my life. And I was just, you know, I couldn't understand the potluck dinners and the stuff around it. There were so many questions that couldn't be answered for me."

It wasn't better doctrine that she wanted at all; in fact, it was the opposite. "There wasn't enough, you know, getting beyond doctrine, getting beyond Bible. You know, talking real stuff from the heart and really talking to people that wouldn't have necessarily have gone to a church, you know, really wise people, wisdom people. You know, that's the stuff that grabbed me."

Hal Meyerson says his biggest struggle came when he went away to college, leaving his Jewish friends from high school behind. Before long he had fallen in love with a Catholic girl. "I guess it was over Thanksgiving my freshman year in college," he recalls. "I ran into someone who had always attracted my fancy who was not Jewish. She was Catholic. We carried on a torrid relationship for a year and a half and had two families abso-

lutely cringing. And I think we broke up because of religion. I can still remember the evening at the time, and it was devastating on both of us. It
was a cognizant, conscious, mental decision. It was not a decision of the
heart."

Living with Patty and JoAnn

For some of the people we talked with, social movements and public religious figures also served as landmarks in their journey. Few of these movements or figures had made a profound impression on anyone, but some
people had refined their sense of themselves in relation to such movements and figures. The civil-rights movement, the campus turmoil of the
1960s, the death of President Kennedy, and the assassination of Martin
Luther King Jr. are sometimes mentioned as pivotal occasions.

Raman Wilkins provides one such example as he recalls the unrest of
the 1960s. At the time, he was working for United Airlines as a sales agent
and was sharing an apartment with two stewardesses. He had quit attending church, but his religious upbringing was still a part of his identity
and he was continually coming to terms with it. His apartment mates were
more religiously involved than he was, and their involvement rekindled
some of his own interest but also helped him realize that he preferred to
stay on the fringes of churches and religious movements. Raman gradually moved out of the religion of his childhood and into a more personal,
inclusive—one might say, secular—form of spirituality. His story shows
that he did not simply respond to one particular event but renegotiated his
own identity by interacting with a variety of people who brought particular aspects of the wider culture to his attention.

One of these cultural influences was evangelicalism. "The two girls
that I lived with, Patty and JoAnn, they were born-again Christians," Raman recalls. "They were Catholic, but the born-again Christian movement was very big in the sixties. JoAnn had Roger going crazy. He was Jewish, and he was part of a group called Jews for Christ. That was big in those
days. There was a revival of some sort about religion when I was working
with United Airlines as a salesman. Like I said, I used to turn on all the religious stations. I used to spend all my time listening, because I wanted to
know, I wanted to find out what it is that perhaps I'm missing about reli-

gion that I should know. So I listened to all of them: Reverend Green, Jerry Falwell and the Gospel Hour, all of them. I just kept it on that station."

Raman himself did not become a born-again Christian, but he says the experience of seeing others do so "made me hopeful." He explains: "I'm always hoping that the spirit of Christianity—morality and good will—will become contagious and make people become better people."

Raman's responses to the civil-rights movement also illustrate how people renegotiate their identities. This part of his story does not relate specifically to his religious identity, but it shows how he actively, creatively, and selectively negotiated his identity as an African American during the civil-rights period. Raman did not participate in the civil-rights movement the way people generally think—by sitting in at lunch counters or marching in protests, for example. But as the first African American to be hired by United Airlines as a sales agent, he found himself in a position to interpret the civil-rights movement to his white coworkers and to rediscover new aspects of what it meant to be black.

He says he became convinced in these years that black people were fundamentally conservative. What impressed him most, watching the civil-rights demonstrations on television, was that black people could be kicked, knifed, and beaten, and still "come back and lick a white man's feet." He adds, "They'll turn in black people to get the praise and recognition from white people."

He also found that his identity as a black person, having become more objectified ("out there") as a result of the public debates generated by the civil-rights movement, was an identity that he could now play with. For example, he used to "put on" his white customers by telling them he was suing the government because he had been employed by the CIA and they had done plastic surgery to make him look black when he was really a white man. He found, too, that white women were responding to him in a new way. It was a heady experience for him, he says, to violate the taboo he had learned as a child against interacting with white women. Looking back, he says, "There's just a lot of things I learned. I grew up."

If Raman still favors religion as a result of having grown up, he has come to do so more on his own terms. "I don't believe that it's a big deal that God gave Jesus as his only begotten son," he asserts. "I'd say there's mere mortals that have given their only begotten son, only begotten daughter in war, or some street crime. And being God, he could have all the sons he wanted."

He says he has doubts about the story of God's getting mad at the children of Israel, too. "When I hear the story about Moses going up there, and then he comes back down and God gets mad because the people are worshiping the idols. If he's already God, He already knows it! You're going to tell me he's all-knowing, all-present, and everything. How can you be disappointed when you already know?" Summarizing his beliefs, Raman adds: "I want to be comfortable in the way that I believe. I think it's important that I kind of accept God and Christ, but in *my* way."

On the surface, the assertions of belief that characterize Raman's spirituality are not dissimilar from the ways in which many other, more deeply committed religious followers talk about their beliefs. Indeed, a characteristic that runs through many people's accounts of moving out of their childhood faith is using a common language to talk about their current beliefs. This language encourages them to express some belief in the transcendent and some interest in spirituality. It discourages them from blatantly rejecting the sacred and may even permit strong affirmations of belief, but it allows them to tailor their views — make *their views* personal — by saying that they have disagreements with or questions about some of the things others believe.

Becoming More Enlightened

Idiosyncratic beliefs can nevertheless be the basis for striking a particularly personal bargain with God. Raman, for instance, remembers vividly the day he suffered his heart attack. "I was *sincerely* talking to God," he recalls. "I didn't recognize it as a heart attack. It wasn't conscious. I was upstairs, and I said, 'God, I know what this is. It's this,' and I was pointing to my cigarettes. Wasn't saying I had a heart attack, but I'm saying, 'This is caused by this. I will keep this out of my mouth if you get rid of this pain.' So I made my way downstairs. I sat on that chair. I said, 'Hey, this is serious.' Then I started sweating. Then I started saying, 'It *is* the cigarettes.' And I kept saying, 'God, please let me get out of this.' Now that I'm scared, 'Please take this away.' I'm really talking to God."

Having made this bargain with God, Raman finds himself interacting with God from time to time, but mostly on his own terms. A couple of days ago, for example, Raman decided to smoke a cigarette. He prayed, "God, I know that I said if you take the pain out of my chest, I'll never stick this in my mouth, but please go along with me. I think you got a sense a humor. Let me enjoy this little deviation."

Unlike some other people, Raman does little on a regular basis to practice or deepen his spirituality. For him, relating to God is sporadic. Indeed, it occurs so irregularly that one might ask what keeps spirituality alive for him at all. The answer is the continuing conversation in which he engages with his past, especially with the memory of his father.

Raman remembers when his father was dying. "I really feel the presence of God through my dad," he says. "When my dad was dying, he accepted where he was going a couple of weeks before he died. He was already communicating with his brothers. He wanted to leave. And he's almost conscious, telling us that he's ready to leave. That's very beautiful, and I'm always hoping that when I pass, I want to believe that when these people say that there's a light that they go in, I want to take that part of religion."

But the conversation with our past is often less conscious than this and less easily tied to a specific event. Raman remembers how his father talked to God from day to day and sometimes, without fully realizing who he is imitating, Raman talks to God in the same way. Being poor, he and three of his six brothers shared their father's bedroom. Raman recalls, "I used to hear him talking, murmuring, muttering to God." As a result, Raman knew his father was "filled with God." In fact, his father told him repeatedly that "he couldn't make it without God."

It is by comparing himself with his father that Raman has developed his own form of spirituality. Raman attributes his unwillingness to believe certain religious doctrines to having had more options than his father and to not having lived "in ignorance" as much as his father. "I think in some areas of the world, I've been more enlightened than my father," Raman explains.

He says he "aspires to become strong in my convictions" like his father, but he also admits that his father "had to have faith" because of the hard life his father lived. "He had to have something very, very significant spiritually in his life to have kept him together those many years. My father's life was not easy, and he always seemed steadfast in his conviction in God."

For Raman, then, turning to God when times are tough—during his heart attack, for example—is consistent with the way he understands the circumstances that reinforced his father's faith. When things are going well, Raman feels less need to follow particular spiritual practices. He also extracts some of the behavioral traits he admires in his father and says these are the part of his father's faith that he wants to retain. "He was an honest man. He was a good man to other people, a very good man, and if I wanted to imitate any of his qualities, those would be his qualities."

Locking On to Something

Some of the changes Raman Wilkins experienced are also evident in Lillia Rizzo's journey. Although her life has been relatively orderly, she has put distance between herself and the church, and yet has developed a more personalized style of faith through a continuing, inward dialogue with her memories of her mother.

She began moving away from the Catholic church psychologically while she was in high school, even though she has remained a member all her life and still lives within a few miles of where she grew up. She thinks she may have had a personality disposition that caused her to question things, but she is sure the church's stand against birth control was a decisive factor in distancing herself from it. She and her husband started dating when she was fifteen and he was eighteen. Lillia was a virgin when she eventually got married at age twenty, and she gave birth a year later; within three years she was a mother of three.

After that, she began practicing birth control. When the Pill was introduced, she was one of the first women in her neighborhood to start using it. Like her mother, she went to church when she really wanted to go, but there were times when she found herself too busy and tired. The word she uses to describe her spiritual journey is thus "searching." She says she has always been "coming and going, always trying to get back to tradition, always searching. I think my whole life has been a process of searching."

But as she searched, Lillia always remembered the past: hearing her mother pray, going to church, the sense of "belonging" she had at the parochial school and among her extended family. She says, "I knew there was more out there," and she felt empty.

These feelings reached a climax when she was approaching her fortieth birthday, and she remembers them vividly: "On the outside, it seemed that I had everything: a good husband, a family, a home, a job, enough to eat. By most standards, I should have been satisfied that my life was taking a nice course. But at that point I knew there was something missing from my life. I didn't know exactly what it was, but I knew I was wandering around with that feeling inside me." She says she had been through enough changes in her life and done enough searching that she "knew enough to know I didn't know anything."

In the midst of her search, Lillia started observing the woman next door and wondering why this woman seemed to have such a deep faith. The woman sparked further memories in Lillia's mind. "I'd always been taught to live a Christian life, and I looked at her, and I said, 'Gee, I wish I had that kind of faith.' I saw how she handled situations and how she prayed." Lillia tried to grasp more effectively the belief in God she had learned as a child, but was unable to "lock on to anything" for a period of six months or more. Toward the end of that time she decided to try to quit smoking, and at a nonsmokers' clinic met a woman who invited Lillia to accompany her to mass. It would be "uplifting," the woman said, especially the music and the message.

Lillia recalls, "She took me to mass at another parish and it was a charismatic mass. And the minute I'd gotten there I just knew that there was a difference here. I didn't know what it was, but I knew there was a difference. I said to my friend, 'Gee you know I'm so happy you told me to come, and it's wonderful. I really would like to, I'm happy I'm going to church, but in our tradition I wanted to receive the Eucharist.' And I hadn't been to church or to any of the sacraments for so long, so I said to her, 'Gee, I really would love to go to Eucharist, but I haven't been to church or confession or anything from our tradition for so long.' 'No problem,' she said. She called this priest over and asked him to hear my confession. So he said, 'Oh, yes. Come here.' Takes me aside and holds the whole mass off and everything, so I can go to confession, because he knew, she told him, in my heart I wanted to receive the Eucharist more than anything else that night.

"So that was wonderful. I was a little, like you know, everything was taken onto me so quickly, but I said, 'Great.' I went to mass and received the Eucharist, and there was a prayer reading first, and when we left there I knew that somewhere, somehow, someday, through an involvement with this, that I was going to find everything I was looking for. I was going to find this God everybody talked about. This personal relationship, faith, and trust that you know is genuine and real and something that's going to change your whole life.

"That was a Wednesday night and the following Sunday, I said, 'I have to go to church now. I really have to go this Sunday.' So I went to our parish and I looked in our church bulletin, and here we had a charismatic prayer meeting that I didn't even know about every Wednesday night. And for some reason I went that Wednesday night, and for the past eighteen years I've really been learning about God and faith and trying to live that life. It's just so wonderful to have this in our church, it really is."

For Lillia, attending the charismatic prayer meeting every week has been her way of returning to the tradition she had learned as a child but doing so in a way that is personally meaningful to her as an adult. "It brought me back to the church, and taught me how to have a personal relationship with God from within my own tradition. I realize that this is what I was looking for. I was looking for faith and trust. And I was looking for God."

Her faith has thus become more personal, but in the process she has also been able to rethink her past and to discover a deeper reason for being involved in her church. "If you get to know God, you have a relationship and you communicate, and so you're going to want to go to church, just to communicate with him and to communicate with your community. So it's nice to be involved in church services, because you're really sharing with other people." She adds, "I've really been able to focus in on who I am as a person, to see my whole background, and to see my life—to see the areas that need to be changed or let go of or worked with."

Lillia's ability to move forward with her life has required her to remember her past, to reconstruct it, taking more responsibility for it and learning from it. "You start reviewing your young life, your whole life, because you have so many years behind you now. You start taking responsibility for your own actions." She calls this process "the healing of memories." For example, she has been able to remember more clearly her relationship with her mother and her godmother—her aunt—while she was growing up; doing so, she has dealt with some of the guilt she has stored away about feeling closer to her godmother at times than to her mother, and she has begun to appreciate more deeply how much she benefited from both these women's love.

The most touching consequence of working through her childhood memories and of "healing" them was a closer relationship between Lillia and her mother during the last two years of her mother's life. As her mother gradually succumbed to cancer, Lillia was able to communicate with her more openly than she ever had before. The two women were able to talk frankly about cancer, death, God, their feelings, and their families. A few days before she died, Lillia's mother asked Lillia to pray for her. "She said, 'I tried to live as long as I could, for your father and for you and your sister.' And she said, 'Frankly, I can't take it anymore. I am wiped out.' She said, 'I can't take the pain, I can't take anything. So now what I want you to do right now,' she said, 'I want us to just be real quiet, and I want you to pray.' She said, 'I want you to ask the Lord to come and get me, because I'm tired and I just want to go home.' So I said, 'Okay.' It was so wonderful to be able to pray with her, to be together, and just to pray and ask the Lord to come and get her."

Principled Conflict

For some people, moving away from the religion of their childhood occurs gradually but then surfaces rather abruptly. Although they may have entertained misgivings for some time, some particular event triggers their decision to drop out, switch, or begin investigating other venues. Often, these points of departure are literally that: the moment when a young person leaves home to attend college, serve in the military, take a new job, or marry. Of these, marriage—along with the dating, sexual activity, decisions about child rearing, and relationships with family members that surround it—is especially likely to serve as a point of departure. Why? Because religious organizations have tried harder to police marriage than virtually any other rite of passage and thus precipitate conflict with people who disagree with clergy rules.

Peter Arno, the man who felt distant from the Catholic parish he attended as a child, provides an instructive example of how marriage can come to be a point of departure. He found an active parish when he was in college, and thus felt more fully integrated into the church by the time he graduated than he had ever felt before. However, he then fell in love with a woman who had been married previously, and this relationship precipitated conflict with the church.

"She had been briefly married before and had been divorced. I didn't realize it, but that of course causes a tremendous problem in the Catholic church, because you're not supposed to be married if you're divorced—I still don't understand the exact rules—and supposedly they can give dispensations for these kinds of things. I didn't realize what a complicated process that was. It seemed very straightforward to me. That relationship was hardly a marriage to begin with, and it was very short lived and it was not a good situation. It seemed very clear to me that religion should be able to deal with something like this, and the Catholic religion couldn't. They just said basically, 'Well, you can't get married with our blessing,' and I finally got so disgusted with the whole thing I said, 'Fine. Who cares.'"

Peter and his wife were married in an Episcopal church, and when they started raising a family, decided they would become active in an Episcopal parish rather than try to return to the Catholic church. Peter says the liturgy is similar enough that he feels more like he's made a "transition" than undergone a conversion. Although part of him remains angry at the Catholic clergy, he has been able to gain some perspective on what it means to grow up religious as a result of this experience. "Religion is something that's supposed to be a constant in people's lives," he asserts, "a constant source of morality regardless of whatever else changes." He appreciates that stability, viewing it as a point of origin that is valuable for children to have. But he also feels it is necessary for adults to live in the real world, where "you are going to have conflicts within your own principles." No matter what one's religion is, he feels adults need to think through their own principles and then participate in a religious community that is capable of respecting their decisions.

Meeting Jewish Girls

Ezra Feldman was greatly influenced by his grandfather. Still, his early experiences with Judaism filled him with ambivalence. On the one hand, there was something solid, if mysterious, about his grandfather's faith; on the other hand, Ezra felt distant, both from that faith and from the rituals in which he participated at the synagogue. There was something warm, intimate, and comforting about his grandparents' home life, but as a child Ezra felt like someone peeking through a curtain into a world he did not understand. His own home fell somewhere in the middle, occasionally offering times when being observant made sense but then violating enough of the rules that it left him confused ("I always felt my father was making up the rules as he went along; there was no consistency, like there was with my grandparents").

When Ezra was a senior in college, he started attending services at the Jewish student center. "I wasn't particularly interested in spiritually uplifting experiences," he says. "My primary interest was meeting Jewish girls." Soon after, Ezra did meet a young woman with whom he instantly fell in love. They dated passionately for six months, talking a lot about their attitudes toward Judaism, exploring what kind of Jewish home they would like to establish, and occasionally hinting at marriage. Eventually the woman broke off the relationship, but it had awakened a new interest in Judaism in Ezra. As he pondered what it would be like to be an adult, to be married, and to be embarking on a career as a biologist, he discovered that he was becoming personally interested in Judaism in a way that was different from his upbringing.

He enrolled in a Hebrew class, became more active at Hillel, began tutoring bar and bat mitzvah students, purchased a set of phylacteries, and began praying. He explains: "There was something I wanted to connect with. I didn't know what it was. Somehow, what had happened in my own household wasn't terribly attractive to me. I don't think I really understood what it was until later in life, but at the time it was just kind of unattractive to me. In my family, I was being made to do it, but now I was wanting to do it on my own. I had a sense that there was something there I wanted to connect with, that God was out there somewhere."

Over the past fifteen years, Ezra has continued to search for God: at times he has felt closer than at other times. For a while, he was able to participate in Shabbat in the home of some friends who made him feel like part of the family. Eventually he married a Protestant who converted to Judaism, and together they gradually became more active in their spiritual seeking. They have attended a number of different temples, and are currently members of one, but Ezra says it is mostly a matter of "convenience" because they feel the need for someplace to worship.

What has meant most to Ezra in recent years is observing the Sabbath with his family and praying alone each morning. These activities remind him of the past—of his grandfather and of the many generations preceding him—and, even more, they give him a chance to stop the bustle of everyday life long enough to reflect on his life and regain some control over it. He explains observing the Sabbath this way: "We don't do any commerce on Saturday. We don't work on Saturdays. If we have to do shopping, we either do it before or leave it until afterwards. It changes the whole way I experience my life. For one thing it feels more like *my* life and less like something that's driven by the world around me. Sometimes I actually feel like I'm in touch with God."

Open the Doors

Jess Hartley attends a church that is almost like the one he attended as a child, and he says his values are no different from his parents'. He takes his daughter to church and teaches her some of the same prayers he learned growing up. He has nevertheless been engaged in an extended period of spiritual exploration. As soon as he was old enough to drive, his parents let him skip some of the services at their church because he had athletic practices to attend; then, in college, he traveled with the gospel choir on Sundays rather than attending any specific church. The day after graduation he returned home and resumed working for his father. Jess's uncle had become pastor of the church his parents attended, but there was dissatisfaction in the Hartley family about how the church was being managed; Jess took the occasion to start shopping for another church, and some Sundays he didn't attend at all. It was personal contacts, more than anything else, that kept him involved.

He remembers: "Corner of Colson Street and Broadway, one block over from Ellis Avenue. I started going there. The fellow that had the community choir, his mom was the pastor. Loved his mother. She was like another mother to me. I've had four women who have been pastors in churches who have been very, very dear to me. She was one. There was another lady, both of whom have passed away. And then there were two others. One of whom I sat under as a pastor because that's where my wife was going. And another who's up in another state, who ironically was one of the people who, unknowingly, helped to start to turn me back around to being more in touch with my spiritual life. She was an evangelist. She came and brought a service to this church off of Colson Street one Sunday. I just sort of went in for Sunday service, and went through the motions. I was going to leave and go do whatever I wanted to do. They had dinner afterwards, and this place was very small. Pews and all, maybe it was the size of my living room. So when it came to dinner, they had a little kitchen, and they just put folding tables up in the front and you sat there.

"They said, 'Brother Jess, aren't you going to stay for dinner?' 'Oh, I don't know, I think I'm just going to go ahead—' 'Oh, you don't have any place to go.' 'Okay.' So I sat there having dinner, and this lady was sitting across from me. It was like I'd known her for my whole life. I mean, we just [he snaps his fingers] hit it off, just like that. To this day, we are very, very close friends.

"It was through her that I met Pastor Della Tentley and started going to some of her evangelistic meetings. She'd come up to me, 'How is my friend?' and look at me, and I knew that I hadn't been living the way that I should have. It was like she was looking right through me. 'How have you been? How's life treating you? Are you attending church? Where are you going now?' Things like that. And just looking in this lady's eyes, I'd feel so much conviction, as if I knew that I hadn't been living like I should have.

"She was just so sweet. She died of a massive heart attack at her home, at her ironing board. My dad knew her, too. We came home from work and we had our regular thing where I'd pull up, let my dad off, back up to the back door, take everything out that we weren't going to use the next day, put everything into the van, pull it back up to the back of the house so we'd be ready to go the next day. And I'd always go in the house. So this one day, I left my dad off, did everything, came back up and went to walk in the house. And he's standing there at the door. He never was standing at the door to open it for me. We'd seen each other all day, and he's standing there looking at me. I'm like, 'Yeah? Why are you standing there?' And he says, 'Listen, I have something to tell you.' I said, 'What?' He says, 'Pastor Tentley died of a massive heart attack today.' I just fell against the door, standing there looking down, like 'Nah, this has got to be a bad dream.' I just couldn't believe it. It's just one of those relationships that there wasn't a lot said, wasn't a lot done together, but when we did see each other and connected for the little time that we had to speak, I just felt a real, real closeness to her."

After Pastor Tentley died, Jess drifted in and out of churches for several years, eventually marrying, and then began to feel pressure from his wife to affiliate with a congregation. Each of them did "a little visiting here and there" on their own. Jess remembers finding a church he wanted to join. "So, unbeknownst to my wife, on Sunday when the doors of the church were open, I got up and I went up and joined."

By chance, Jess's wife happened to be there, too. "And she's there crying like crazy, because she was so happy. She told me later that she had prayed to God and said, 'We really need to do something, and if it's your will for us to be here, let Jess join today.' And sure enough. And we hadn't talked about what I wanted to do. I was actually praying and saying, 'If it's your will, Lord, let the doors of the church be open today.' Because in a lot of our churches, opening of the doors of the church isn't just something that's arbitrarily done. Somebody needs to voice to the pastor, 'I would like for you to open the doors of the church so that I can become a member next Sunday.'"

What kept him in the faith community in which he had been raised was thus a network of friends and relatives. Despite times when he was uninterested in church, he continued to shop around, met people who took an interest in him, and they put him in touch with others. Internally, he was also undergoing a change. "I've read more on my own to get a better understanding as to what God really is to me," he says. "It's just deeper rooted. Rooted might be the wrong word, because you think of what was put in way back, but it's more real to me now than it was when I was younger. Being an adult now and having the ability to choose what I want to do and when and where, it means so much more to me. That's why I can appreciate what I learned growing up, even more now than anytime ever before."

Talking with Institutions

Whether or not people stay in direct contact with the religious institutions in which they were raised, it is evident that those who grew up in such institutions carry on a continuous conversation with them. Their congregations remain in their minds, and as they make shifts in their own views of spirituality, they interact with these images, reinterpreting them in ways that help make sense of where they are going.

Clearly, some people have more opportunity to move away than others do. For example, a woman who met her husband at church when she was fourteen and married him three years later had little time to explore other options. In fact, she observes, "I wanted to wander. If I hadn't been church going and a Christian, I think I would have been wild, really. But then I met my husband, and he was from a strict background, too, so we were never out doing anything bad."

But most people have the chance to move out if they wish. That many of them do so should not be surprising. Deeply religious backgrounds are no guarantee that people will remain in the same faith as their parents. What will become more evident in the next chapter, however, is the extent to which this faith goes with them, even when they move.

→>-<-

CHAPTER 8

Remembering the Past

ALTHOUGH PEOPLE MOVE AWAY from their childhood religious understanding as they mature, they also carry that understanding and their related religious experiences with them, doing so partly because it is never
possible to escape the past entirely. One poet captures this ongoing influence of the past when he writes of mothers as the ones "hidden inside the
clothes of our body."[1] In other cases, remembering what it was like to have
grown up religious is done intentionally, reflectively, in order to learn
from the past. It is through the deliberate attempt to remember that memory becomes anamnesis.

Curiously, the act of moving away has been accorded much greater le-
gitimacy in American culture than the act of remembering, even though
both are important. For instance, adults are supposed to grow and to move
to higher stages of faith, just as they are supposed to become self-sufficient,
leaving their parents' home, finding their own career, and fulfilling their
own dreams. In contrast, focusing on the past is denigrated as nostalgia or
as an unrealistic desire to live in a time that no longer exists.

The stories in this chapter are examples of anamnesis. They show how
the past becomes a living memory when people take the time to reflect on
it. Memory is then, as Frederick Buechner has so aptly written, "more
than a looking back to a time that is no longer; it is a looking out into another kind of time altogether where everything that ever was continues
not just to be, but to grow and change with the life that is in it still."[2]

For most of the people we talked with, the past conjures up ambivalence. People who grew up content in their religious traditions have sometimes come to realize how secure they felt only in retrospect. Some of them have returned home in the sense of having greater appreciation for their religious upbringing. Others have come to see more clearly that their upbringing was filled with pain or that it was excessively restrictive. In some cases, people have become more aware of physical and emotional abuse. Although the details vary, the common dimension is that deliberate conversations with the past play a vital role in the hard work of spiritual development.[3]

Looking over One Shoulder

When Stephen Fukuyama graduated from college, Uncle Sam congratulated him with a letter from the local draft board. It was 1969. American soldiers were dying by the thousands in Vietnam and new recruits were sorely needed. Having heard so often his parents' stories of the internment camps during World War II, Stephen had mixed feelings about serving in the military. For a few days he contemplated fleeing to Canada like so many of his friends were doing. But his parents had instilled in him the belief that Japanese Americans needed to try even harder than European Americans to demonstrate their patriotism. Stephen decided not only to serve, but to serve as an officer, a decision that was to prove pivotal in his religious development.

He had attended church for as long as he could remember. Both sets of grandparents had come to America shortly after the turn of the century, and they believed firmly that "being a Christian is part of being a good American." By the time World War II broke out, both grandfathers were dead. Stephen's parents were married but had no children. They, along with the two grandmothers and several aunts and uncles, were sent from California to a relocation camp in Arizona. After a year, some people from a Methodist church signed papers saying they would be responsible for Stephen's parents, so they were allowed to leave to attend a Methodist college in the Southwest. Stephen's father served with General George Patton in Europe immediately after graduation and then entered seminary. It was thus that Stephen came to be raised in a series of Methodist parsonages.

Looking back on his youth, Stephen says it reminds him a lot of *A River Runs Through It*, the story of a Presbyterian minister's family. Stephen's parents were strict, loving, hardworking parents who expected the best from their children. Stephen was the "good son" who went to Sunday school and youth group, said his prayers, and read his Bible. His brother was the "bad son" who rebelled against the pious ways of his parents. The brother was killed in a motorcycle accident when he was a teenager. Stephen remembers the little wooden dog tag everyone was given one summer at a Methodist youth camp. The youth leader said that you were close to Christ whenever you wore it. Stephen's brother was wearing his when he died.

After his brother's death, Stephen increasingly questioned the religious beliefs of his parents, even though he still sat quietly in the pew each Sunday morning. President Kennedy's assassination confirmed his growing cynicism toward God. Then, during college, Stephen noticed that his small cohort of friends from high school was gradually getting smaller. One day he learned that a friend who had been on the football team had been killed in Vietnam. A few months later, word came that the brightest student in the class had also been killed.

Despite the risks, Stephen's own dream was to become a pilot in the air force or navy. Neither would accept him because of his eyes. The army didn't care how well he could see. "They needed grunts, foot soldiers," Stephen explains. He took basic training at Fort Ord and officers training at Fort Benning, Georgia. By 1971, he was a combat platoon leader in Vietnam. "They said, 'Infantry are a dime a dozen; their lives are limited and they die very easily, so we need a lot of replacements.' I was a replacement platoon leader for the 101st Airborne Division. I kept pleading and telling them I didn't jump out of airplanes. They corrected me and said, 'We no longer parachute out of airplanes, we take helicopters and jump, repelling with ropes, or we'll put you on the ground close to it.' So I was a platoon leader in Vietnam for approximately eight months. Nixon was sending troops home at the time, and so I was transferred out of the jungle into a truck outfit for a month or two, running ice cream and bullets out to fire bases. From there, I got out of the service, in '72."

While he was riding helicopters, Stephen had time to think about what he wanted to do next (if he lived to do anything). He says he had always done what people told him to do, just assuming he had no say in the matter, but now he realized he was going to have to make some decisions. "I realized, sitting in the jungle, that I was getting letters from home from these people all over, saying, 'I hope you're doing okay.' And cookies. You know, they didn't forget me. I realized right there that I kind of just took everything for granted. Never making solid decisions, just saying, 'It's automatic, there are certain ways you have to act and do.'" Suddenly it dawned on him that he had already made a crucial decision of his own in choosing to be an officer. He said to himself, "I'm going to have some say about it. This is a battle I'm going to meet. I will have some control over it. I'll lead people into battle, and I'll have some control over the living and the dying."

That realization prompted him to start thinking, "If I get out of here alive, what do I want to do?" He read his letters and ate the cookies from home. "I was moved by those people," he recalls. "They were supporting me and accepting me without asking anything in return. They were just doing it out of their spiritual commitment." Stephen decided he, too, needed to "do something to the best of my abilities." He applied to medical, dental, graduate, and law schools, and eventually chose to go into law. And he vowed that if he succeeded, he would return to his roots. "I will come back and stay permanently, I will find a little Japanese church. As my commitment to God, I will support those people. With the little bit of talent I have, I will use it to my utmost. So that's what it is: a payback."

He says people at work kid him, saying he just felt guilty. Having practiced law now for nearly twenty years, and having been an active church member all that time, Stephen thinks he was motivated by more than guilt, however. "I have this theory," he explains. "As you go through life, you should always look over one shoulder. If you do, you'll see the people who helped you get where you are. You'll see these humble people supporting you all the way. They may be the people of God. That's why you've got to look back."

Lessons from the Past

With varying details, Stephen Fukuyama's story emerges again and again in our interviews. To remember the past is to connect it with one's religious upbringing and thus to interpret events through religious eyes. For those who have grown up religious, it is virtually impossible not to see the religious meaning in events. And this meaning is often clearer in retrospect than it was at the time.

The growing awareness of a person's religious upbringing is heightened by virtue of living outside that tradition for a period of time. Stephen Fukuyama realized more keenly than he had before how much the Methodists he had grown up with meant to him while he was away from them in Vietnam. Absence makes the heart grow fonder, the saying goes. But there is a more important dimension to this awareness. Stephen's image of looking over one shoulder to the past is instructive, for it suggests that only part of a person's attention can be guided by the past if that person is still to move ahead.

The way in which other people speak of their past helps to sharpen this insight. Part of them interprets events, especially public events, just like everyone else. And another part of them sees the religious significance of these events. On the one hand, television and newspapers, or politicians and friends at work, are the sources of one's interpretations. On the other hand, the languages one has learned from religion supplies another set of interpretations. In this way people start sensing what it is like to live in two worlds.

Vern Gordon, for instance, was in high school when Martin Luther King Jr. was killed. His most vivid memory is that the school play he was in was canceled. He also remembers feeling endangered because he had to ride a bus from one part of town to another; he recalls windows being broken and bricks being thrown. At one level, then, his experience of these events was like everyone else's. On another level, though, social and political events have special, spiritual significance that only those with spiritual eyes can see. Vern says that the civil-rights movement came to be interpreted within his family and his church as a spiritual struggle. Of the freedom marches, for instance, he says, "Spirituality had to play a part in it for the people going down there, because not only did they have to believe seriously in what they were doing, but they had to have thought that God had to be on their side, because they were going into the eye of a storm." For him, the Vietnam War also carried a religious message. It reinforced his belief that people should place their ultimate faith in God because, "If you put your faith in American leaders or human leaders, there will be something lacking."

His memories of the civil-rights movement and of the Vietnam War are thus divided, giving him a clearer sense as he grows older of being somebody with a religious past as well as a person who simply has experiences like everyone else. Raman Wilkins's story of how the civil-rights movement influenced him and Delmer Schwartz's memories of the Vietnam war illustrate this same heightened awareness.

Looking back on their childhood, many of the people we talked with also say they lived in very homogeneous settings—religiously and often racially or ethnically as well. For them, heightened awareness is often associated with some ambivalence about the degree of this homogeneity. They generally view the breakup of these homogeneous enclaves as a positive development. They value having greater freedom to make their own choices, believe it is good for people of different kinds to mingle, and say they are glad to see more tolerance toward other groups. But they also talk about what has been lost.

When they were little, they could simply take for granted that their own group was right. Even the specific customs of their church or ethnic group could be practiced without questioning them. Now that there are more choices available, it takes more effort to get along in the world. Many of them have developed a second language for commenting on the sources of their primary religious affinities. People learn to talk about those affinities as accidents of birth and as products of the times. They say that one must distinguish the core principles of faith from the ways in which particular groups talk about their faith. In short, remembering the past has required developing a language in which to describe it.

Vern Gordon also exemplifies these ways of talking. As he looks back on his experience in the African American community and as a Baptist in the 1950s and 1960s, he sees how the wider society forced him to live within a relatively homogeneous community. "All our involvement back then was in the black community," he observes. "We didn't have the freedom to go and do things that white kids would do. So we were pretty much immersed in it, legally, and otherwise, too. I remember quite well going to a bus station and I can remember the colored and white signs. I never had any thoughts about going to that other section. Your mind set is such that the thought never even enters your mind, because you know, 'Hey, I can't even go to that area.' So there's a lot of things that never even enter your mind. We were only in an environment that we were put into."

He says the same things about his religious heritage. "The whole environment had always been Baptist. That's the kind of upbringing we were around. If you are constantly around an environment and that's all you see and that's all you hear, then you follow suit. It was very much a homogenous group there. Definitely no Jewish people, and I don't recall Catholics in our environment either."

As he talks about it, Vern describes this environment as a relatively safe, sheltering place in which to live, and it is only with greater exposure to the wider world that he understands just how sheltering it was. "Back then," he says, "I had not been in an environment where I had seen broken homes. I guess my grandparents did keep me sheltered from a lot of things. I had never even known a family that was broken or didn't have love or even seen violence, because back then, even watching TV, you didn't see violence. The first couple of years we were in the very rural area, so we didn't come in contact with anyone. Then moving to what we thought was the big city, which compared to the city nowadays is still very small, we were in a house with neighbors maybe fifty feet or so away. But didn't come in contact with them that much, other than we'd see them on a regular basis. There was no thought, in fact, about people getting divorced. So I pretty much thought that all families were the same as ours and like the Cleavers. Everybody just loved everybody and you always had the two parents. I was not exposed to negative things. I can understand better now about some of the things they were praying for that wouldn't happen to their household."

He also has more understanding now of other forces making the society he grew up in the way it was. For example, he says it did not strike him until many years later that the church was still the most segregated of all institutions in the 1950s and 1960s. In retrospect, he thinks it is strange that religious people are mostly talking about the same God and the same heaven but refuse to worship in the same churches. He also remembers that the pictures of Jesus that he saw as a child were always of a "white man with blue eyes and a goatee." He thinks black children learned implicitly that white was good and that black was bad. "If you have negative views of yourself," he says, "then there's just no hope, especially for yourself and your culture. There's just no hope." Reflecting on the pictures of Christ he was raised with, he says, "And even going to church, you would see an all-white Jesus, so it's like you were doomed. You're just negative from the start." He says he's glad that things have changed. He points to black beauty pageants and to the Kwanza celebrations that have begun in African American communities since the 1970s as examples.

Vern is himself aware of the ambivalence expressed in his comments about the past. Interacting with people in his church, family, and neighborhood was especially important because of the affirmation this interaction provided. Yet his parents also encouraged him to interact with the wider world. He says, "The society told us we were inferior, but our family gave us values that strengthened our positive attitude toward ourselves. I think we felt more comfortable within our own group. But we were also taught to mingle and not to be clannish. If you aspire to any kind of position, you really have to be able to interact with everybody. And you can't be clannish, because if you are, then you more than likely will not advance. So it's very hard. It's kind of like walking a tightrope."

Growing Up

People grow up religious, and then do it all over again. The first growing up takes place in their families and congregations when they are children. The second growing up occurs in adulthood as they gain a clearer understanding of the messages they received in childhood and as they learn to move beyond these messages. The second growing up may take as much effort and extend over as many years as the first.

With adult vision, some people come to realize that their parents may have also been more ambivalent about religion than they were able to recognize when they were children. This is especially true of people who realize now that their parents wanted them to follow timeworn customs but also valued doing whatever it took to assimilate and be successful. Hal Meyerson puts it well as he describes his parents' attitude: "We weren't living in the shtetl anymore, in the village in Europe. We were living in America and we had to make our way among Americans and be like them. You had to assimilate, in other words. They knew that we had to fit into America, get jobs, get work, be successful. Yet they didn't know how to have us maintain our Jewish values as we were assimilating. This was the great problem."

Other people have come to realize that their parents were ambivalent about some of the traditions of their congregation or that their parents had been unable to give expression to their needs within the tight community in which they lived. For example, one man talks about an older brother who had been wounded during World War II, became addicted to the pain medicine, and eventually took his own life. The man remembers that his father, a leader in the local church, quit attending for several years. At the time, the man thought his father was angry at God, but he realized later that his father could not bear the shame of facing people he knew at the church.

Another example is Karen Stacy. Like a number of people, she has come to realize more fully that religion was a source of family conflict at the same time that it undergirded family unity. She is surprised, in retrospect, that she did not know her paternal grandparents better, because they lived only about a mile from her parents. She thinks there was probably a lot of conflict between her grandfather and his daughter-in-law (her mother). She remembers how he used to order both her grandmother and her mother around ("'Woman! Do this.' And, 'Woman, do that.'"). She thinks it probably "drove my mother bananas." But because they were all "very churched people," nobody ever talked about it.

For some people, part of growing up the second time has also been learning to respond differently to old stimuli. The messages people carry in their heads are sometimes very powerful indeed, especially when they have been reinforced by biblical teachings. As adults, people are able to respond differently to these messages only when they have become more aware of what the messages were. Lillia Rizzo talks about "playbacks" and "old scenarios." "You know, you play these scenarios in your head." Many of these scenarios are unconscious, instilled in her by the way she'd seen members of her family and congregation respond to one another. As she has participated in her prayer group in recent years, gone through counseling, and reflected in private about her past, Lillia has been able to move beyond these playbacks. She has done this by repeating them often enough and consciously enough that they no longer haunt her from the corners of her memory and by putting new voices into these conversations, voices from her present self that say, "Yes, but I see things differently now; she also loved me; she was doing the best she could," or whatever. Lillia says, "The difference is that your thought processes change and you don't play those same old scenarios in your head anymore."

Coming to Terms with Abuse

Although most of the people we interviewed speak fondly of their child-hood memories, a few offer examples of the negative consequences of some kinds of religious upbringing. They were physically abused, disciplined so severely that they had difficulty developing a positive self-image, or taught to fear a domineering, authoritarian concept of God. A woman now in her seventies, for example, remembers her father's beating her as a child. "He always attended church," she admits, and "he loved to sing, had a beautiful voice, played the violin." But she also kept as much distance from her father as she could. "It's so vague," she explains. "I'll tell you, with my father, I don't remember too much about him, because I was actually afraid of him. He was so stern and hot tempered and all that. I always kept a low profile, out of his way. I always felt that I'd be punished for something even though I didn't do it."

Our interviews were not designed to test systematically the differences between abusive upbringings and other environments, but other research suggests that *fundamentalism* is a distinguishing factor. One psychiatric study of abused children found that they came from all religious back-grounds, but that a significantly large number came from fundamentalist homes characterized by rigid, authoritarian beliefs.[4] In another study, re-searchers systematically compared the attitudes of parents who had physi-cally and emotionally abused their children with the attitudes of parents in five control groups chosen to represent different religious traditions, in-cluding fundamentalist Protestant. The abusive and fundamentalist par-ents were found to be statistically indistinguishable, while parents from liberal Protestant and Jewish backgrounds were the most different from the abusers.[5] Research has not probed the reasons for such findings suffi-ciently but suggests that fundamentalism legitimates physical punish-ment by adopting a literal interpretation of biblical verses encouraging this kind of punishment, that fundamentalists emphasize the sinfulness of children, and that the self-esteem of parents themselves may be low in such settings, making it difficult for them to nurture positive behavior in children.

The people we interviewed who had experienced abuse as children confirm some of these suppositions and suggest other factors as well. A working-class man in his fifties struggles to find appropriate words to express his feelings about the harsh, discipline-oriented, conservative Protestant tradition in which he had been raised. "Sometimes I think religion makes you a weaker person," he ventures. "You know why? They beat it into you that, 'Oh, God's going to punish you for doing this or doing that.' Then you, 'Oh, wow! Why'd I do that? God's going to punish me.' You have like a shroud over your head."

He continues: "That's the way the old folks used to say, 'God's going to punish you for that.' Makes you maybe insecure sometimes. It depends. It depends on what kind of upbringing you have." Trying to explain why he feels this way, he adds, "It's like when we were young and our sisters would tell us ghost stories and scare us a little. Now, when you grow up, you're afraid to walk through the woods or you're afraid to walk down that road. You're scared. Now my kids, I never scared them. They think nothing of walking down to the woods. That's how I relate religion. But maybe I can't blame it on the religion, maybe I have to blame it on the people I was brought up with."[6]

Other people have painful memories of being physically punished in ways that might be considered abusive but that were justified in the name of the Lord. A woman in her late twenties who grew up in a fundamentalist church, for example, says it was just common in her family for parents to spank their children. Her grandparents spanked both her mother and her father, and her parents spanked her. "My father hit us," she confesses. "I'm not going to lie. My father did hit us." She says her brother got hit the most.

One time, she recalls, her brother opened the fire hydrant and got his new shoes all wet. "My brother was all wet and my father hit him, and he had marks like for three days on his legs. And I think my father got like in shock, and he promised him he will never hit him again. My brother was like ten years old, and since that day my father has not touched my brother." In recent years, she has also been able to discuss these times more openly with her father. "Like my father says, 'I hit you guys. Sometimes I used to hit you guys and I don't even know why, and it's because when you're young you think that because your father hit you, that's the right way to reprimand your children, thinking that it's the right way and it's not.'"[7]

Jess Hartley illustrates a certain kind of abuse as well. He received severe spankings as a child, and yet he knew his parents were not simply
striking him because of anger, and so he is able to look back on it with a
sense of humor. "You know what a switch is?" he asks. "Branches. And the
worst part about switches was when your mom sent one of your siblings to
get one and they brought back a tree trunk! I remember how that used to
happen all the time, and Mama would say, 'I just want to give him a spank-
ing, I don't want to kill him.'"

Sometimes it was the combination of physical punishment and not
knowing when or why one was being punished that was the most trouble-
some. One woman says she'd had her mouth washed out with soap as a
child, not for saying bad words, but whenever her parents decided she had
been "disrespectful." A man recalls that he had learned to "clam up" and
say as little as possible to his parents, because even a reasonable discussion
would sometimes result in a board's being applied to his rear end. Another
man remembers having his mouth washed out with soap for calling his
mother "Mommy." She and his father insisted that she be addressed as
"Mother."

Some of the household chores that children were expected to do would
perhaps border on abuse as well, although hard physical labor was not
seen that way at the time. It was a duty that one fulfilled for a parent who
demanded respect. The biblical injunction, "Honor thy father and thy
mother," gave chores a kind of religious austerity.

A man who grew up in a family of staunch Calvinists in the 1930s remembers vividly how he spent his Saturdays: "Saturday you had to do all
of your chores. My chores consisted of mowing the grass, which was
around three acres of grass. We had to do the front part, which was about
a half acre, by a push mower, reel-to-reel push mower. And in the back we
had to run an eighteen-inch power mower. I had to trim the hedges, and
we had hedges all around the house. I had to do that. Weed the garden.
Weed the truck patch, which was about an acre truck patch, had to keep
that weeded.

"Had to clean our room. Had to scrub the dining room, living room,
kitchen floors, and that was the size of the whole downstairs of this house.
We lived in a big home. My older brother and I were supposed to do it
together, but he was older than me and bigger than me, and he usually

wouldn't do it. We had to get down on our hands and knees and scrub that floor. We had linoleum floors. Just didn't have a choice. Had to help my mother with the wash, and that was the old wringer-type washer.

"Every night we had to wash the dishes and dry them. And if we went to bed and it wasn't done, and my dad would come home, midnight, one o'clock in the morning, if he was out, and if it wasn't done, he'd come and get us out of bed and take us downstairs, 'You didn't finish the dishes,' and we had to finish the dishes." In retrospect, the man says these chores were always linked subconsciously in his mind with God. "It was always, 'You will do this because I said you will do it. You will do this because it's expected of you. You will do this because it's what's right in the sight of God.'"

Besides abuse that may have been associated with parents' religious beliefs and practices, children who grew up religious were sometimes abused because their lives were exposed to much of the same tension and dysfunction as people from other backgrounds. Some were reared by a deeply religious parent who was married to someone with no religious convictions, and some of the religiously oriented parents were nevertheless alcoholics or mean spirited.

Abuse was then part of a much larger set of problems that drew the entire family into its vortex. Sharon Olds, writing of her alcoholic father, has captured this experience well. "Our lives slowly disappeared down the hole of his life," she observes.[8] Under such circumstances, the special events that created fond memories for some people became nightmares for others. Family devotions were clouded by sudden temper tantrums, or holiday celebrations would be shattered by drinking and violence.

One woman paints a graphic picture of how her family usually celebrated Christmas. "My father was always out drinking on Christmas Eve and then it would be time to put up the tree. We had these big clunky Christmas lights that they don't use much anymore. It would be my father's job to put the lights on the tree. My brother and I would kind of make a bet as to what time Dad would come home this year, drunk, and wrangle around with putting the lights on the tree. This is partly why it was hard to respect my father, because my mother would open the door at the top of the hallway when my dad would be coming in and yell, 'Cheezit, here comes the grouch!' We would all run in different directions so we weren't there when he came upstairs, because we never knew what kind of mood he was going to be in or whether he would just kind of keel over on the floor or what. And the smell, I'll never forget. But he would come home and do these lights. Inevitably, he'd be up half the night, swearing and yelling because they would get all tangled up, and it was just a nightmare. He had a volatile temper. The tree wouldn't always be decorated that night if he gave up in the middle of the night. Sometimes he would pass out or go to bed before he finished, so we would finish it and put the tinsel on." Sometimes she would sit in church on Christmas and break into tears. Only later did she fully come to understand why.

Dying for Acceptance

Apart from overt abuse, the hardest part of growing up religious for many of the people we interviewed was feeling they were never quite good enough. This feeling stemmed directly from the parents' idea of what it meant to lead a godly life. Children learned early that they were wicked, incapable of pleasing God, and yet expected to do their very best to live as God wanted them to. These parents were strict disciplinarians who spoke with such authority that their children often confused what their parents said with the voice of God.

A woman I'll call Madeleine Dunn talks at length about her struggle to gain acceptance from her father and from God. Her father was a brilliant, eloquent, godly man who read the Bible to his children, prayed with them every day, spoke often about God at church, and talked about God a great deal at home. Indeed, he quoted and paraphrased the Bible so much that Madeleine was sometimes unsure whether the words were his or God's. She knew that God and her father were often displeased with the way she behaved and that her mother always took their side instead of hers. When asked what she remembers her parents said to her about God when she was little, she responds, "My parents talked to me about God's discipline and God's rules and God's wrath and what God expected of me." When asked what else they said about God, she asserts, "That's about it." And when asked what she thought God was like, she says, "I thought God was like my father."

The connection she drew between her father and God was that both were interested mainly in her wrongdoing. "They were one and the same, on the same discipline team; both were disciplinarians. I imagined God as someone who corrected me when I was wrong, who made my path diffi-cult when I was doing something I shouldn't be doing, and who forgave me if I cried enough and was genuinely repentant and admitted I was just completely wrong, and I'd start all over and try to do better. Which is the same image I had of my dad. My earthly father and my heavenly father were very similar."

Madeleine had good reason to worry about displeasing God. Unlike children who thought God would overlook their misdeeds, she was sure to receive a scolding from her father. "I worried about disobeying God be-cause that would mean I was disobeying my dad, which meant my life was going to be miserable, and I would be called into these little meetings with him and have to repent and show visible remorse. I knew there would be repercussions. It was a strange kind of triad: Me thinking that if I dis-obeyed some of God's general commandments, and knowing that my dad would see it. And because he saw that I was disobeying God, he would then discipline me kind of in place of God."

The infractions were typically not of specific rules, such as playing in the street or abusing the dog. Instead, they were of broader and more ab-stract mandates, such as being a good person or having a good attitude. Breaking them was thus an indication of some deep-seated personality problem, not simply a temporary failing. Madeleine felt that it was *she*— her very being—that was not good enough. "If I was selfish, or if I was not kind to someone, or if I didn't accept authority, then that, to my dad, was a sign that I wasn't pleasing God. I was displeasing God, so I had a person-ality trait that needed to be corrected and changed. And my dad would take care of that for God. Certainly in action things. I was fearful enough of this displeasure that there were no drugs, no alcohol, no sexual activity. Nothing visible. It was mostly personality traits."

As Madeleine matured, she gradually realized that no matter how hard she tried, she would never be quite good enough. Whenever she thought about dying, she imagined herself arriving at the pearly gates and being told, "Well, I'll let you in because you're a Christian, but we're disap-pointed with you and, by the way, here's a list of things you still need to work on." Somehow, she could understand that sort of attitude from God, but she found it harder to accept what seemed like constant disapproval from her parents. Her high school sweetheart (whom she dated in secret) became her only source of unconditional love. And when he died from a sudden illness, she worried that God was trying to send her a message. At least she was sure her father would not have approved of her boyfriend.

A decade later, having established herself in a career, Madeleine still found herself unable to please her parents. She remembers on a visit to her parents making an offhand comment about a misunderstanding with a mutual acquaintance that was causing her some inconvenience and frustration. "My dad said, 'I need to talk with you. We need to sit down and talk,' and that meant in his office. This is what had happened all my life. Every time I had done something wrong or maybe he had seen something in my personality he thought needed to be changed, he would say, 'We need to sit down and talk.' That meant, my dad, my mother, and I would sit and we would hash this thing out until I admitted I was wrong and I cried and said, 'You're right. I'm wrong. I love you. I'll try to be better.' This happened like twice a month. So here I am, I'm almost thirty, and he wants to talk with me. So I come to the office. He says, 'Sit down,' and he starts talking to me about how I need to work on this attitude. I have a terrible attitude problem. I don't know how to deal with frustration as a Christian.

"I remember thinking to myself, it wasn't necessarily what he said, but the fact that I think I had kind of always thought in my mind that at some point in my life I will become good enough that he will stop doing this. He'll reach a point and he'll say, 'Madeleine has arrived. She's good enough. My job is finished.' But I realized that day that this was never going to stop, that I was never going to 'make it,' I was never going to please him. I remember how devastating that was to me to think, 'This is never going to stop.'"

Madeleine ran out of her parents' house and drove away in desperation. She was not seriously contemplating suicide, but all she could think about was dying. "I remember thinking, 'You know, if I was dead, people would come up to my dad at the funeral, and they would say, 'Madeleine was such a wonderful person. You know, she helped my daughter. She was so encouraging. She was this. She was that.' And he would finally reach the point where he'd say, 'Yes, maybe Madeleine was a good person.' I remember thinking about how to kill myself so that he could finally realize, 'Well, maybe she was a decent person.'

"The thing that stopped me was this: after people tell him that I was a good person, then he'll think, 'But look at this stupid thing she did. If she was here, I would sit her down and tell her how stupid that was, how selfish it was.' So I was thinking about killing myself because he would finally get it, yet what stopped me from doing it was the fact that it still wouldn't work!"

She also realized that she could no longer reach out to God for help. "I got to the point where I couldn't even pray to God, because all I could see was my dad and God on this other side. And I couldn't see how I could have a problem with my relationship with my dad and not have a problem with my relationship with God, because it seemed like if I had problems with my dad, that meant something was wrong. Therefore I couldn't reach God either. That was the real dilemma."

At that point, Madeleine decided she needed professional help and sought a pastoral counselor who understood the kind of upbringing she had experienced. The counselor helped her see that she had seen only the disciplinary side of God rather than the love of God. It helped especially when she was able to recall that her father had interpreted love to mean discipline. "He said, 'Love is discipline, and that's what I'm doing.' So that was the perception I had of God's love. It meant he disciplines us." It also helped to disentangle her images of her father and of God. She started realizing that she might never be able to earn her father's complete approval but that God's love was unconditional. A decade later, she is still struggling to understand that realization.

Beyond Nostalgia

Historians are often critical of sociologists who write as if there were some golden age that has now been lost. Stories of physical punishment, abuse, and emotional distress like that experienced by Madeleine Dunn show that growing up religious should not be regarded as a golden age. In light of such revelations, the nostalgia for lost worlds that some of our interviewees exhibit may seem to be a similar misrepresentation of history. But remembering the past, even with fondness, is not the same as glorifying it.

For instance, when Stephen Fukuyama counsels us to look over one shoulder to the past, he is suggesting only that the love one may be able to see in retrospect is indeed love worth remembering. Similarly, when Hal Meyerson bemoans the loss of Jewish tradition, he is not saying that things were better in the past than now, he is asserting the importance of remembering the past and of keeping its traditions alive.

Hal Meyerson's father, Samuel, is helpful in this regard. We were able to speak with him at length during one of his periodic visits to his son's house. Samuel is the one Hal credits with having explained the Torah to him, with having taught him to pray fervently, and with telling him stories about his ancestors. Many of these stories demonstrate that the past was scarcely a golden age. For example, Samuel's grandfather was working in the field one day near the shtetl where they lived in Russia when the Cossacks swooped in on horses, rounded up all the men, women, and children, and shipped them off in boxcars to work on the Trans-Siberian Railroad. Twenty years later the Red Cross located him and brought him to the United States. He was the only survivor from the village.

Samuel's father had already come to the United States as a teenager, so he missed the worst of the pogroms in Russia. But Samuel remembers how difficult it was for Jews in the United States during the 1920s. "It was an atmosphere," he says, "where from the day of your birth you fought for your existence." The major industries routinely refused to hire Jews and blacks. Catholics and Jews went around in gangs to protect themselves from each other and from Protestants. By the time Samuel graduated from high school, the Depression was making it hard for anyone to find jobs. He worked temporarily in Yiddish theater, traveled through the Midwest with a huckster who seized mineral rights in exchange for farmers' gambling debts, and eventually made it through college playing football.

By the time Hal was born, Samuel and his wife had settled in a section of the city known locally as Jew Town and Samuel and his father operated a construction firm. Samuel says it was a "ghettoized community" populated mainly by Jews, who lived within walking distance of the synagogue, and a few blacks and Catholics. It was not a pleasant place to live, he admits, especially because it was overcrowded and some of the people were "rowdy." There was also constant discrimination in business, in country clubs, and in schools and colleges. Samuel says, "I came to realize that there wasn't much difference between me as a Jewish man and the guy next door as a Christian man, and I couldn't understand why he didn't trust me and I couldn't trust him."

This was the environment in which Hal was raised. The reason he cherishes the past is not that it was wonderful but that Jewish tradition was embedded in this past and he is convinced it is worth preserving. As Hal says, he will sit shiva with his father when he dies, and Hal will remember Samuel's words about tradition: "We are a conduit through which passes all of the traditional rituals, precepts, and practices of the older generation. The traditions pass through each generation, being carried on to a new generation for the purpose of making that one a better generation than the ones that have gone before."

The Lasting Significance of the Past

Remembering the past has lasting significance when it creates enough of a vacuum that people feel inspired to work harder to fill that vacuum. Nostalgia, conditioned with ambivalence, points to the importance of carrying on the practices that have been embedded in traditions even if it must be done in innovative ways.

For Hal Meyerson, the sense of loss is quite profound, and yet it prods him to move ahead with a greater appreciation of the precariousness of life. When he was growing up, he says, "ninety-nine percent of all Jews were tied to the central Jewish functions: the synagogue, the community center, the ghetto. Now it's hard to have thirty-five percent of the Jews tied at any one given moment in time to their Jewish background." His most heartfelt comments are like this. He paints images of a world that has been lost, a world not only of Judaism in decline but also of happier times that are now impossible to recover. For instance, he talks animatedly about the fun he used to have at United Synagogue Youth conferences, including the hotel where he and his friends used to look forward to meeting girls from other temples; then his smile fades as he describes how the hotel is now boarded up and waiting for the wrecking ball. Speaking words that convey a deeper meaning, he remarks, "It's depressing to think about something that is so vital and alive in your memory and then realize that there is nothing left."

But he also believes spirituality is even more important to him than it was to his father and grandfather. "It's in my soul," he explains. "To them it was meeting the criteria that they needed to meet to make peace with their maker, and to them that's traditional Judaism, more than it is spiritual. I feel that my spiritual Judaism says that if I'm a good person and I treat people well and other creatures on the face of the earth, that God knows that I'm a good person and that's part of my spiritual communication with him, and *that's* what's going to be my salvation with him. Whether I light candles on Friday night is going to be less important than how I treat my fellow man."

He nevertheless attends services three or four times a month and he talks to God all the time. Having learned as a boy to pray, he still prays, and he lives within a kind of spiritual framework. Faced with hard decisions at work, he says he does everything he can, and then "I just sit back and talk it out with God." Doing so gives him inner strength and compassion. "It takes compassion from somewhere deep within my soul," he says. "And God helps bring that out."

Reinforcements

The rest of Vern Gordon's story is worth telling, too. His musings on the past make him realize that things often stay the same, even when they change. Much about race relations in American has stayed the same, despite the dramatic changes Vern has witnessed in his lifetime. Much remains the same about the Baptist church, even though he no longer adheres to it as faithfully. Growing up the second time has convinced him of the need to move and yet to find reinforcements.

Over the past twenty years, he says, "I sort of feel that I have not done as much from the standpoint of going to church and maybe vocalizing my commitment to God as I should. I think that is one area which I need to improve upon." He adds, "My basic beliefs have remained the same over the years, but in physically showing commitment, I've not done as much as I think I should or could do." As he talks, he notes on several occasions that "the physical actions and going to church have changed."

Partly, what he is talking about is a change in his *attitude* toward church. When he was a child, all his relatives and friends were Baptists. He says they would have been greatly disturbed had he decided to become a Presbyterian, let alone a Catholic or a Jew. Only Baptists were the true believers. As an adult, Vern is more inclined to think that denominations are just "traditions" and that Christians at least pretty much all have the truth, whatever their denomination may be.

He remarks, "From my knowledge of some of the other denominations, there's maybe one or two beliefs that are different and hence you have a different denomination. I think all of them, at least all the Protestants and I guess Catholics, too, want to get to the same place. They have the same belief in heaven and doing, quote unquote, the proper thing, that you will go to heaven. So I don't think there's that much of a difference within the denominations. It's just that the Baptist is something that my family has always been involved with. It's just a tradition."

Emphasizing the "proper thing" means that the teachings of particular churches matter less. But, for Vern, that also means, as he says, less physical involvement as well. "Since I became an adult, I have not been involved with the activities in the different church groups as much as I was before." He says he attends religious services "but not on a regular basis." Several times he has made New Year's resolutions to become more active but has not carried through on these promises to himself.

He also admits that religious organizations have not played any formative role in his spirituality as an adult. He explains, "the church environment is a good environment for the most part, but one that is not needed to carry out the functions that God has for us on earth." Speaking more broadly about his spirituality, he also asserts, "It's not how many times you go to a religious institution, but it's how you carry yourself and how you treat others." In contrast, he says, some people say, "Hey, I went to this institution once or twice every Sunday, and so therefore those other six days I'm home free."

If being in a church environment is unnecessary for being a spiritual person, Vern nevertheless remains convinced that certain practices in daily life are essential for reinforcing one's faith. Talking about the tracts and devotional booklets that his mother and grandmother carried in their purse, for example, he says, "We all need reinforcements in whatever we do. Even if it's the love we have from our parents, it's good to have that reinforcement. Even though you know your parents love you, to hear them say that, I think, means a lot, or a spouse, or what have you. I guess maybe reading just reinforces one's views spiritually. Some people have positive feelings from reading the verses from the Bible. It helps to reinforce what we already believe."

CHAPTER 9

The Move to
Spiritual Practice

How do people who grew up religious move from the taken-for-granted world in which they had been raised to a more deliberate, intentional approach to faith? Many people, of course, do not make this move at all. People from the most intensely religious homes sometimes lose their interest in spirituality, either from sheer boredom or because they found such upbringing oppressive. Others continue on, perhaps claiming to believe what they always did and even attesting to the centrality of faith to their lives, yet doing little as adults to deepen their spirituality. The people I am interested in are the exception to both those patterns. They are the ones who decided at some point that spirituality was a quest worth pursuing actively, a pursuit requiring time and energy. They can be understood better, however, by beginning with an example of someone who did *not* choose this path.

Something Higher

Sandra Barton, age forty-nine, works part-time as the office manager for her husband's roofing business. This is her second marriage. Shortly after graduating from high school she was married the first time. Three years later her husband left her. She then dated a man for nine years, who died, leaving Sandra devastated. She says her present husband "pursued" her for a long time before they got married. Sandra and her husband attend the Presbyterian church in which she was raised.

Growing up, Sandra attended services every Sunday, went to Sunday school and youth group, participated in vacation Bible school, attended her denomination's summer camp, memorized Bible verses, and ate lots of fried chicken in the church basement. She continued attending faithfully until her father died five years ago. Now, even though her mother disapproves, Sandra attends church only when she feels like it. She figures she probably is there about once a month. And it does not bother her to miss. She says she knows it is possible to be a good Christian without being compulsive about church.

In these ways, she is fairly typical of the American public. At least sixty percent attend religious services about this often. About seventy percent identify with a particular denomination or religious tradition. And more than eighty percent say it is possible to be a good Christian without actually participating in any religious organization.

Sandra Barton is also typical in her religious beliefs. She says that these beliefs hold a fairly important place in her life. They are, she explains, the foundation for her values. They keep her from doing bad things. For instance, she says it would never occur to her to spray graffiti on an overpass or subway wall. She believes in God, though she isn't sure what God is like. Indeed, she thinks it is impossible to know. But she says there has to be something "higher than us" because the world is just too complex to have come into being by itself. "Even if everything just evolved," she muses, "who got it started in the first place?" She also believes in heaven. The present world, she thinks, is "a living hell." So it comforts her to believe that everything will be better after we die.

When asked how religion or spirituality enters her everyday life, therefore, Sandra Barton insists that there is an important connection. She says religion is just part of her outlook on life. It prevents her from having to think about her values. And it gives her confidence that "somebody" is in control. Especially when things are going badly, she feels better knowing that she can ask God for guidance. Sometimes, as she sits in church, she even experiences a brief feeling of serenity.

But Sandra Barton does not engage *deliberately* in any spiritual practices, other than attending religious services sporadically. She does not pray or meditate. She does not read the Bible or any other religious or inspirational books. She does not watch religious programs on television or listen to religious music. She says she prefers to "keep quiet about that," rather than talking about her faith or spirituality with other people. She says that trying to forgive others is not an issue for her. And she expresses no interest in becoming more disciplined about her spirituality.

Yet she does provide a valuable clue about spirituality. The reason she does nothing actively to pursue spirituality is that such practices are not intrinsically rewarding for her. That is, spirituality offers a kind of vague hope that things will turn out better in the end, but as long as things are going okay at the moment there is little need for it. This view, in fact, can be traced to her childhood.

After describing the various religious activities in which she was engaged as a child, she volunteers that her favorite one was attending vacation Bible school. The reason is that the children received P's (as in "Presbyterian") for attending, for memorizing verses, and for doing good deeds. The children with the most P's won a prize at the end of the week.

Whether it stems from this kind of inadvertent religious instruction or some other experience, Sandra's approach to spirituality has remained much the same as an adult. Asked why she attends church, she admits that desiring to please her mother is still an important motive. If nothing else, churchgoing helps keep peace in the family. Asked what she likes best about the congregation, she says, "I grew up there; I have friends there." And, in talking about what she gets from attending church, she chuckles and admits that her husband sometimes gets paid for fixing the roof and gets referrals to repair other church roofs in the area.

Practice as Practical Wisdom

The obvious contrast to someone like Sandra Barton would be someone with an explicit, systematically theological understanding of God and of his or her relationship to God. Someone like this would go beyond saying that God is simply someone or something "higher than us." He or she would proceed to give a full account of the nature and attributes of God, as well as a doctrine of creation, the origins of evil, the possibilities of redemption, and the reasons people should believe in certain tenets about immortality and eschatology.

We found no living examples of such people, despite the fact that some of the people we interviewed are clergy, the children of clergy, or have received extensive religious training. A few can point out books to read that provide such theological understanding, but they deny that these books adequately reflect what is most vital about their own faith.

The better contrast to the nonpracticing Sandra Bartons are people who live inside of a faith commitment, actively praying or meditating, reading devotional materials, or demonstrating their faith in deeds of service.[1] Their understanding of spirituality is more practical than doctrinal, providing provisional insights about what to do and why to do it rather than being composed of full-blown statements about the nature of truth. Indeed, some of the people we talked with claim they have a better understanding of God as adults than they did as children, but most admit they have grown to understand God less. One writer, describing how well she had understood "Mister God" as a child, expresses this movement clearly by saying, "Mister God keeps on shedding bits all the way through your life until the time comes when you admit freely and honestly that you don't understand Mister God at all."[2]

By focusing on practice, I do not mean to imply, however, that all truth is relative or ultimately unknowable. People may be painfully aware that it hurts when they accidentally put a finger on a hot stove. And they may hold certain tenets that are less easily verified yet are regarded as absolutely true (for example, that God exists or that justice is good). Even if they hold such tenets, most people nevertheless live in complex circumstances where it is not readily apparent how these truths apply. We have to apply them in the course of our practice of life itself. For instance, a fundamentalist who believes that every word of the Bible is literally true still has to figure out how to apply these truths in daily life, just as someone who believes only in freedom of conscience does.

Deciding how to live, moreover, is always more complicated than simply determining that an abstract principle or rule pertains or does not pertain to a given situation. Many more considerations enter into moment-by-moment decisions than we can consciously consider. We often respond, as it were, automatically. Or we weigh our options carefully but then decide without being able to articulate every consideration that went into our decision. This is why we depend on our practices in daily life. We learn to respond to complex situations by becoming habituated to such decisions. We absorb bits and pieces of information in the process of training and as we engage in our practices over time.[3]

To say that some people engage deliberately in spiritual practices, then, is to suggest that they have chosen to undergo training, and in most cases to continue such training, just as a person may do to keep in shape physically. What such people have discovered is that spiritual practices are neither automatic nor easy, but that there is, in the words of psychologist James Hillman, value in "staying with tough stuff in a time of the fast fix and the quick buck."[4]

Specific spiritual practices differ from time spent working, sleeping, conversing with friends, or relaxing. "Our daily life in office and home, in cars and airplanes, at parties and conferences, while reading magazines and watching television, while looking at advertisements and hearing radio, are in themselves continuous examples of a life which has lost the dimension of depth," Paul Tillich observed. Such a life "runs ahead, every moment is filled with something which must be done or seen or said or planned. But we cannot experience depth without stopping and becoming aware of ourselves."[5] Spiritual practices provide time to reflect on life by allowing one to remove oneself temporarily from the busy activities of the everyday.

These other activities are nevertheless influenced by spiritual practices, often through the implicit processes of making decisions. In this sense, the practices are not only deliberate but internalized and habitual. Writer Reynolds Price, who thinks of his writing as a spiritual discipline, illustrates clearly how practices become internalized, habitual, when he observes, "I really don't go into my room thinking, 'Today I'm going to do something that makes the human race more merciful than it used to be,' any more than a horse thinks, 'I'm going to walk across this field and jiggle that barbed wire fence because I'm a horse.'" He adds, "It's the nature of my mind, and it's what my parents reared me to be, and it's the operation of grace in my life and in my work that lets other people feel that this is the result."[6]

Learning to Practice

For those who continue on a significant spiritual journey as adults, the pattern we observe repeatedly in our interviews is one of gaining distance from religious organizations through a process of discovering a more personalized style of faith. Gaining distance does not mean that people necessarily quit participating in religious organizations but that they expect to receive less from these organizations, often become willing to *give* more of themselves in service to these and other organizations, and learn more effectively how to communicate with God in their personal lives. Spirituality comes to have greater meaning in their everyday lives because it includes insights gained through experience, prayer, and devotional reading.

Often, growing up religious has provided models for these spiritual practices—for example, memories of adults who seemed to pray with special intensity, or simply the habit of family devotional rituals—but it becomes necessary to rediscover these models and sometimes to transcend them in order to take greater responsibility for one's own spiritual development.

A woman who grew up in a Protestant family that attended church every Sunday offers a valuable example. Spirituality had been so much focused on Sunday school and church services that she had never felt a need to pray or read the Bible on her own while she was growing up. But after college she was asked to teach a Sunday school class. At that point she decided she needed to be getting something out of her spirituality if she was to have anything to impart to her students. "I can't give from something that's empty," she thought. So she began reading the Bible, more or less at random, and praying for a few moments in the morning.

She tried to do this every day, but generally missed two or three days each week. Nevertheless, she found the experience rewarding. She had a sense of "gradually growing" and of "getting to know [God] better." Now, more than twenty years later, she still reads a few verses from a devotional guide and prays nearly every morning. She feels more of a personal relationship with God and is more reflective about how she lives. "It's something that is personally beneficial for me," she explains. "I just think God was leading me, directing me to do or say a particular thing. On my own, I would have done something different, but I know that it was his spirit guiding me."

Although the specific practices may vary, the common dimension is that people start to take responsibility for their own spiritual development and thus begin to acquire personal knowledge and skill that goes beyond what they have learned simply by being a member of a congregation. For some of the people we talked with, religious music was the avenue by which such development took place.

For example, Alan Threadwell learned to play the organ in high school and then took a volunteer position as children's choir director at his church. As he selected hymns and taught the children to sing, he became increasingly aware of the theological significance of the hymns. He says, "Hymns clearly state what your position is in relation to God. They are also a means of defining who God is. A hymn that deals with praise will clearly articulate what the theology of the church is as it relates to the Trinity. You also have hymns of doctrine, hymns that deal with justification, hymns that deal with stewardship, hymns that deal with mission, hymns that deal with the Nativity, the nature of what was the Resurrection. They will define what the church is, so that when a church has hymns that are of sentimentality, it produces a theology of sentimentality."

Whether it is through music, reading, or just meditation, the focus of such practices, people tell us, is increasingly to reflect on God rather than simply learn new skills or resolve personal problems. For example, Alan Threadwell also spends time praying and meditating as a way "to really understand the magnitude of God's goodness." Alan recognizes that his life has been relatively comfortable, compared with the way many people live, and so his thinking about God helps him remember that these comforts are "gifts" that he does not necessarily deserve and that he should use to help make other people's lives better. He thus tries to be of service by working on church committees, by living frugally, and by donating time and money to charities.

In other cases, people remember the exact words of prayers they had learned as children but as adults start praying them with renewed interest and meaning. The naturalist Edwin Muir, for instance, writes in his diary of finding himself one night repeating the Lord's Prayer over and over with greater fervency than he had ever said it as a child: "It was late; I had sat up reading; I was sleepy; but as I stood in the middle of the floor half-undressed, saying the prayer over and over, meaning after meaning sprang from it, overcoming me again with joyful surprise; and I realized that this simple petition was always universal and always inexhaustible, and day by day sanctified human life."[7]

Another recurrent theme in our interviews is how a newly conceived relationship with God enables people to reshape their interaction with friends and family members. As they recall their religious past, it becomes more evident to them that they were *children* in that remembered world. All relationships were asymmetrical, other people being on top, and them on the bottom. Their relationship to God was thus like that to their parents: one of dependence, perhaps fear, involving a need for obedience, and in turn supplying comfort and security.

As they rethink these memories and as they seek a new understanding of themselves spiritually, they often come to see God more as a friend or confidante and their peers more as brothers and sisters. They are thus able to relate more as equals with their peers rather than feeling they are still children who need to receive comfort from other people (or perhaps resenting the fact that others treat them as children).

Lillia Rizzo's relationship with her mother, for example, shifted to the point that the two were able to relate more as peers than as mother and daughter. Lillia also observes that she has been able to think of her own children in a new light. As they have matured, she is able to think of them as "brothers and sisters in the Lord." She is able to treat them more as adults and to detach from some of their problems.

Many of the people we talked with have learned the importance of following certain techniques in order to cultivate their spirituality more intentionally. Before considering those techniques, however, it is important to realize the extent to which the spiritual practices of adults, like those of children, are embedded in social relationships. Whereas these relationships are largely a result of family and congregation for children, they are likely to be more deliberately chosen by adults. Nevertheless, the latter often reflect the former. Indeed, people's descriptions of their spiritual practices show that the specific techniques may vary from one month to the next but the practices themselves are part of a continuing spiritual journey, which in turn is part of a changing understanding of one's relationship to God.

Looking for Love

Judy Sutherland is a woman in her middle forties whose spiritual journey has taken her from the Presbyterian church of her childhood, through

Billy Graham meetings, the sixties' counterculture, and periods of deep distrust of God, to an identity as a born-again, charismatic, evangelical Christian. Her story is especially helpful as an example of how memories of the past play a significant role in shaping one's religious identity as an adult.

As a child, Judy attended the Presbyterian church just down the street from where she lived. It was a church of about three hundred people, most of whom were doctors, lawyers, business and professional people, and others of the upper middle class. Judy felt slightly out of place because her father was a machinist and her mother worked as a retail clerk. Still, she had friends at church, attended Sunday school and Sunday morning worship services every week, sang in the children's choir, participated in youth group, and went to church camp in the summer. Judy's father was a lapsed Catholic who had become so disillusioned with religion that he refused to attend church or have anything to do with religious discussions. So her mother was the driving force in her spiritual life, making doubly sure that Judy and her sister learned about God at church.

Judy did learn about God. She learned that God created the world and watched over it, and she learned that Jesus was God's Son, who had come to earth, been crucified, and rose again. She also learned to say the catechism, went through confirmation class, and absorbed much of the ambiance of church by sitting each week and staring at the beautiful stained glass windows, candles, and altar. But Judy feels in retrospect that she never quite understood what she was learning and thus found it more of a chore than a fulfilling experience. "It was kind of like God was over here on Sunday morning and the rest of your life was separate. It was nice to do all these activities and have social times together and be do-gooders in the community, but it didn't seem to have a connection to me. So even at an early age, I apparently sensed that."

In Sunday school, Judy remembers a very dedicated "motherly" teacher who told Bible stories and who devised activities for the children, such as "cutting out pictures of Joseph and pasting them somewhere." Judy liked the woman but admits "nothing was clicking." In the Sunday evening fellowship groups, Judy also found herself wondering what was happening. Typically, the meeting was in the church basement or at one of the parents' homes and included volleyball, refreshments, and a discussion of some topic.

Judy says, "My remembrance of the material covered is vague. We sometimes would discuss problems that some of us were having. It would be a discussion group. I don't remember it being related to the Scriptures. The meetings were pretty informal, mostly social. If we did Bible things, it was kind of perfunctory and it apparently didn't make an impact on me." Her worst memory is of catechism class. "It was studying church history, learning the Apostles' Creed. To me it was just like schoolwork. It was boring and dull and did not connect with real life. It was kind of an unpleasant experience. It was, in my mind, a formality that had to be gone through to join the church, and so I did it."

Judy's childhood image of God was thus of someone she did not understand and did not feel close to. God was church property. And in the absence of a better grasp of God, she began to imagine that God must be like her father: someone to be feared. Judy's dad was an alcoholic. So was her mother, but his drinking was more out of control than her mother's, and he was sometimes physically and emotionally abusive. She says her view of God "certainly wasn't a biblical one. I thought of him as an angry father." About the only times Judy thought about God was when she did something wrong; she was sure God saw her misdeeds and she generally felt guilty whenever she thought about God. "Obeying God was just a burdensome thing, so I put it out of my mind as much as possible."

Judy could just as well be talking about God as she describes her father's sitting in the dark, drinking and her trying to sneak past him to go to bed. "I remember how many times I went down that hall not knowing where he was at, if I had done something wrong or not, always being afraid I had, afraid I was going to displease him. I remember shirking, pulling back and kind of ducking, just in case. He was ready to backhand me as I went by. That was his method of discipline. I just don't remember him being a part of our lives much except in that kind of way."

Her mother was often at work when Judy went to bed, so Judy has no memories of her mother's praying with her, reading her Bible stories, talking about God, or saying grace at meals. Judy's experiences of feeling close to God were thus limited to rare occasions. Once at summer camp she slipped quietly out of the dorm at sunrise and walked down to the river by herself. For a few moments, she felt transfixed. "I guess it was a kind of spiritual experience," she says. "It gave me a sense that God was real, a sense I'd never had in church."

Another memory is less positive. "My mother had very bad stomach ul-cers, and they broke one evening at home. I was about eight years old. All of a sudden my mother was screaming in the back bedroom. My sister ran up the hallway, and I picture this vividly, that she was crying and scream-ing things like, 'Oh my God, Mom's going to die!' I saw my sister kneel at the kitchen counter and so I just followed suit and we cried and prayed that my mother wouldn't die." Her mother did not die, but she underwent emergency surgery and took a long time to recover.

When Judy was in junior high, she had another momentary encounter that brought her close to God. It was at a Billy Graham revival meeting. "I heard this Billy Graham fellow in very clear terms explain to me who this Jesus guy was, for the *first* time. Who he was and the fact that I was a sinner and I needed a savior. And that God isn't some horrendously punishing person, but he does require justice, and his grace is combined with justice by the gift of Christ. Billy Graham put it all in context for me and said, 'This is a personal thing. This isn't something you get while you go to church. You can't be saved and go to heaven just by attending church or being confirmed or going to catechism or singing in the choir!' It was like, 'Oh my gosh!' All of a sudden, things started to fall into place. 'This makes a lot of sense to me.' So he said, 'If you've never done this, you need to do this. You need to become born again.' I had never heard those words."

In language that she has come to understand only in later years, Judy explains what happened next. "He asked each person to get out of their seats and walk down in front of the stage in order to pray what they call the sinner's prayer together and become born again. It was at the end of the service and there was music in the background and it was very emotional. People were flooding up to the front and crying. They had counselors and workers who had been trained to help the people as they came and make sure you're not standing there alone. He then had you repeat the sinner's prayer after him. That consists of admitting you are a sinner, just agreeing with what God says in the Bible, that you believe that Jesus is the Son of God who came to save you from your sins. He is God's payment for all sins, and you just accept his gift of that payment. You give your life to God, you make a commitment to Jesus Christ and ask Him to be Lord of your life. He shares the Bible verses and explains that you have now become born again. Prior to this, your spirit that God created was dead and not con-

nected to God. When you're born again, you're born of the spirit and re-
connected to God. You have reestablished the connection that Adam and
Eve had before the Fall. Christ has made that possible."

Judy was instantly taken with the idea that God could be personal and
loving rather than distant and punishing. "I was crying and crying and crying and I could hardly see by the time I got down to the front. But I knew
it was something I had to do. The following week our youth group talked
about what had happened. The leader said to me, 'Now, Judy, why don't
you share with the group what happened, because you went down.' So I
did, and everyone looked at me like I had three heads!" The event turned
out to be a momentary experience for Judy. In retrospect, she thinks she
might have grown closer to God had she been in a church that helped her
do so, but she was not.

During high school, Judy stayed involved in the church because her
mother wanted her to and because there were some cute boys in the youth
group. Then they quit going, and she did too. "I was looking for love in all
types of places," she says. Not only was she seeking the love she felt lacking
in her childhood, she was also compensating for a steadily deteriorating
situation at home. Having no money to attend college, Judy got a job and
lived at home. Every penny went to pay for her father's drinking habit, so
Judy finally insisted he move out. A few months later, Judy's mother had
to be placed in a long-term nursing facility because her own health was
failing badly. Judy moved to a cheap apartment and tried to establish some
direction in her life.

Over the next three years, Judy interacted infrequently with some people at work who called themselves born-again Christians. Judy thought
they were pretty bizarre, because they told stories about food in their
house multiplying miraculously, but she was mildly attracted to the idea
that it was possible to have such an intimate relationship with God. Still,
she was even more interested in having an intimate relationship with
man—a specific one who rode with a motorcycle gang and smoked marijuana. Judy began riding with the gang and drinking but never felt that she
could really be part of their lifestyle.

Judy spent the next several years "running from God," as she now puts
it. She and the man she was living with moved temporarily to the Southwest, and there Judy met a woman who also called herself a born-again

174 ➤ MOVING AWAY

Christian. The encounter brought to Judy's mind her own "conversion experience" at the Billy Graham meeting. "Oh my gosh, God is after me
again," she realized. Through some other friends she was drawn into a
prayer meeting, where on several occasions she felt her own prayers were
being answered. God started to seem more "real" to her, someone who was
personally interested in her and who was trying to meet her needs.

A few months later, a girlfriend of Judy's persuaded her to "rededicate"
her life to Jesus, and Judy started attending an independent gospel church
with this woman. The people were very demonstrative, Judy remembers,
expressing their love of God in highly emotional ways and asking God to
meet their every need, including their desire for material things. Judy was
impressed by how loving the people were, seeing in them how she could
relate intimately with God. She was baptized and symbolically turned
over a new leaf, breaking off her relationship with her boyfriend and becoming actively involved in a small Bible study group that met in her girlfriend's home.

After spending two years in this group, Judy decided to quit her job and
move to be closer to her sister (their mother had died while Judy was away).
The move forced Judy to find a new church. It was also an independent
evangelical congregation that emphasized personal relationships between believers and God. But it was more biblically based, Judy felt. As she
reflected on the church she had been attending in the Southwest, she realized that it was "very self-centered" and taught a "very self-absorbed slant
on the gospel." At the new church, she was able to be demonstrative during the worship services, but there was also a sense of God as King or Lord
rather than his simply being there to meet people's needs. Shortly after
joining the church, Judy met a man who had religious views similar to
hers, and they fell in love and were married. The past decade has been the
happiest one in Judy's life. She feels she's found the love she had always
been seeking.

Judy's story is thus one of moving away from a certain kind of religious
upbringing to a different style of faith and in the process gaining a more
nuanced understanding of God. The idea of a transcendent God that was
distant, external, powerful, and capable of evoking fear came naturally
from the environment in which Judy was raised. Because her exposure to
teachings about God was entirely in church, rather than at home too, she

found herself *knowing about* God—much like she knew about geography and history—rather than feeling that she really *knew* God. She did not see her mother pray, so Judy had no idea how to talk to God, and her father's erratic, alcoholic behavior left her with the impression that God was also unpredictable and wrathful. Lacking parental love, she was attracted by the warm, intimate, loving God she heard about from Billy Graham and at the church she attended in the Southwest. As she has learned more about her faith, she has moved toward a more "balanced" view, in her words, that combines both the transcendent and immanent aspects of the sacred.

It is also clear from this story how strongly recollections of the past figure into a person's self-understanding of spirituality. Judy's memories of her religious upbringing are not simply an accurate rendition of what happened but a selective reconstruction that allows her to make sense of where she is and where she is going. She paints her religious upbringing largely in negative terms and in so doing is able to explain why she was without faith for a number of years and why she is now in a different kind of church from the one in which she was raised. Yet it is also evident that her religious upbringing was the occasion for learning Bible stories and for thinking about God in a way that would forever frame her search for love in religious terms. Her continuing sense of God's being "after her" was firmly rooted in the half-understood stories of God that she had learned as a child. Thus, she says, "I'm grateful that my mother made me go to church. It set the foundation for my seeking God."

Permission to Be

If Judy Sutherland's story shows that a relationship to God is central to understanding spiritual practices, it is equally important to recognize that practices also develop in conjunction with changing social relationships. I suggest that childhood spirituality is rooted in authority relationships with one's parents and with God. The fact that people move in their spiritual journey thus has implications for the parent-child relationships that are so important in spiritual development. Not only do people reconstruct their memories of their parents as they themselves mature, but also their parents may well be changing as they grow older. Seeing how parents change, especially in relation to a person's memories of who they were when she or he was growing up, can be a powerful message about the nature of religious faith, and it can heal the very relationships that may have gotten in the way of a better understanding of God.

A woman in her thirties, who grew up in Ohio, tells a moving story about a change in her parents that had influenced her perception of herself and of God. She had been raised in a second-generation Catholic immigrant family that had very deep misgivings about Protestants. As a child, she attended mass every week with her mother, learned the catechism, and was warned repeatedly about interacting with Protestants. Her mother was a talented musician who prayed faithfully and was greatly admired by her daughter. Her father was a businessman who traveled a great deal, and so she saw him less, felt emotionally distant toward him, and seldom saw him go to church, although she knew he believed in God and read the Bible and prayed often on his own. As a teenager, she was instructed in no uncertain terms by both parents that she should only date Catholics, that sex before marriage was wrong, and that abortion was an unspeakable sin.

Feeling quite devoted to her faith but also feeling stifled by it, this woman went away to college, started questioning the distant, critical God who seemed so much like her father, and quit attending mass. She also became sexually active, was raped by her boyfriend, became pregnant, and had an abortion. Of course she kept it a secret from her parents. Several years later she fell in love with a man from a good Catholic background, someone her parents approved of, and had a big church wedding. She had confided in her future husband, and together they agreed never to tell her parents about what she had experienced in college. But a few years later someone else managed to leak the story to her parents and they confronted her. At first she denied that there was any truth to the story, but later she felt so guilty and alienated from her parents that she paid them a visit and confessed everything.

Her mother was furious, exclaiming that they would never have given her a big church wedding if they had known about her sordid past. The woman was utterly shaken by this response, although she soon realized it was consistent with the rigid religious training she had received as a child. Her father's response, however, was different. Despite the distance she had always felt between them, he was in tears by the time she finished her story. She still remembers his words, "I feel so sad that you couldn't tell us and that we couldn't be there for you." Repeating them a decade later, she also breaks into tears.

"There was such liberation in his words to me," she explains. "That was a real significant part of my journey; it helped liberate me from the task master God who always said that if you screwed up you were finished. To have screwed up in one of the worst ways that a father can see his daughter screw up, and then to hear him say 'It's okay. I'm just real sorry that I couldn't have been there for you,' it was amazing."

She adds, "It says in the Bible that 'nothing shall ever separate us from the love of God.' Through my father's actions, I knew that nothing that I could ever do would ever separate me from my dad's love. I knew that if my father, given his background and given who he was, could do that, then God had to do that so much more. And that gave me a real freedom to explore and grow and question. It was permission. It was permission to be who I was and nobody else but me."

Daily Discipline

This woman, like Judy Sutherland, has come to such a rewarding relationship with God that she seldom questions the value of praying or engaging in other devotional activities. In contrast, some of the people we talked with find it necessary to follow rigorous routines in order to stay in tune with God in the way they feel is right. They deliberately set aside time every day, usually in the morning, to pray, meditate, and read.

Lillia Rizzo is one example. In addition to reading Scriptures and devotional books, she meditates on creeds, recites formulaic prayers, practices breathing slowing, does exercises, and writes in her journal. She is especially fond of the "journaling" she has done. "I journal on everything, because you can never recapture that thought or feeling, the exact words, a few years later. So every time I want to lock into an idea, I'll take out my journal."

For instance, just a few days ago she has written in her journal, "I have a picture [in my mind] of the Sacred Heart of Jesus and my heart beating as one and he said, 'Let me put this in your perspective.' And it was as if we were dancing. We're always dancing or doing something. And he'll use words from songs and there was a song he used last night. It was an old song from years ago, 'Two hearts gently beating and murmuring love. My darling, I love you so.'"

Because she prays and writes in her journal every day, Lillia has also been able to visualize her relationship with God in much more meaningful ways. For instance, she says it helps when her husband holds her to imagine that God holds her in the same way. One time this blending of the two became quite real to her: "I was listening to a love song in the kitchen and all of a sudden it was as if the Lord was there. And he said, 'That's how it is with you and me.' And it got to the point that I envisioned him and my husband and they were blending to be one and then he was taking me in his arms as if my husband would."[8]

A woman named Stel Edwards, age thirty-three, who lives in Mississippi and works as a short-order cook in order to support her main interest in life, which is racing her motorcycle, also illustrates that spiritual practices take time. A couple of years ago her boyfriend left her and she was—in her words—a mess. In hopes of helping her out of her doldrums, her mother sent her a devotional book. Stel got up every morning and read the book and prayed. As she read, she would sit quietly, reflecting on her life. She says the book helped her remember that what she was going through was not the end of the world.

As she looks back on it, Stel says "this practice" helped her tremendously. For six months, she did it "religiously." She says she missed it when she stopped. The reason she stopped was that she found a new boyfriend and started racing her bike again. Instead of spending half an hour meditating, she simply got up and rode off on her bike. She still thinks of herself as a spiritual person. She believes in God. And she prays. But her prayers are not a practice in the same sense as they were.

In contrast, Ezra Feldman is one of the people who has become more disciplined in recent years about the way he practices spirituality. He typically prays for fifteen minutes every morning. There were many years when he did not pray at all, and even now he does not find it easy to pray. But prayer is a discipline, a deliberate practice, that he has chosen to do, partly because it is commanded in the Bible, partly because it is a way of connecting with his Jewish heritage, and partly because he finds it a positive experience.

"It really does change my life," he says. "When I'm doing it, I feel significantly different. I feel almost like I'm lost in time." His routine each morning is the same. "Almost without fail, I wake up, shower and get dressed, and then spend about fifteen minutes doing the standard morning liturgy from the prayer book, before I eat and go to work." What he gets from it varies. "Some days it's just something I have to get through before I go to work because I've decided I will do it every morning, do it regularly. Other days, it's like time stolen away from everything else. I suppose that people who meditate feel it pulls them out of their normal stuckness. On good days, it has that kind of elevating sense for me. On other days, it's just part of my routine in the morning."

Besides prayer, spiritual practice typically includes some kind of reading or study aimed at expanding one's understanding of the sacred. Ezra Feldman also exemplifies this aspect of practice. Besides morning prayers and observing the Sabbath, he and his wife have been reading through the Book of Psalms lately, in Hebrew. "I think there's a tremendous amount of stuff that we learn about ourselves from reading Scripture," he observes. "By 'ourselves,' I don't mean individually so much as archetypal human nature. I'm really attempting to understand what I talk about when I'm talking about God, and ultimately I guess that's what's important to me."

Another man who has become more disciplined about his devotional practices is Delmer Schwartz. He admits that when he "got serious" about God, nothing much changed. It took him three years to recover from being in Vietnam. He was emotionally wounded and it took time to be comfortable around ordinary people again. Eventually he married and started farming, praying all the time that God would keep the creditors from his door. But agriculture has not been good for the Schwartzes; they have come close to bankruptcy several times.

Being serious about God, nevertheless, is more than a slogan for Delmer Schwartz. He prays and reads the Bible every day. "I can't say the Lord tells me that I need to do this or that," he admits. "I'm more of a reasoning kind of person, I guess. I trust the Scriptures when they say that God is in my life. It's like the stories of David or Paul. You just pray and figure that God is with you. You try to turn things over to God."

Asked what he prays about, Delmer responds, "I say, 'Lord, I need your wisdom here. Not only do I need more spiritual insight, but I need to have more knowledge and how to use that knowledge, too.' So that becomes a prayer at times when things really get pretty strenuous. And there are times when, all of a sudden, I have to stop just in my own thinking, and say, 'Lord, look, things are getting way out of hand. I don't know where I'm at.' It's a very short kind of conversation, and yet I know that the Lord is with you every moment, that you can voice those things or you can overlook them."

Delmer says that trusting God reminds him of his parents. You made your request and then you shut up. The answer was yes or no, but it didn't help to plead. When he prays now, he doesn't plead. "I sort of voice [my prayers] to myself now, knowing that God already knows my situation." He thinks his understanding of prayer has been growing.

When he first started getting serious about God, he thought it was important to pray every now and then when you were thankful or when you needed something. More than a decade later, he says he now thinks of prayer as a kind of reminder. It helps him remember that God is in charge. Delmer says he is able to enjoy life better as a result. "There's an underlying kind of presence," he explains, "not that things will be all right, but that life is precious. Whatever happens, the Lord can handle it."

Recycling

Most of the people we talked with who are trying to practice their spirituality in a deliberate, regular way have given themselves permission to do what they can amidst busy lives rather than being too rigid with themselves. Indeed, people who had been raised to perform religious duties often acknowledge that the biggest problem is getting over the idea that they "should" be doing something and moving to the point that they want to.

A woman from a conservative Protestant background tells us she had such high expectations of what should be done devotionally that she seldom managed to do it. "I kind of felt like there was a specific way it was supposed to be done, yet nobody really told me how to do it. I was just supposed to do it. I thought, 'It's got to be right, or don't do it at all.'" For example, she thought she should read a whole chapter of the Bible or of a devotional book every night before she went to bed but was usually too tired to do so. "It's been very difficult for me," she admits. "I think of it as something that needs to be this huge, monumental event. If I don't do that, I might as well not do it at all." Lately, she's been able to ease up on herself, reading a shorter devotional passage, perhaps earlier in the day, and being satisfied if she does so a couple times a week.

In this respect, Ezra Feldman is far more dutiful than most. A more typical example is Elaine Margolis, who said she tries to pray and read something devotional every day but often falls short. Her way of getting in touch with God is by remembering that there are cycles in all of life. Thus, each January she regards the new year as a time of renewal, as a season of fresh resolve, and during the ensuing winter months, when the days are shorter and there is less yard work to be done, she reads part of a devotional book each day and spends about fifteen minutes each morning praying and reflecting on her life.

To stave off boredom, she uses this time in different ways, sometimes by scribbling thoughts in her journal, sometimes by free-associating biblical words, and sometimes by reviewing her thoughts about herself. She describes these activities as "a great time of recycling for me." It helps her to start over again, changing some of her thought patterns from the previous year and looking inward. "Having that time in the year to concentrate on study and to nourish oneself," she says, helps prepare her for the work that has to be done.

After a month or two, she has usually become too busy to keep to this schedule, but these deliberate times of prayer have oriented her to be more in tune with God in her daily life. She explains that she is more or less in a constant state of prayerfulness. For example, "If I hear my kids laughing together in the TV room, I say, 'Lord, thank you so much for letting me hear their laughter. Thank you for this gift.'" She is also more attentive to nature, thankful for its beauty, and nurtured by its serenity.

She is not at all sure she understands prayer or is even sure that God answers her prayers, but she prays anyway and feels more in touch with God as a result. And if these practices are provisional and rooted more in personal experience than in elaborate understanding, they are nevertheless foundational. She explains, "I wouldn't want to think what life would be like if there was no God. I'd probably kill myself, because there would be no hope without some sense of the world's being greater than the deep sadness and deep evil that I see."

Whether they succeed in being regular about their devotional practices or not, the people we talked with insist that it is important to be intentional about these practices. It is easy to become absorbed in other activities; thus, devotional time requires effort. It becomes a conscious commitment to create a space in which to focus attention on the sacred. One man explains it this way: "I tend to be very busy in my work and I want to devote a lot of time to my family. I get so involved with those activities that I feel like my own private spiritual life is unraveling. So I need discipline." He typically rises at five o'clock each morning in order to read from a prayer book and to meditate for about twenty minutes. "It gives me perspective," he says. "It reminds me of what's important and what isn't."

Part of being deliberate about their faith, too, is making a conscious effort to create a place in which to pray and to be close to the sacred. Church may become more remote as people live further away from fellow parishioners; ethnic customs that tie people to their congregations may fade into the past. For one woman who has experienced these changes, the way to remain spiritually oriented is to create a sacred space in her own house. "I have the Lord's Prayer on my wall and I have a plate of our church on the wall. I call it my inspirational corner," she laughs. "I say that jokingly, but it means a lot to me so I put it up in my home." She explains, "When I see it, it gives me strength."

Don't Lose Your Enthusiasm

For people like Elaine Margolis, spending time alone with God has become the central aspect of their spiritual practices. Relating to God in this manner has become increasingly meaningful, even though they often feel more detached from any religious institution or congregation now than while they were growing up. Many people, however, have remained involved in a congregation of some kind. They demonstrate that spirituality can become more personal and yet be nurtured and expressed through active involvement in a congregation.

Indeed, we observed some fascinating cases in which greater involvement in a religious organization becomes the route to a more individuated faith. The ways in which this happens vary, but often the process involves identifying with the organization as an *adult* (moving past one's sense of being a child within the congregation) and thus feeling closer to the pastor or another adult leader. This sort of identification then provides a basis from which to hear about spirituality in a new way and to internalize its implications for one's personal life.

Janet Arbuckle is a woman in her early thirties who attends a Presbyterian church. She was raised as a Presbyterian, going to church and Sunday school every week and learning to pray by observing her mother at home. She has experienced a deepening of her faith just in the last three or four years, a change that she attributes to God but that was also shaped by her involvement in church and by her pastor.

The change began when Janet was chosen by her congregation to serve on its board of elders. She says she had always gone to church for selfish reasons, hoping to receive some blessing from it, but now she started to think of it as a place to serve others. She also became better acquainted with the pastor, which gave her greater freedom to talk with him, and she became more interested in what he had to say during his sermons. Not long after this, Janet's mother became ill and died, her brother's alcoholism grew worse, and her husband lost his job. Rather than blaming God for these difficulties, Janet listened all the more closely to what the pastor had to say about God.

One Sunday, Janet was especially moved by the pastor's preaching about enthusiasm as a feature of the Christian life. She recalls, "I left the church, I got into my car, my daughter was in the backseat, and I turned on the radio. I was just listening to some music. And on the way home I thought about how I did not have any enthusiasm at the time. My daughter looked at me from the backseat into the mirror and tears started coming down my face and she said to me, 'Mommy, why are you crying?' And I said to her, 'Well, I'm crying because I don't have any enthusiasm.' And she goes, 'Well, Mommy, you got to be happy. Why are you crying?' I go, 'I guess the minister's sermon just got to me because I just don't have any enthusiasm in my soul whatsoever.' So I cried all the way home. But of course, by the time I got home I dried my tears. I didn't want my husband to see that I was crying."

The reason Janet didn't want her husband to see her crying was that he was near despair himself because of the loss of his job. Determined to be more enthusiastic, Janet scanned the newspaper that afternoon and spotted a job opening. She says, "I said to my husband, I said, 'John, I want you to go after that job and I want you to go to that company, I want you to give it your all and in your mind I want you to say, 'John, I'm going to get that job.' And I encouraged my husband and I feel that I gave him strength, and at that time, even though I didn't have any enthusiasm, I gave him my enthusiasm for him."

John went for the interview and "gave it his all." Janet explains what she was feeling inside: "I knew in my heart that he was going to get that job. I feel like crying right now because I knew he was going to get that job." She breaks off, sobbing. "I'm sorry," she says after a few moments, "but I have to continue this story. I just want you to know that what happened after this is my husband did get the job and it was with the world's largest company. I mean, he's making a lot more money. It's like God gave us a miracle."

Some would criticize Janet, saying that she was just using her faith for her own ends. She, however, believes firmly that God was speaking to her through her pastor that Sunday and that her encouragement was helpful to her husband. She feels strongly that God was teaching her a lesson. "It was like God was trying to tell me something. I think he was trying to tell me, 'Don't ever lose your enthusiasm, no matter what happens, because bigger and better things will happen to you.' I think he was trying to tell me, 'Don't ever worry about tomorrow, live for today, and you have faith in me and I'll take care of you.' You know what I mean?"

Since then, she has been paying even closer attention to her pastor's words. One Sunday, he preached on angels, for example, and Janet had just been reading a book about angels. She thinks it was more than mere coincidence. He has also been preaching lately about prayer and about being compassionate. Janet is trying to apply these ideas in her job.

"Every day that I work, I need God's strength on my job to get through my day and I'll tell you why," she asserts. "Because I'm a customer service rep for an insurance company. I deal with people that scream at me all day long. I take about two hundred phone calls a day, and to get through the day you need a lot of strength. You need not only strength, but you need to be somewhat of a professional as far as telephone techniques are concerned. You have to know how to handle people in such a way that you don't want to say anything wrong in order to lose a person as an insured and you want to direct them to the proper department and, if they have a complaint, to the proper person. It takes strength because all of these people that call me in the course of a day, they're all screaming because their car insurance is too high or because we're charging them 946 dollars for an accident or so forth."

She prays during the day, almost as automatically as she breathes. Doing so gives her the poise she needs. "I feel that God is making me stronger each day," she observes, "and I feel as though, even when these people are screaming at me, I feel like I have the strength to take it on and not to feel overwhelmed by what they're saying to me. Just strength and wisdom." She figures it is the same strength her mother relied on and perhaps even what it took for her grandmother to come to the United States as a young woman and to survive the Great Depression. She hopes her daughter will understand some of this when she grows up.

Staying Connected

We also found in our interviews that even people who are not actively immersed in a congregation seldom perform their spiritual practices entirely alone. As many writers have observed, practices of all kinds—playing chess, gardening, playing the piano—are always social, whether or not they are done alone or in the immediate presence of other people. Spiritual practices, even the ones that people pursue by themselves, are social in the sense that these activities are carried on in conversation with the congregation in which people have been raised, in comparison with their parents and siblings, and with the help of resources supplied to them by other people, such as devotional books, hymnals, and tapes. It is not unusual, therefore, for people to identify themselves with a wider subculture even when their practices are solitary.

One Catholic woman captures this idea nicely as she talks about meditating on the Psalms each morning. "It's a form of praise and also a prayer that I join in unison with all my brothers and sisters throughout the whole world. Even the Jewish people are praying the Psalms. So when I pray the Psalms, I see myself as part of a worldwide community of God's people offering praise and thanksgiving."

In addition, a number of people point out specific ways in which they have stayed in live contact, as it were, with other people, even though these people may not be part of the same congregation. For example, a woman who has moved several times in recent years and who feels alienated from the people at her current church offers the following as an illustration of how a soul mate—in her case, a friend from high school—can remain an important part of one's spiritual journey, even at a distance.

Her friend had been struggling with cancer for several years when, quite unexpectedly, her husband died of a sudden heart attack in the middle of the night. "So my friend and I had this conversation by phone as to why God would allow that to happen to someone who was serving him, who already had suffered, who already is suffering—why God would allow one more area of suffering. My friend and I talk about once a month, about what to pray for each other, and we pray together."

Counseling is another way of staying connected. For example, Madeleine Dunn, the woman who was dying for acceptance, finds that counseling helped her both to think more clearly about her upbringing and to give her new messages about herself and her relationship with her father. On one significant occasion, she felt that these new messages were opening the door so that she could pray and, in turn, hear God's voice speaking to her in a new way.

She was driving alone when "it was almost as if God came into the car and wiped my heart clean of all the things my dad had done and literally forced me to forgive him. And it wasn't a coercive force. It was just a wiping clean of all this hatred and all the memories of all these things that he had done. And it was so powerful and so overwhelming that I remember having to pull the car over and I just sat there and cried. It was like a load had been lifted off my head. I didn't ask for it to happen. I didn't want it to happen. It just happened."

In her case, as in many people's, staying connected with her parents, long after she has moved out of their house, has been valuable. A few years ago, she was able to sit down with her father and explain how she had experienced his upbringing and what she felt was lacking. "We had a long conversation where I tried to explain to him some of the frustrations I had felt, and what I needed from him. And he admitted to me that, yes, all the time I was growing up that he viewed me as someone who needed to be reined back, controlled and shaped, because I never looked as if I needed encouragement. And he admitted that he didn't interact with me that way, nor did he up until that point, but admitted that he should have and that he would."

She felt "tremendous" as a result of this conversation, because she knew she hadn't just imagined everything. "He got the message that what I need from him now isn't discipline, but love, support, and encouragement." Her father also acknowledged that he is hard on himself and often does not know how to get the encouragement he needs.

Madeleine, in turn, was able to realize, "Okay, I'm an adult, and I want him to look at me as an adult. I have a responsibility to encourage him and to thank him when he has done something well. He said, 'If you could share with me some of the things you're struggling with, I would know how to pray for you.' So I mentioned some of the things I was struggling with. And he said, 'Maybe if it's all right with you I can pray for you, and you can pray for me.' I said, 'That's great, but I have no idea how to pray for you. You've never asked for prayer. We've never prayed for each other in our house. I don't know how to pray for you.' So he went on to share some things about his struggles, which was amazing. It was a real change for him to assume that I could pray for him."

Spiritual retreats are another way of having some contact with other people who are trying to cultivate their spirituality. They vary enormously but generally encourage people to devote at least an entire weekend to silence, prayer, and contemplation. A woman we talked with who participates in a retreat once a year describes her experience this way: "I really need that time to be refreshed by God. It takes me away from the world. And it's a wonderful privilege and grace to be able to back away from all my responsibilities and just have time to be."

She emphasizes that retreats are helpful because they give her time to be by herself but they also put her in contact with other people. "To just be in the presence of God without a lot of distraction" is what she cherishes most. And yet she experiences "a tremendous amount of love and faith in being in the presence of others in prayer." Her retreat lasts three days, during which she hears homilies twice a day, talks to other retreatants at meals, but otherwise remains silent, praying the rosary and meditating on God.

Spirituality and the Political Person

Although spiritual practice is often regarded as a kind of devotional behavior that puts people in closer touch with God, some of the people we talked with insist that it should also be more than this. They think spirituality should influence their behavior, not only by making them friendlier or harder working, but also by encouraging them to work for the betterment of their communities. Their religious upbringing taught them that the church was a resource, a place to learn, a point of origin, rather than an end in itself or a closed community. As they matured, they have become lifelong learners, as it were, seeking to grow spiritually through their reading, attendance at seminars, and conversations with friends, and in the process have found a way to connect this inward sense of spirituality with community and civic involvement. The people who are able to make these connections are rare enough that it is helpful to consider how they do it.

One of the more interesting people we talked with is Dave Volkman, age forty-three, a man who grew up in a Methodist church in Illinois and who now teaches English at a community college. Both his parents were active in the church, teaching Sunday school classes and serving on committees. Dave enjoyed going to church as a child. He credits it with sparking his interest in the Bible and with planting the idea that one should be of service to one's church and community, not simply a passive participant. In high school, he withdrew from participating, as many teenagers do, but was enough of a bookworm that he continued to read the Bible and the various religious books in his parents' library. He was increasingly fascinated with literature and realized that many of the poems and stories he was reading had religious overtones.

In college, Dave majored in English literature and took part in the campus protests and peace marches of the period. He then worked in a variety of short-term jobs, traveled, and did graduate study before settling into his present career. He became interested in theology for a while, but he views it as an intellectual discipline, which he distinguishes sharply from the practice of spirituality. He asserts, "I suppose I'm a person that intellectualizes things, but that's not what gives life to my sense of spirituality. I've always been predominantly interested in how private spirituality and the practice of spirituality feeds and nourishes a person and energizes him or her to get out and do things and practice those beliefs in community.

"My sense of personal spirituality is tied into how I view myself within the community and within the culture and as a political person as well," he explains. "I think it's very hard to talk about religion, politics, and other important areas of life as mutually exclusive. I think they're mutually encased and they encroach on each other and overlap each other. What you do as a political person only makes sense in terms of you as a religious person or as a person living within the culture. It just seems to me everything is part and parcel of other things."

This understanding of spirituality has been confirmed by the reading Dave has been doing over the past twenty years. Mystics, saints, poets, and writers, he finds, help give expression to the things he somehow already knows. "I've done a lot of reading in the literature of spirituality," he says, "again, not for the intellectual experience of it all, but toward personal enrichment. Things like Teresa of Avila and a lot of Thomas Merton and literary people who are like crossovers. The English poet William Blake; another English poet by the name of Robert Herrick; Henry Vaughn, another English poet. I read a lot of Tolstoy over a period of years."

Dave says his reading has "basically confirmed all the things I had come to believe when I was a child." He cites a passage from G. K. Chesterton that says "Christianity confirms all those wonderful things you learn in the nursery." Dave explains, "All my religious instincts, which I had bred in me when I was young, were simply confirmed by the things I was reading: Tolstoy, as an old man, saying that you stop gathering things to yourself at a certain age and you start pushing those things away and giving up and sort of reducing to your basic, elemental, spiritual self. That made sense to me."

What he learned as a child was that the church was a familiar, comfortable place, but one that essentially required people to be part of the world, with all its flaws, working to build community and helping to serve the needy and the outcast. He remembers how his father would do volunteer work in an all-black neighborhood and how his parents invited people over for dinner who, he learned later, were homosexuals. Rather than believing God was waiting to punish him, Dave came to understand God as a source of strength, actively engaged in helping people develop their natural instincts for community and service. His summary of his father's faith is very similar to his own: "God was the basic gyroscope for his entire life, the central factor in his life which gave his life balance and direction and directed his instincts and his actions."

Over the years, a dynamic tension has existed between Dave Volkman's political activities and his experiences in church. Sometimes one pulled the other along. Later, the situation might be reversed. For example, Dave's political involvement left him at one point feeling the worship services he attended were too passive. He and his wife started attending a Catholic church, and Dave realized the liturgical mass was what he needed. "It was the experience of watching people go forward to take Communion. Most Methodists take Communion seated in their seats. They get served Communion sitting down. Catholics, of course, stand and go down the altar and take Communion. It made sense to me that you don't sit in your seat and wait for God to serve you. You get up and you go and you go as a group. You go together. And you seek out the Eucharist. You get up and go *to* it. That ties into the fact that you've got to get up and move politically. You've got to get up and act."

For the past several years, Dave and his wife have been attending services at an Episcopal church. They appreciate the fact that people still go forward to take Communion but feel more comfortable about the role of women than they did at the Catholic church. Dave now sings in the choir. He admits he doesn't have much of a voice, but singing has become another way of connecting his devotional life with his sense of political engagement. "As our choirmaster says, 'When the choir is singing at its best, you don't hear yourself singing, you just hear the choir. You just hear the ensemble.' That seems to me to be central to real religious experience, that sense of anonymity or self-effacement. The harmonization of all those voices seems particularly symbolic."

Symbolic of what? Dave explains his present understanding of spirituality—one he says he learned as a child but has learned to express better as an adult: "God is immanent and here and incarnate in people, and inside you, yourself, but you only get to that central part of yourself where God lives by giving up yourself and going out and living in community and working in community and serving in community. I have always looked at myself as essentially a Christian person who does things politically or reacts politically or votes politically, basically in terms of what makes the most sense to me religiously or spiritually."

Dave Volkman hardly considers himself a saint. He feels, however, that his private spirituality is genuine only if it spills into his public activities.

He tries to practice "generosity of heart," as he puts it, by living simply, giving money to charitable causes, and helping the needy. He tries hard to raise the political awareness of his students even though he is not teaching courses in politics. He knows from previous experience that he could make more money in business but regards his teaching as a calling. At his church, he has been leading an effort to get parishioners to think more broadly about stewardship to their communities and to the environment. Right now, he also spends a lot of time with his two children, trying to show them the value of caring for others. "I believe that God dwells inside you," he summarizes, "and that you need to prepare your heart for him. I believe that you should live in accordance with those preparations you do, as you relate to other people."

The People Who Practice

In all these examples, spiritual practices would not be conceivable without some vibrant sense of the sacred. Being in contact with God, worshipping, communing with the divine, and gaining a renewed sense of transcendence are all central to the ways in which people practice their spirituality. In each instance, the person who practices is also connected with other people, often by participating in a congregation or by interacting directly with friends and family and sometimes through such indirect means as remembering the family or congregation in which one was raised.

It is nevertheless *people* who engage in spiritual practices. Indeed, one of the virtues of focusing on practices is that people once again take center stage. This is often not true in discussions that focus on religious organizations, theological doctrines, texts, or even communities. These are all abstractions that take our attention away from people. In contrast, practices are always performed by people, either individually or in cooperation with others. Practices are the deliberate activities by which people relate to their world and make sense of it, and spiritual practices are the activities by which people come into a closer relationship with the sacred.

Words like *self, individual, doer, actor,* or *agent* are key to any discussion of practice.[9] So much has been written in recent years about the scourge of excessive individualism in American culture that it is difficult (perhaps especially in religious circles) for words such as *self* and *individual* to be emphasized without seeming to imply a return to such individualism. Yet it is true in the cases we have considered that people had to individuate themselves in order to gain a fuller appreciation of the very communities in which they were involved. Spiritual practice does not connote self-sufficiency, but it does involve taking responsibility for one's spiritual development rather than expecting that participation in some congregation will excuse one from having to take such responsibility.

To a considerable extent, it is still possible to describe American religion in terms of its congregations and institutions, but increasingly it appears that people are recognizing that participation in these entities may not be the same thing as practicing spirituality. If nothing else, the multiplicity of options available for guiding our spiritual practices now places a heavy responsibility on individuals, alone or in the company of others, to make choices. Beyond that, spiritual practices have always been recognized in religious traditions as the core around which any life of faith must be built.

It cannot be emphasized enough that spiritual practices are like cultivated tastes. Even for people who have been raised religious, they often do not come naturally. They require time, effort, and personal discipline, and the insights or feelings of wholeness and holiness that result generally come later rather than being the occasion for such dedication.

Madeleine L'Engle, who likens praying to playing the piano, writes, "If I stop going to church, no matter how mad church makes me, if I stop praying at home, no matter how futile it sometimes seems, then 'real' prayer is never going to come."[10] The thirteenth-century Sufi poet Jelaluddin Rumi expresses the same idea this way: "When you quit meditating, the layers of rust eat into your soul-mirror. There's no sheen."[11]

Most of the people discussed in this chapter learned to cultivate their spirituality by engaging in such deliberate, regular practices of devotion, worship, and service. Following certain routines has helped them be more serious about their spirituality, and in some cases using particular techniques for inspirational reading, prayer, and meditation has also been helpful. Few have become addicted to these techniques, however. Indeed, the ones who engage most fervently in spiritual practices are most likely to admit that the spirit of God is more encompassing than any human practice could adequately express.

More than a century and a half ago, none other than Jonathan Edwards voiced the same idea. Concerned about the rigorous and sometimes stultifying church services and devotional practices being advocated by his fellow clergymen, Edwards observed that "some have gone too far towards directing the Spirit of the Lord, and marking out his footsteps for him, and limiting him to certain steps and methods." The Spirit of God, Edwards counseled, is too unsearchable and untraceable to be known through any human techniques. "Nor does the Spirit of God proceed discernibly in the steps of a particular established scheme, one half so often as is imagined."[12]

Interestingly enough, theology itself does not surface often in people's remarks about their spiritual practices. Yet it is not entirely absent, either. For people who have been in congregations much of their lives, reading and listening to the Bible, theology is the doctrinal webbing that holds them up when they start falling into intellectual doubt. They can rest assured that God exists and that the Bible is true because someone, once in a while provides a coherent sermon on the Trinity, the canon, the Resurrection, or the theology of miracles. Knowing that, they can feel more confident about God's role in their own life.

Here is an older woman, a widow, who was married to a pastor for forty years and who has been active as a church leader all her life. When asked to summarize her religious beliefs, she says, "It's just simply believing in God. That he is a sovereign God, Creator of all things. And the wonder of it. The older you get, the more you see the awesomeness of God and what he has done, and you say, 'What must heaven be like?' I see his power. I know that he could heal."

She continues, "The power is the same. Jesus healed people, blind people, raised Lazarus. That power is still there. I believe in a personal relationship with God. I really don't know what people do without the Lord. And now when I lost my husband, I still say, 'Well, Jesus, if you see him, tell him I love him.'"

PART IV

E Pluribus Unum?

CHAPTER 10

→►◄←

Bridging Diversity

THE PRECEDING CHAPTERS have emphasized the particularity of religious traditions, paying special attention to the distinctive local practices that encouraged people to feel that it was special to be growing up Jewish or Irish Catholic, to take pride in being African American Baptists or Asian American Presbyterians. How then is it possible for people from such diverse backgrounds to live harmoniously with others?

The Process of Blending

One answer is that the experience of particular traditions is always situated within an awareness of other traditions. People are more likely to grow up feeling that their religious tradition is best *for them* than they are to think simply that it is best. Loyalties are thus local, embedded in the customs of one's family and community, and their localism is evident to participants even at an early age.[1]

For example, Hal Meyerson feels he has always been part of a multicultural society. There were about a hundred students in his class in high school. About a dozen were Jews. About a dozen were African Americans. Another dozen were Polish Catholics. There were some Italian Catholics, Irish Catholics, Presbyterians, Methodists, and Baptists. "No clear majority," Hal says.

Attending a high school like this had a profound impact on him. He was a member of AZA, a Jewish fraternity, in high school, and most of his close friends were boys who attended his temple. But he also enjoyed and respected the other students. When he went to college (at a large state university), he sought out a mixed fraternity. He is proud that it included blacks and whites as well as Jews, Catholics, and Protestants.

He certainly recognized the differences between himself and his Protestant or Catholic classmates. But he also learned to draw a line that took them in. This line distinguished people who shared the same moral values, whatever their particular religion, from those who had not received proper training in morality. The people at his temple prided themselves on being devout—some (like Hal's mother) retaining their commitment to Orthodoxy—and they sometimes felt more affinity with devout Christians than they did with Jews in the same community who attended a Reform temple.

A story illustrates how Hal drew the distinction between those who were properly religious and those who were not. One of the boys in his class at school was commonly known to be the illegitimate son of a mob boss. One day the mob boss came into his grandfather's liquor store and said, "This is no longer your store. It's ours." Another time the boss's gang burned down a structure that his father's company was building, because his father refused to have dealings with the mob. On still another occasion, they shot his father's foreman. Hal says it was very interesting to be in school with the boy, knowing that all this was happening. He says he did not dislike the boy. But there was a clearly printed map of moral geography in Hal's mind. Those who lived by deep religious principles, whether Jewish or Christian, were honest and law abiding; those who did not live by religious principles were different.

For many of the other people we talked with, the challenge of living with racial, ethnic, and religious differences is nothing new. Indeed, they have made adjustments repeatedly in their thinking that show them how Americans can get along better with one another while retaining their commitment to distinctive traditions and, in many cases, to an underlying religious faith.

Alan Threadwell is a vivid example. Growing up in a community of many different religious and ethnic groups, he was well aware of the tensions such differences could cause. Religion often aggravated these tensions; for example, he tells how he and his friends in high school would have heated discussions about whether Catholics and Jews could go to heaven, and he was aware that Lutherans remained divided to the extent that Slovaks and Norwegians might have little to do with one another.

But during the 1960s he saw many people in the churches rethinking these traditional boundaries. "We were redefining American life. We were redefining religious life, and the churches were not immune to it. Was it the ethnic bond or was it a theological bond that was going to be most important?"

For Alan, one thing led to another. Seeing the turmoil taking place among fellow Lutherans over what the church should be inspired him to learn more about Martin Luther and the Reformation and then to volunteer for a denominational committee concerned with reorganizing the church. Marrying a woman who was a staunch Calvinist also forced him to rethink some of his ideas about religion, as did a stint in the military, which put him into closer contact with people of different backgrounds.

At present, Alan mostly draws a distinction between people of faith and other people. Referring to the various lay people and clergy he has met over the years, he says, "We have our theological differences, of course. But on balance people of the church—I'm talking about the 'big church' here—are heads above the rest when it comes to caring and ministering to needs."

As people grow older, many of them also realize that their particular religious traditions embrace an inclusive ethic. As a matter of principle, people learn that they are supposed to love one another, even when they belong to different faiths. They may internalize slogans about God's loving everyone and about all people's being God's children. The latter slogan especially conjures up affinities with people of other religious backgrounds. As long as they are raised religious, they can be regarded as legitimate members of God's kingdom through a kind of covenant that includes children in devout households. As in any household, diversity, in principle at least, may be regarded as a strengthening element.

Mary Shannon illustrates these ideas. She thinks the growing diversity of American society is a good thing, and she believes this for religious reasons. "I think it's wonderful," she says, "because diversity brings to us all the realities that there are of God." Noting that she is especially pleased to see new immigrants from cultures that are "more focused on God" than American culture often is, she adds that diversity "begins to complete the tapestry of who God is. It's like weaving all those threads instead of the threads all being one or a few colors. I think it adds the richness to life that God intended."

She takes this argument a step further, asserting that increased ethnic and religious diversity is also likely to make America stronger spiritually. "The fact that others bring to us another reality of God, another vision, another aspect of him," she says, is especially interesting. "I think we're limited in what we know about God, and I think, through cultural diversity, we're going to come to know a more complete God." Underlying the differences, she believes, there is also a common sense of God and of human experience. "I have found just how much more we are alike than how much we are different," she says. "I think the more we get to know people of other cultures, we're going to find we are so much more alike than we are different, but yet the differences will help to enhance that vision of who God is and the reality of him."

A Muslim man, describing how he prays, provides another good example of the affinities that religious people may express toward one another, even toward people of other faiths. The prayer he recites thirteen times a day (twice in the morning, four times in the afternoon, and seven times in the evening) is intended, in his words, to "tell God to save you and to give you the sort of knowledge you need to be a good person. You ask God's help in being a good person and in dealing with your community, your family, and so on. And you thank God for giving you your arms, your legs, your body, your whole person."

He says "a good Sikh or Hindu or anybody could feel comfortable saying it." In talking more broadly about his religious views, he also says: "The Christians, they believe in Jesus, the Jewish people, they believe in Moses, so you see there is a unity between the people through the messengers of God. But it's unfortunate that we are divided with a lot of customs and rituals and traditions."

At a very practical level, people from different religious backgrounds have increasingly had to accommodate to pluralism because they are unable to control what goes on within their own families. For instance, most of the people we talked with say their parents were consciously trying to raise them in a particular religious tradition, usually the one in which one or both parents had participated from an early age. They are, in this sense, saying only what scholars have often observed, namely, that one of the most cherished of all human values is the desire to share our deepest values with our children. Yet many of the same people acknowledge that it is less certain that their own descendants will share their values. These people know it is unlikely that their children or grandchildren will grow up to embrace the same particular religious community in which their ancestors had lived, and so they have broadened their definition of what is acceptable, conceiving themselves as part of a broader subculture of people who share common religious and moral values.

Mary Shannon is candid in expressing her views toward her children in these terms. "I think it's in the Lord's hands," she observes. "I can continue to be an example to them, and should they want to talk to me, I'm happy to do that. But I think it's their journey now, and they're not journeying in the way I did. They're not involved in the Catholic church right now." With some sadness, she adds, "I would like them to have religious values that help them to love themselves and love other people. It doesn't necessarily have to be my own."

Another man illustrates a related way in which people have had to broaden their definition of what is acceptable. This man's children are still young, and he is an evangelical Protestant who believes strongly that they should be brought up religiously and morally. But these are his step-children through a second marriage, and so he has been forced to acknowledge that the way they were raised in their first home is a sufficient moral foundation on which to build. "I have not had the chance to mold them," he notes. "But I do feel that there are some things that really are universal to any children if they had a strong upbringing, which these kids did."

Another factor that is having a serious impact on the experience of growing up religious is intermarriage between people of different faiths. Even among those raised in the most religious homes, a substantial and apparently growing number of people marry into different denominations or faiths. And those who do intermarry are less likely than those who don't intermarry to remain active in the religion in which they were raised. Nevertheless, a different consequence of religious intermarriage must not be overlooked: a substantial number of those who were raised religious and who intermarry make a decision to remain committed to one partner's religion or to become active in some other religion. For these people, growing up religious is an important reason for deciding to remain religiously active, and remaining active reinforces their sense of being part of a single religious subculture. Rather than identifying only with the ethnoreligious enclave in which they were raised, they feel more akin to others who were also raised religious, and in the process they come to a deeper understanding of religious pluralism.

An especially vivid example of this process is provided by a woman in her forties who was raised in a devout Christian family and then married a man who was a Hindu. At first she felt extremely uncomfortable with Hindu religious practices, especially the many gods that Hindus worshipped and their custom of what she could understand only as "idol worship." She agreed to have a Hindu wedding but privately vowed that she would have nothing to do with Hinduism.

She had to rethink this vow when her first child was born. More than anything else, she wanted her daughter to have a strong religious upbringing, and she knew this could not happen unless she espoused her husband's religion. So she mentally "converted," symbolizing her change of heart by having a second wedding ceremony. She now sends her children to the Hindu temple, where they take classes and participate in a singing group. She also attends classes and has learned to celebrate the holy days.

She looks for parallels and points of agreement between Hinduism and Christianity, such as their emphasis on helping the poor and the way they stress devotion to God. She observes: "No matter which religion you're praying in, you're still praying to the same God. God knows exactly what you need, so you just pray wholeheartedly and God answers your prayers." For her, the important fact is being religious, and she finds common elements in the way she and her husband were raised.

She has also come to understand religious pluralism as something that can exist within her own family and inside her own soul. The out group is no longer people of another religion but people who have not been taught religious values at all. "I don't think people have God in them anymore. Look at the way a lot of kids are now," she complains. "They don't respect their parents; they talk back to their parents; they'll even smoke a cigarette right in front of their mother. My kids, they respect me. They have good values."

The Character Thing

To some extent, this sense of acceptance is evident in some of the evangelical Christians we interviewed, too. Although they feel they have a special relationship with God, they emphasize that Christian maturity involves looking out for the welfare of others rather than standing up for one's rights.

Judy Sutherland puts it this way, "You may know that they're wrong. You may know that what they are doing to you isn't right, and you may have a right to say so or to speak out about your own rights. But Christianity isn't about our rights. The Christian response is that you realize what's happening and you allow that person to have their way instead of you having yours, without becoming bitter, resentful, or taking revenge. Not only that, but that you can live with it with a clear conscience, knowing that God is growing you up, maturing you. This is a character thing."

An attitude like this can be condescending, of course, but for somebody like Judy Sutherland, who has experienced a tortuous journey in her own relationship with God, there is likely to be some appreciation of the struggles others are experiencing. She explains, "Being a Christian means that you allow other people to have the upper hand if they want, if it's that important to them. In a lot of cases, you allow that, but you also are able to love them anyway. You're able to set your own pride and your own needs aside. Not be a doormat, not that extreme at all. But you place it into God's hands, he takes care of it. They may or may not apologize, but it doesn't matter. You accept them where they're at."

The ecumenical movement in the 1960s and 1970s also played a big role in creating a more tolerant atmosphere among religious groups. Through interfaith dialogue, as it was called, religious organizations that had once drawn high walls around themselves began to explore common ground with other organizations. The result was no lessening of conviction about the importance of the sacred but a greater understanding of what in fact might be bases for shared understanding. For people who had grown up in some of these organizations, the ecumenical movement was thus evidence that other people, who had also grown up religiously, might be part of the same world. Indeed, the transformation in attitudes was sometimes remarkable.

Elaine Margolis had been raised to fear Catholics. Not only did her father march in the annual Orangemen's parade, but all her aunts and uncles and cousins gathered periodically at her grandmother's house and exchanged scandalous stories about "the other side," as they called Catholics. That was in the 1950s. But during the next two decades Elaine's parents were deeply influenced by the ecumenical movement. Her mother became more universalistic in her understanding of God, and her father started working with an ecumenical organization to promote better relations between Protestants and Catholics. When he died, a Catholic school instituted a scholarship in his name to honor his ecumenical work.

Samuel Meyerson has witnessed enough hatred between religious groups that he is not optimistic about their ability to live in harmony. But, despite his commitment to the preservation of Judaism, he has also been working actively in his later years to promote interfaith understanding. In fact, he organized a group called Bridges for Peace that encourages cooperation between Christians and Jews. Some of his friends criticized him when he did, worrying that the Christians would convert him. "If they do," Samuel responded, "it will be only because my own faith is not strong enough." In the process, he has never been tempted to convert, but he has come to see some basic points of convergence between Christianity and Judaism. "It's my belief," he asserts, "that the only basic difference between Christianity properly carried out and Judaism properly carried out is the timetable. We as Jews representing the Old Testament believe that the Messiah is going to come when we're ready for Him. The Christian, if he believes properly, is not anti-Semitic, but he believes that Jesus was the Messiah, and He came, and he's smart enough to recognize that the world wasn't ready for Jesus, so they're waiting for the Second Coming."

The more private, personalized spirituality that many people describe, compared with that of their parents and grandparents, is also a way of adapting to a multicultural world. The assumption in many of the discussions of such privatism is that it represents a withdrawal from the institutional church and perhaps from community as well. Our interviews show, however, that private spirituality serves a different function. People can remain in their institutional church and yet tolerate its flaws better because they distinguish it from their personal spirituality.

Congregations thus become a vehicle for service and a way in which to experience community. But spirituality boils down to a more essential understanding of the sacred. People can regard their understanding of the sacred as being true, at least for them, given what they have read and experienced. They can appreciate what they have learned from their congregation but also realize that other congregations and even other faiths may be acceptable alternatives for those associated with them.

Dave Volkman has come to think of spirituality and the church in these ways. He considers community to be very important, and he serves the wider community through his political activities and is active in his congregation as a way of worshipping with others. Yet, in comparing his spirituality with that of his parents and grandparents, he says his is much more private.

He explains, "My sense of God is less a sense that's wrapped up with the institutional church, I think, than theirs was. Also, I've studied and thought about things that they never had the opportunity to study and think about, like comparative religions and Buddhism and African religions and so-called primitive religions and things like that. So my context for fitting in the Christian God is a much broader context. For me to say to them that the ancient Babylonians had a creation myth that was very like to the Genesis creation myth, they would have said, 'What's this supposed to mean?'" His private spirituality is thus connected to his awareness of religious diversity.

Denominations Are Human Inventions

In contrast to people who have become more tolerant in their views as a result of ecumenical involvement or higher education, other people we talked with have arrived at a similar position because of the implicit messages they picked up from their friends and acquaintances. In these cases, people are seldom able to give elaborate reasons for their views about religion, but they have come to be relatively open-minded, even if there are definite limits to what they can accept. They have typically become spiritual shoppers at some point, switching denominations or faiths, and eventually settling into a pattern of religious commitment rooted less in absolute truth claims and more in what feels comfortable.

This outlook can be illustrated by telling the rest of the story of Walt Brubaker. He grew up in a Union congregation that gave him some sense as a child that denominational boundaries were permeable. He also cherished the social support from people at his church perhaps more than he did its religious doctrines. As a fatherless child from an impoverished family, he looked to the church to bolster his confidence in himself. When he went away to serve in the army, he was stationed in the Far East, and during this time he started to question the tenets of Christianity. Many of his closest friends practiced Buddhism, Taoism, Shintoism, or Hinduism. Walt was unable to imagine that God was going to send these people to hell because they were not Christians. He decided that agnosticism was the best position to take toward religion but did so less in a skeptical vein than as a way of affirming that God probably loved and accepted everyone, even though we could not be sure.

When he returned, he married a woman who lived about twenty miles from his home community. She was Catholic, the daughter of a Catholic mother and a Lutheran father. Walt and his wife lived with her parents because they had little money of their own, and Walt alternated between attending the Catholic church with his wife and the Lutheran church with his father-in-law. Feeling not quite at home in either, he eventually joined a United Church of Christ some distance away. When his work schedule permitted and he wasn't too tired, he went there; if he was pressed for time, he attended the nearby Lutheran church. This went on for several years. After their son was born, Walt and his wife started quarreling over how to find a church that they could both feel comfortable in as parents. Each agreed to attend the other's church for a time to see how it felt, and Walt's wife eventually gave in and joined the United Church of Christ.

From Walt's description of these years, it is evident that his orientation toward religion had become that of a spiritual shopper. He was taking his cues from the people around him and from considerations of what was intuitively to his liking. No longer in the presence of Buddhists and Taoists, he was comfortable settling into the Christian community. But he had no strong loyalties to any particular church or denomination. And as he tried to find a place in which to feel comfortable, he placed less emphasis on doctrine and more emphasis on whether or not people were friendly. He also found it increasingly difficult to make up his mind and settle into a single congregation as he had done as a child.

Walt signaled his restlessness to various people he met at work and evoked a remarkable series of encounters with people trying to sell him on their own brand of religion. One day the Mormons came to visit; Walt greeted them warmly, listened to their message, and then decided he couldn't quite "buy" it. Another day some Baptists called on him, but he decided the chemistry wasn't quite right for him to consider their church. Through an Amway salesman, he learned about an independent fundamentalist church and started attending services there on Sunday evenings, while still going to the United Church of Christ on Sunday mornings. That church seemed a bit too intense for him, especially when they started asking him whether he was born again and believed in the imminent return of Jesus. The encounter that he speaks about most animatedly was an invitation to attend a concert by a country gospel singer. Walt and his wife went, not knowing what to expect and figuring it would be a "turn off," but they were impressed by the huge number of people that had come to hear the concert. It was as if the popularity of the event was a reason to take it more seriously. Walt was flattered, too, when the person who had invited him managed to introduce him to the singer.

Over the next few weeks, the same person invited Walt and his wife to his church, an independent charismatic fellowship, and to a Bible study group sponsored by the church. Walt was impressed by how friendly everybody was and by their upbeat attitude. He started telling people at the United Church of Christ about these encounters, and to his surprise—he'd always considered the UCC a liberal church that embraced many different views—found resistance to the idea that these charismatics could be genuine Christians. "That offended me," Walt recalls. "My belief is very strong that you can worship God in many different ways and that the denomination should not be a deciding factor. Denominations are man's invention, not God's invention."

Walt left the UCC congregation and joined the charismatics partly because the latter were friendlier but in large measure because they were more tolerant of people from many different denominations and backgrounds. For the past fifteen years, Walt and his wife have remained involved in the charismatic congregation. They like it because it is only a five-minute drive from their house, because it seems "solid" to them, and because Walt is in a men's group that makes him feel at home. As he describes it, he makes it sound very much like the youth group that meant so much to him in high school. He is not a man who cares very much about theology or the historic reasons for different denominations. He just feels it is important to have God in his life.

Without quite realizing it, Walt Brubaker has become part of the religious subculture in America that is both intensely loyal to its own local situation and fairly capable of living in the pluralistic environment of the wider culture. His local attachment is that of a shopper who has tried out Chevrolets, Toyotas, and Fords and who has settled on one because it is just as good as the rest. He is comfortable enough and so has little incentive to keep moving. He is a Christian because he was raised as one and because the people he knows in his community express their relationship to God in Christian terms. It just makes sense to him to think this way. Were he suddenly back in the Far East, he might think differently. His faith, he explains, is pretty simple: he knows that one day he will be with God; meanwhile, he prays to God to meet his needs and praises God for what he has received. He is glad he can know God in an emotional way, without having to give much thought to the nuances of Christian doctrine. For him, following the Bible means living a good life. He takes the Bible seriously, of course; indeed, he has been "delving into it" more lately. Sometimes he isn't sure whether the Bible is leading him to do one thing or another; if he can find two or three verses that point in the same direction, he feels more confident about it. He has enough of a shopper's mentality that it reassures him to know that his congregation is popular, drawing new people who move into the community, and that there are lots of people around the country whose beliefs are like his. In fact, he's convinced that "in reality religion is becoming more important now than ever."

As he thinks about the wider society, he is happy enough to embrace its diversity. He is open enough to other world religions that he doesn't worry much about Jews and Muslims; they are finding God in their own way. "All people are children of God," he asserts, "and we can learn to live in harmony, irrespective of our differences." If people who have no faith cross his path, he is willing to tell them how he has found happiness by following Jesus. But he isn't going to make an issue of it. To be sure, there are enemies in his world. He has little use for homosexuals, abortionists, and liberal government bureaucrats. But they are a distant threat, something to complain about to his friends rather than anything to spend time fighting himself. As an elected official, he could well be drawn into the religious controversies that have divided some communities. But he says that most of the issues he faces are gray areas rather than matters of right or wrong. Compromise, he believes, is the best policy. From a religious perspective, he thinks God simply gives him choices and then helps him make the ones that are best for the community. He figures you shouldn't get involved with things unless you feel "led by God" to do so. Thus far, God has been leading him to work hard, be considerate of his friends and family, and meet with his men's group on Tuesday evenings. As he says, "God is your friend. Whatever you do, it's pretty much just between you and God."

An Embattled Remnant

Americans who have grown up religious often recognize an affinity with one another, because there are many links connecting their particular tradition with people in other traditions. Intermarriage, personal contact with schoolmates and army buddies, life in the same neighborhood, ecumenical efforts, and beliefs about the oneness of God and the similarities among all religious traditions are enough to forge these links. And yet these links are not the only basis on which people feel they have something in common. They also feel this way because they sense that religious people are an embattled remnant. The same feelings of loss that they express concerning their particular background are ones they extend to people of other backgrounds.

Ethnic groups have always become more aware of their own identity when members feel their cultural influence is declining. When the old ways start to erode, people decide it is time to write histories of the past, preserve the ancient traditions, record the recipes, and organize to protect themselves. The sense of decline that many of the people we interviewed feel about their religious past helps strengthen their interest in religion. Some have fought harder against the moral decay they see threatening American traditions. Others express more optimism about the future but see themselves increasingly as a cultural remnant.

Asked about the strength of religious traditions, Dave Volkman gives a particularly revealing answer. "The prevailing narratives of the faith aren't being passed along in the same way. There is a general falling off in biblical literacy or Christian cultural literacy." Still, he feels confident about the future. "If the faith has validity, if it, in fact, has the kind of deep resonance that it has always claimed to have, then it will prove that by continuing in the people that practice it. So I'm not bothered. The Old Testament prophets said, 'Okay, if you want to shoot the civilization in the foot and send it off to hell in a handbasket, go ahead. That'll be fine. And a Syria will come in or a Babylonia will come in or the Persians will come in, and there'll still be a remnant out there that are doing the right things.'" He thinks a remnant that takes its faith seriously may be better than a large majority of people who simply participate in religious institutions because it is the stylish thing to do.

Similarly, Delmer Schwartz is glad he grew up attending church and he's happy that both his boys recently joined the church. But he feels this is unusual. "I think there's enough families who have not brought their children up in the church, so when there is a need, they don't know to call on God." He says he was able to see a "deficit" in his life after his father's tractor accident and "go back and draw on some of the things I was taught." People who have not been reared religiously have nothing to fall back on. "If you don't have that, it leaves a lot."

Another man puts it this way: "Part of spirituality is morality. I think we're seeing more and more of an acceptance of the idea that it's okay if you get away with it. And that's from the top on down, and somewhere it's just going to lead to more serious problems. It's very uncomfortable, I think."

This idea is also voiced by another man, who laments that the religious life of America is "falling apart" because of what is happening to families. "People working and there's no discipline. Being that there's no discipline in the family, they can't get their kids to go to church. Kids don't listen to their parents as much as they used to or [as their parents] would like them to."

Part of why people sense they are an embattled remnant is also that they feel guilty about their own adherence to tradition. People recognize that times have changed, but they also worry that they themselves are not doing what they should to keep the faith of their fathers and mothers alive. A Protestant man in his fifties remarks candidly that he likes to think spirituality is central to his life but he knows this is not a completely honest statement. He remembers how his father and mother prayed and read their devotional book every day, and he feels guilty that he does not follow the same practice. He says he is too busy, but thinks he would make time for spirituality if it were really that important.

The Next Generation

The most significant challenge facing people who have grown up religious is whether their identity will carry forward with the next generation or whether family patterns have changed so substantially that this identity will soon become a relic of the past. Of course, the sense of generational decline has a long history, especially as it pertains to fears about whether or not children are receiving proper religious instruction. Writing in the fourth century, for example, John Chrysostom complains that "every man takes the greatest pains to train his boy in the arts and in literature and speech [but] to exercise this child's soul in virtue, to that no man any longer pays heed."[2] Nevertheless, the current concerns should not be dismissed simply because they have antecedents.

There are many indications, in fact, that people who have grown up religious are not subjecting their children to the same kind of upbringing. Polls suggest that fewer young people are being taught to pray and read Scriptures at home than was true a generation or two ago, and many teenagers and young adults appear to have received little instruction in religious traditions while they were children. Nevertheless, church going and personal prayer among adults has shown little sign of diminishing over the past twenty or thirty years, suggesting that people are somehow rekindling religious interests even if they are not learning as much about religion while they are young.

As with most religious trends, the future of growing up religious has more to do with subtle changes in the character and quality of religious training than with easily observed markers in public opinion polls. Those changes are difficult to assess, but some inferences can be drawn from what we have seen in previous chapters. Most important, growing up religious in the past meant spending a great deal of time at home, as well as in religious organizations, performing activities that brought the sacred into the family and into the lives of children. The holiday feasts, daily prayers, and extended preparations for Saturday or Sunday services took enormous time and energy. Moreover, these activities were effective instruments of religious training because they included grandparents, aunts and uncles, neighbors, and friends. With fewer people living in ethnic neighborhoods or in the vicinity of family members, these ties are much more difficult to sustain.

Nevertheless, memories of the past are important to most of the people we interviewed, and their current views of spirituality are deeply influenced by these memories. Most people look back with some ambivalence on their religious upbringing, but very few regard it strictly as a negative experience that should be forgotten and transcended. As people mature, the more personal approach to spirituality that they generally adopt gives them a new perspective on their religious upbringing. They regard the specific customs as rooted more in ethnic and denominational traditions than as essentials of spirituality itself. Yet they also recognize that spirituality cannot be simply generic but must be learned in particular contexts and with the tangible reminders of the sacred close at hand. Thus, they want their children to grow up religious, even if this can not happen in the same way it has in the past.

Most of the people who talk about their aspirations for their children say they want them to have some exposure to religion and to share some of their own religious values. One man offers a fairly typical response when he observes that he would like his son to "share some of the basic beliefs that I have about how to treat other people, how to feel about himself, how to feel about himself in relationship to God, and so on." He does not want his son to grow up hedged in by religious rules or having religious dogma forced down his throat, but he and his wife are taking their son to church regularly and encouraging him to make friends there and learn about their faith.

If this man's views prevail, the future of America's religious culture is likely to be characterized more by an underlying belief in God, some understanding of one's own tradition, and exposure to and tolerance toward other traditions, rather than intense, communal, and familial involvement in a single tradition. People will perhaps have fewer stories to tell of the Saturday evenings they spent polishing shoes for the next day or the elaborate feasts their families prepared for religious holidays, but they will continue to be raised with a sense that it is special to grow up in a religious tradition and believing that there is value in praying and learning to serve others. For those who wish their children to develop a deeper understanding of spirituality as adults, it will also be necessary to encourage participation in classes and other formal religious activities that may have been lacking in their childhood. The fact that many Americans recognize the value of having grown up religious but have also moved toward a more personal understanding of spirituality is probably the surest indication that spirituality will remain a significant feature of American life.

Indeed, one of the most important reasons people are embracing others with religious roots is that they are desperately seeking answers to the complex questions they and their children are facing. The mother of a fifteen-year-old illustrates the difficulties involved in finding answers to these questions. They are not abstract, metaphysical questions about how to understand the universe. They are practical questions about how to behave from day to day. This woman was raised Catholic, attending mass, Sunday school, and a parochial day school until she went away to college. She has entertained many doubts about the church over the years but still attends sporadically and looks to it for guidance. She holds a high-paying job as a financial analyst, and her husband is a successful business executive, but she has also witnessed the turmoil of contemporary life. Her older brother was a drug pusher. Her husband's sister is a drug addict. She helped a close friend find an abortion clinic and sat with her after the procedure. When the doctors told her that her own baby might be brain damaged, she considered having an abortion herself. Now that her daughter is approaching adulthood, she talks with her regularly about sex and drugs, faith and politics, and careers.

This woman believes the world would be much worse off without religion. She says, "I think religion, like the law, is the glue that holds society together. I think it makes people behave in appropriate ways, in ways that are nonoffensive and nonhurtful to other people. I hate to say this, but I think a lot of mankind, given their druthers, would do their own thing, lead a hedonistic life, be selfish and not worry about the other person, given no laws and no religion. I think religion's the fiber of society."

Yet she also looks more to the religious teachings of her childhood than to anything else, even the church, to help sort out her own answers. She asked a priest recently if he still believed in absolutes or if everything was gray. "He told me that he thought everything was gray. I said, 'Does the Vatican agree with you on that? Are there no more absolutes left?' And he said, 'No, the Vatican still believes in black and white.' But he as a priest did not." She herself thinks there are absolutes, and she is trying to communicate them to her daughter, not by preaching sermons to her, but by talking about events as they happen. She thinks other people have to do the same, and she hopes they can reach into their own background for religious teachings. As for herself, she says she can only communicate what *she* believes.

Even the most devout seem to feel uncertain about how best to teach their children to have a regular devotional life. Going to church and sending their children to Sunday school are easy by comparison. Prayer is more difficult, because people are reluctant to use the simple, formulaic prayers of their own childhood; yet they seldom heard their parents pray spontaneously, so they do not know exactly what to say. A telling example comes from a woman who has become more devout in recent years as a result of illnesses and financial difficulties in her family. She had been taken to church every week as a child and has a vague sense that her mother prayed when things went badly, so she has recently been praying that God will help them sell their house so they can move to a new location where her husband can get a better job.

The woman is using the occasion to teach her daughter, a nine-year-old, how to pray. "I said to her, 'Allison, I think what you should do is, when you pray to God and you ask God to please help us try to get another house, pray like this, "Dear God, please help us to get another house. We'd like to get another house," and then when you end your prayer, I want you to say, "I ask this in the name of thy son, Jesus Christ. Amen."' And the funny thing that happened after she said that prayer is somebody put a contract on our house. I said to my daughter, I said, 'Allison, do you know I really think, Allison, the reason that these people signed a contract on our house is because you did pray and you asked in the name of thy son,

Jesus Christ.' And she says, 'Yeah, Mommy, I think that's true, I think God really tried to help us.' But the nice thing about it is she believed that God really helped us. I saw my daughter having faith in God, and I thought that was beautiful."

The story isn't over, however. The woman can only laugh as she adds, "But unfortunately what happened after that is the contract did fall through." As if to express her confusion about what to convey to her daughter, she mumbles, "Oh, boy!"

Money Crucifies Jesus

People who have grown up religious are by no means uniformly pessimistic about the future of American religion. Yet it is valuable to listen to their laments. Few of them want to return America to an earlier time when bigotry may have been more common or when standards of living were lower and health care less available. Having lived part of their lives in sheltered worlds, they nevertheless are able to view the wider culture with greater detachment than many people can.

Esther Sikous is deeply troubled about her grandchildren. She came to the United States in 1939, from a small village in Greece. A year earlier she was carrying a jug of water home to her parents, feeling sorry for herself because the villagers were jealous of the job she had gotten weaving rugs, when an American stopped her and asked for a drink. She told him she did not have a cup, but he found out who she was and a few weeks later gained her parents' consent to marry her. A month later, the American embassy asked all American citizens to leave because of the impending war in Europe. Esther was finally able to join her husband by taking the train to Le Harve and then a ship to Ellis Island. On its return voyage, the ship was sunk by a German torpedo.

Looking back on her own childhood, Esther appreciates more than ever the centrality of the Greek Orthodox church. "We used to go to church every Sunday," she says pointedly. "Every holiday during the week, we have to go to church." She pounds her fist on the table for emphasis. "And you can't do nothing the night before. If let's say today's Saint Apostle's Day, the twelve Apostles day, last night we're not supposed to do nothing. We have to celebrate. It was very religious, those years."

Mothers took their religious responsibilities very seriously. "Every single holiday during the week, including Sundays, the mother has to take us to church." Again, she pounds the table on each word. "We have to go to church. My mother used to go to church every single holiday, and she used to go before the priests, and get up early. And she used to go before the priests and she wait outside the church for the priest to come to open the church. That's why we learn, I learn from my parents to go to church."

Esther had less opportunity to observe her father, but she insists that he too was a very religious person. "I tell you, the style used to be the man in different room and the woman, even in church, in different room. And they got a partition, one room to the other, and the women on this side, the men on the other side. Every Sunday, everybody used to go to church. And on the holy week, and the forty-eight days before Easter, every day, every night, church, every night church. Wednesdays and Fridays, morning and night. The people was in the field all day long that time, they come wash their face a little bit, and go to church."

The congregation consisted of the eighty families who made up the village. Esther says the church was "like our own home." And her own home was like the church. "Every day we prayed. Before we go to bed, that's the rules from my mother and father. Before you went to bed. 'Hey, you went to bed already?' 'Yes, Mom.' 'You say your prayers?' I say, 'Yes, Mom.' 'I don't see you.' I say, 'Mom, honest, I do my prayer, I say my prayers.' Before we sit on the table for dinner or whatever, 'Come, Jesus and holy mother, come to eat with us,' like this. And 'Our Father,' and then we sit down and eat. On the end, my mother watching us if we say, 'Thank you, Lord, what we got on the table.' Every day."

Jesus came to Esther when she was ten years old. She remembers it well. "One day, month of May, the roses blooming. We used to have a lot of rosebushes, and my mother send us to pick up the roses. We sought to make the perfume. So one evening my mother said, 'Tomorrow you have to go pick in the fields, to pick up the roses, and then you're going to go to work.' Okay. I get up five o'clock. I went pick up all the roses and besides I got some weeds for the animals, to bring home for the nanny goats. I was scared to death, all by myself, to walk one hour. On my way home, but a couple blocks from my field, there used to be church, Saint Victor's. I stop in front of the church to exchange the heavy load from one arm to the other. Across from me there was a cherry orchard. I see Jesus underneath the cherry tree, the way he is on the altar. Exactly the same in life! And he's got his hands like this to me. With a nice smile. But I was only ten years old. I got so scared and I run. The walk is one hour and I probably make it in twenty minutes!"

When Esther got home, her mother knew something was wrong. "My mother see me, I don't know how I was looking. She say, 'What's the matter with you? Somebody touch you, somebody talk to you?' I say, 'Nothing, nothing, nothing.' I just remember the moment. 'Come on, tell me,' she push me. My mother was strict. 'What happened to you? Why you like that?' I say, 'Mom, in front of the church I saw somebody, and he blessed me like this, his finger like this.' She say, 'Somebody else now is ninety years old, he saw in his young days, this is Jesus.' A lot of times, even today, I say, 'Good Lord, why you don't give me the mind to stay, to ask for what I want from you?' "

When Esther's own children were young, she tried hard to teach them about Jesus. "Every night, I taught them to say a prayer to the mother of Jesus," she explains. She also talked to them about God. "I say, 'You have to listen. You have to believe in God. That God is only One. That God makes everybody. That God makes everything. That God makes the earth. That God makes the ocean divide with the land. That God makes the earth in six days and the Sunday is day for relax.' "

Life was slower in those days. "When I first came in this country, you can't find any store open on Sundays. If you miss something, an emergency, you don't find a place. Sunday used to be gathering day, from my young days, up to 1945, before the war stop. After the war stop, lot of money comes around, they forget everything. No gathering, they is working day and night, Sundays and weekdays. They don't realize there is day for gathering."

After her children were married, Esther and her husband invited them to visit every Sunday. She wanted to know if they had been to church. At first they went, but gradually they stopped going. She understands why. It was the pressure of their jobs. It was also the pace of life, driven by the desire for money. "The money ruins the religious," she says, pounding the table. "The money makes the people not to come to churches, because they are working. If they're working days, Sundays, weekdays, why? Why? I wonder why. Honest to God, my God is my witness, the only worry of mine is that I don't see my children at church, because they used to come. I look around, I don't see any of mine. I don't see a lot of others. A lot of the children state they don't come to church any more. You know why? Because they make a lot of money, and the money control the country."

As she thinks about the coming generation, she worries. "They don't know what Jesus is. Why don't people bring their children to have Communion sometime, to come to church, to hear the priest? You know why? They're working, they overdo, working overtime, and they get tired. Of course, they got bodies, they get tired." She pounds the table. "The money brought this catastrophe. The money crucify Jesus!"

✦➤◄✦

CHAPTER 11

Seeing with Four Eyes

A STRONG AND INTERNALLY diverse population of people with deep religious roots has an important contribution to make to the current debate about multiculturalism. Some people at least have been reared with a kind of dual vision that permits them to see appreciatively the distinctive value of their own tradition and that also permits them to recognize common values, such as tolerance and respect for others who may differ dramatically in their own lifestyle. Dual vision of this kind may be difficult to sustain, yet it runs to the heart of what must be realized for genuine pluralism to prevail.

In recent years the question of diversity has, perhaps curiously, arisen as much because of fear that diversity is diminishing as from concern about the centrifugal forces that pull in opposing directions. Indeed, observers of American society have often worried that democracy—the melting pot, the great leveler—is forging a new world in which the very soul of a people is being sacrificed. Dull, boringly the same, colored only by smug conformity, Americans have been accused of impoverishing themselves culturally and spiritually in the name of progress and tolerance. Critics fear that without the distinctive idioms of language and the peculiar dialects of ethnic roots, we will not have the cultural resources with which to build strong character.

A multicultural perspective is consistent with the respectful preservation of religious subcultures and faith communities. It goes beyond the liberal tradition that encourages tolerance of minority religions at the same time that superior nonreligious orientations are being encouraged. It also goes beyond a liberal syncretic view that champions all faiths on grounds that they are all inherently the same anyway or because the enlightened student of religious cultures can find bits and pieces of wisdom in all of them. Multiculturalism respects the truth embodied in different subcultures, at the same time recognizing that this truth may be incommensurate from one subculture to the next. A Baptist who believes that only Christians can be saved, for instance, cannot also be a Muslim who believes that only Muslims are saved. Multiculturalism also recognizes that a Baptist cannot truly be a believer in the fullest sense if deprived of the right to worship freely or to evangelize others. Still, multiculturalism is itself not a faith. It is not a metareligion that asserts the value — as a spiritual matter — of having as many religions as possible. It is instead a social perspective, a view, especially toward government, that asserts the possibility and desirability of cultural and religious groups' coexisting within the same nation or social sphere. It specifies rules of mutual respect, tolerance, and civility as norms for mutual accommodation at the same time that it guards against these norms' compromising the values of the groups it aims to preserve.

The Contribution of Religion

Most Americans from strong religious backgrounds are unwilling to think that every kind of value and lifestyle is of equal worth, but within limits they regard cultural diversity as a positive aspect of American society. They recognize the universalistic character of their own religious tradition, often diminishing its potential for conflict with other universalizing religions, and they are heartened by the thought that people with diverse personalities and from different communities can live in harmony under the same religious umbrella.

I do not mean to suggest that growing up religious is necessarily a formula for tolerance, however. The people we interviewed vary enormously in their tolerance toward other groups. Some feel so strongly that religion's place in American society is being eroded that they are vehemently opposed to groups they think are responsible for this development. For Tony

Martelli, America's slide away from the "religious convictions" of the founding fathers dates from the 1960s, and he thus disparages everything that happened during that decade, including the civil-rights movement, the Vietnam war, the counterculture, and the death-of-God movement. Other people miss the ethnic neighborhoods in which they were raised, blaming criminals, drug lords, or other groups for the demise of these communities. Yet, in other cases, people have developed a strong understanding of intergroup differences and are better able to appreciate other groups by virtue of recognizing the distinctive features of their own.

The interesting question is not so much why some people are more tolerant than others but what can be learned about living in a pluralistic society from those who have experienced the realities of this pluralism in their religious upbringing. In this regard, religion is particularly revealing because it has been an encompassing, primary commitment for many people, and yet it also purports to embrace universalistic principles of love, peace, and justice. Apart from any formal expression of those principles, many people do appear to learn how to be loyal to their own religious traditions but also to recognize broader, unifying experiences among the diverse array of such traditions.

Part of what it means to live in a multicultural society is thus to have a genuine appreciation of the particularity of one's past. Consider what Raman Wilkins says about the African American church. "There is an ethnic connectiveness to black people's religion, because I can go to Detroit and somebody can just drop me in the church, and it'd be no different if I was in Pittsburgh or I was in Newark, because that black thing comes out, all of their culture." He adds: "I think it was the basis of strength for the black community. I sometimes think that if it wasn't for the black church, black people wouldn't have any cohesiveness. I think the black church is the essence of black people."[1]

The strength that comes from identifying with a particular community is balanced by respect for the fact that people come from different backgrounds. Such respect is nurtured by religious traditions that perceive commonalities with other traditions. Members of newer immigrant communities are sometimes the best observers of the unifying potential in religion.

For example, one of the Muslim women we interviewed describes Islam as "universal" and is proud that it embraces Iranians, Pakistanis, Russians, Bosnians, and Chinese. She says her own mosque, in New York, is "international; we have different people from different backgrounds coming here and they want religion. That's what I like best about it." A young man from a devout Muslim family makes a similar point, stating that his parents want him to "be able to deal with everyone, of all nationalities, races, religions, whatever, it doesn't matter, because we're all stuck on this planet anyway, and we have to deal with each other."

Peter Arno, who was raised Catholic and became Episcopalian when he married, expresses a similar idea. "I think people find spirituality in certain ways. Part of it comes from tradition, and I think there's a lot of different religions in which people can speak to the issue of spirituality, and I think for those people, those religions are true."

Even Tony Martelli strikes a balance between loyalty to the particular tradition in which he feels most comfortable and the broader values that are embodied in that tradition. "I always took pride in being Italian," he says on the one hand. "I still do. I still think of Rome as being the center of Western culture. Its history goes back pretty far, and when you look at what the Romans did to culture and civilization in general, and you look back at the artifacts and the history of it all, there's a lot to be proud of there. You talk about architecture, music, science, it's quite a history. They had their act together!" On the other hand, he learned early that a tradition of this kind is somewhat arbitrary and that people from other backgrounds are good, too.

In some ways, he learned this contrast from his parents. His mother exemplified the value of being deeply rooted in a single tradition. His father, having a more private faith that surfaced mainly in fair dealings, taught him to judge goodness in broader terms. Tony explains: "You respected a human being because of the fact that they were a human being. Of course, some people don't gain respect, and you have to act accordingly, but if you act like a human being, I'm going to treat you like a human being."

Town and Country

The people we talked with seldom use sophisticated theoretical language to explain their views of cultural diversity. They shun arguments about

SEEING WITH FOUR EYES   ◄◄   223

rights, interests, equity, and social justice, turning instead to the home-
spun metaphors that spring naturally from their own experiences. A
woman named Barbara Gilroy is able to demonstrate that lessons in multiculturalism can be learned in unlikely places.

As a girl, she lived in a small town in western Iowa that measured exactly seven blocks from north to south and eight blocks from east to west—
she could ride her bicycle anywhere, and she always felt safe. Townspeople ran the bank and the filling station, worked at the cafe, taught school,
and operated the co-op where farmers from a twenty-mile radius came
to market their grain. Her family attended one of the four Protestant
churches in town; there were no Catholics or Jews, and everyone was
white. In western Iowa, she muses, "multiculturalism meant either you're
a farmer or you live in town."

When Barbara Gilroy grew up, she went away to Iowa State University,
where she mixed with people of many backgrounds; then she taught in an
all-black elementary school in the Deep South; now she lives in a large
city and works at an institution that prides itself on cultural diversity. She
recognizes that the United States is becoming more varied in racial and
ethnic composition, a development that she regards as an unqualified
benefit.

Giving minority groups and women more of a political voice, she feels,
will make America stronger: "Hopefully, we're going to get rid of the predominantly male, Caucasian ruling class, and bring a lot of other different
perspectives into decision making. And that's going to affect what kind of
laws are passed." She acknowledges that this is going to be a difficult transition, especially for people in homogeneous towns. "I think people in western Iowa may struggle, because we'll have ethnically diverse people making decisions which affect predominantly white, rural Iowa. I think that
will be tough." But she is confident the transition can be made.

Two aspects of Barbara Gilroy's upbringing account for this confidence. One is the grassroots democracy she witnessed as a child in western
Iowa. Townspeople and farmers had their differences; so did the members
of the four churches. But they came together, held town meetings, hag-
gled, and voted. Even if it is much harder to reconcile differences in a
complex, national environment, the same democratic structures are in
place. The other is her religious outlook. She saw plenty of interchurch
conflict as a child, and she has not yet fully resolved her views about non-

Christians; yet she feels a unifying bond that is stronger than the barriers that divide. Although she loves the denomination in which she was raised, she recognizes its failings, and she sees a need to love other people rather than judge them. It bothers her to think that religious values may be slipping away, but she is heartened by the spiritual searching she sees everywhere. People may not be finding the same answers, she says, but the needs transcend cultural boundaries.

Coal Miner's Daughter

That people can become more tolerant is well established in the research literature; *how* they become so is far less understood. Education, of course, is said to be an enlightening influence. Presumably people learn that it is morally wrong to discriminate or that tolerance is good for democracy. Perhaps they learn that teachers are open minded or that it is unfashionable to use racial epithets. All this may be important, but what our interviews suggest is that people also learn to be tolerant by reconstructing their own life stories. Just as they understand themselves spiritually by reflecting on their past, so they come to think about other groups in new ways by finding aspects of their own background that legitimate a change in attitude. Indeed, most people have examples in their own histories of being hurt by discrimination or, conversely, of viewing acceptance at close range, and when these stories can be remembered, they provide the material for refashioning one's outlook.

Consider the story of Amanda Sapolsky, a coal miner's daughter who grew up in West Virginia, Ohio, Kentucky, and southern Indiana during the 1920s. Her parents were immigrants, neither of whom had attended high school, and Amanda was one of eight children. Family traditions included stories of bitter conflict between Catholics and Protestants in Eastern Europe. The Sapolskys were Protestants, and it was unthinkable for any of them to say a kind word about Catholics. In the mining towns in which Amanda was raised, ethnic conflict was pervasive. Knowing this, the foremen generally housed Protestants with other Protestants, and Catholics with other Catholics. Even the work crews were often religiously segregated. Tensions between whites and blacks were even more severe. Whites resented blacks because the mine bosses often used them

SEEING WITH FOUR EYES 225

to break strikes or as a threat against demands for higher wages. Amanda grew up with a rich vocabulary of racial and religious prejudices.

The legacy of this upbringing has remained with Amanda over the years. As she thinks about the world her grandchildren are inheriting, she is worried. "The crime is so bad and the morals have sunk so low," she laments, "sometimes I think we're worse off than in the days of Sodom and Gomorrah." She does not point to any particular group as the source of these problems, but there are racial and ethnic overtones to her concern. For example, she thinks some of the newer immigrant groups are becoming too powerful, and she thinks it is dangerous when groups focus on asserting their rights rather than trying to assimilate. "I can't hit the nail on the head," she says, "but I just feel it's a problem with these ethnic groups when one is so much larger than the others. I just feel there's problems because they want to force their beliefs on the other group, like in Florida. Did you see that with Miami? The people from Cuba, they want to make the Spanish-speaking language the [official] language."

Despite these concerns, she is nevertheless a strong supporter of ethnic diversity. She feels newer immigrant groups are making the United States a better country, and she favors efforts to combat racism and to ensure equal rights for everyone. Having never received much education herself, she does not express herself in a language of civil rights or social justice or multiculturalism. Instead, she speaks from her own experience. She recalls one childhood memory that has become increasingly meaningful to her over the years. One of her uncles, according to family tradition, had been deeply in love with a Catholic woman back in the old country but had not been allowed to marry her. The woman married a Catholic man, gave birth to several children, emigrated to the United States, and then a few years later was widowed. Meanwhile, Amanda's uncle had also come to the United States and by chance happened to meet the widow, wooed her again, and this time, in the more tolerant atmosphere of the United States, was able to marry her.

The mining towns were so segregated that Amanda thinks she was probably eight years old before she ever saw a black person, but she has also been able to find a story from her childhood that gives her reason to believe in the value of racial harmony. "This black man was working with a white man, and my father liked the black man because he didn't shirk," she recalls. "The black man did his share of the work, and the white man was always snitching on him, telling the foreman that he's not doing his share of work. My father overheard it and went and stuck up for the black man." Years later, when the civil-rights movement came along, Amanda responded favorably to it, her only regret being that it did not accomplish more.

These stories from her past also help her respond to the changing realities of her own family. Several of Amanda's siblings have married Catholics, and her daughter is married to a Jewish man. Amanda wants her grandchildren to remember their ethnic and religious "heritage," as she calls it, and she is content knowing that they will have several heritages to remember. "I'm a firm believer in all this kind of stuff," she asserts. "I always say that mixed marriages make for better people." Greater diversity will make the country stronger, and it will make American religion stronger, she believes. The greatest danger, she admits, is when one religious group tries to "push its beliefs down other people's throats." What gives her hope is the fact that some religious groups are doing more to cooperate with each other. A few years ago her own congregation was approached by a nearby synagogue to help feed homeless people in the community; now there are six congregations from various faith traditions helping with the project. She thinks American religion will remain strong if more congregations can enlist people in these kinds of efforts.

Fundamentalism

If what I've argued holds true for most people who grew up religious, it nevertheless leaves an important question about fundamentalists. Are they not the exception? Of all people who may have grown up religious, fundamentalists are most likely to have taken their early religious commitments seriously, and yet by most indications they are intolerant of people with different religious views and lifestyles. Moreover, fundamentalists may be the one group toward whom other people who have grown up religious find it difficult to be tolerant.

Most research shows that fundamentalists are indeed different from people who hold more liberal or moderate religious orientations.[2] Compared with other groups, fundamentalists include a fairly large number of people who have converted to their faith as adults, either having been raised with little or no religious training or having repudiated their religious upbringing in favor of something they consider more genuine. And converts often become "true believers" to a stronger degree than people who have grown up in a particular tradition. In addition, fundamentalism builds higher walls between itself and other groups, often demonizing other religious groups as wolves in sheep's clothing. Like many people who have grown up religious, fundamentalists often perceive changes in the society that are distressing to them, but rather than attributing these changes to such developments as technology, population growth, and consumerism, they blame particular political and religious leaders, whom they deem to be evil, and they argue that only they understand divine truth and are willing to live by divine principles. In their recent efforts to seize control of governments, schools, and other public institutions, fundamentalists have done more to alienate other people who have grown up with religious sensibilities than they have done to forge alliances with these people. The shrill rhetoric captured in media specials about fundamentalists suggests that they are indeed an alien force.

Nevertheless, media images of fundamentalists are often misleading, especially when fundamentalist worship services are videotaped as a kind of spectacle or when highly edited sound bites are solicited in local situations that have become conflict ridden. In our interviews, we found that fundamentalists are more complex in their views than is generally understood by the media, and that nonfundamentalists are also more ambivalent about fundamentalists than has sometimes been recognized. Especially among people who had grown up in a particular religious tradition, there is often a basis from which fundamentalist beliefs can be understood; among fundamentalists, the fact of having grown up religious is often a basis for recognizing diversity and the need for change.

Nonfundamentalists sometimes express respect toward fundamentalists because of their willingness to take religion and morality seriously. For example, Peter Arno—speaking now as a theologically liberal Episcopalian—remarks that he dislikes and fears fundamentalists who are active in politics, and yet, he says, "You've got to admit one thing, they have a point which challenges those of us in other religions, and that is that they do try to integrate their faith into their lives. You have to respond to them on that level." He disagrees with fundamentalists' efforts to wield political power but feels he can relate to their religious and moral concerns. Other people are less accepting of fundamentalists but are able to draw on their own religious experiences to make sense of them, often by perceiving of fundamentalism as a childlike faith (emphasizing absolutes) that needs to be transcended as people mature. If this understanding encourages them to be condescending toward fundamentalists, it nevertheless gives them reason to believe that fundamentalists are part of their own world rather than from a world occupied only by the demented or mentally deficient.

Fundamentalists themselves are generally very much aware of religious and cultural pluralism. Although they inisist that certain religious experiences (such as being born again) are essential and that certain lifestyles (such as homosexuality) are absolutely evil, they have often pared away much of the religious baggage of their youth or of their present denomination. For example, there is a striking willingness to migrate across denominational lines, switching from church to church as the need arises, as long as a certain style of preaching and worship is present. On the surface at least, there is little evidence of racism, and many of the churches fundamentalists attend are more racially mixed than those attended by nonfundamentalists. Gender distinctions among fundamentalists run contrary to egalitarian ideals, and yet women often exercise a great deal of power in their churches and homes, while men are often devoted husbands, fathers, and homemakers.

The political issues around which fundamentalists have become mobilized, such as abortion and school prayer, make it difficult to identify the common ground they have with other religious people. Yet, insofar as a subculture is understood to be a loosely structured network of individuals and organizations who are themselves quite diverse, the subculture of people who have grown up religious includes both fundamentalists and nonfundamentalists and provides some implicit understanding that keeps conflict between the two from escalating to more serious levels.

Fundamentalists' willingness to use political means to impose their views on others is also limited by the conviction that religion should be private and personal. A woman in her early thirties who says she is "born again" and who attends a conservative Baptist congregation illustrates this view as she talks about a "run in" she had with the pastor when she was a teenager. He became so caught up in antiabortion sentiments that one day he went to Washington, took a position near the White House, and slit his wrists to show how the blood of innocent unborn children was being spilt by the government. The woman remembers being completely repulsed by his action. "That isn't how a religious leader should act," she says. "I told him later, 'I can't follow you as a minister if you're going to do something like that.' It made no sense, it was a stunt. He was just using his position as a pastor. He was using religion to get attention for his political views. Religion shouldn't be something you use. Religion is something you believe and respect and follow."

More than a decade later, this woman remains very conservative in her own views. She, too, is opposed to abortion and she believes that "homosexuality is against God's law." Yet she feels that God places people in different situations for a reason and that everyone must follow the path that God has placed before them. "I feel he guides everybody's path and that everything happens for a reason and we are to learn and seek his strength in what happens, respect his laws, respect people for how they interpret God's law. I've been dealing with that, because I have a friend who's gay. I don't like him any less. It's his burden to carry and I will give him my opinions on it, but I don't shun him or talk down to him. It's his own path." She and her gay friend have "a religious feedback thing," as she puts it. "He'll give me an opinion on how he sees a religious event from his upbringing and I'll give one on how I see it and we try to understand each other. It gets me thinking. I gives me a different viewpoint."

The Last Acceptable Bigotry

Effie Cairn, the seventy-year-old Irish Catholic who cried at Christmas while she was growing up, has also developed a way of thinking about group differences that permits her to be loyal and tolerant at the same time. She describes her commitment to Catholicism (somewhat tongue-in-cheek) as "the last acceptable bigotry." By this, she means she is willing to defend it as a style of religious expression that makes sense to her. She says she likes its structure, its organization, and the fact that it stands for something. In contrast, she says she has little use for charismatic or fundamentalist Protestants, because their services are often too emotional, spontaneous, and disrespectful of church traditions. Yet she thinks it is wonderful that people who have not been comfortable in more established traditions have been able to feel at home in such groups. What also makes her bigotry acceptable, she believes, is that she tells people up front that her background is Irish Catholic.

This example points to the importance of communication. In Effie Cairn's case, the lack of communication in her family so many years ago heightened her awareness that people must talk if they are to overcome their differences. Interacting with people of other ethnic backgrounds and faiths helped, too. She has come to see her own tradition *as* a tradition rather than as having a unique corner on the truth. Although she is happier in this tradition than in any other, she recognizes that other people will be more comfortable in their own tradition. She thinks the biggest difference between her present views and those she was raised with is that she can be loyal to her faith without being so "frightened" about it.

Maintaining a bit of acceptable bigotry is also a way of retaining the right to be critical, sorting out the good and the bad, rather than being entirely tolerant of everything. Effie Cairn illustrates this ability as she talks about ethnic and religious diversity. "We are a nation of immigrants. People bring a lot of wonderful stuff with them. And they bring some stuff that's not so wonderful. I think that some of the Asian cultures put down women even more than Europeans and Americans do. Some of the religions are a little frightening. I keep reading that the Muslims are people who respect all life, and they respect women, and a guest is a treasure, and all of that. And yet that's not the side that keeps coming out. Other religions may reinforce family and clannishness, while making other people outsiders. That certainly helps the people inside the clan but may be a problem. I don't know a lot about the Shintos, the Buddhists, and things like that, so I really can't say. I would think that anything that is nonviolent and family centered could only be a plus, but I just don't know enough." In short, one needs to have knowledge of other groups and to understand that they have strengths and weaknesses, just as one's own group does.

Dual Vision

In larger terms, what Effie Cairn embodies is an ability to see with four eyes. With one pair, she sees the distinctive community that has meant so much to her; with another pair, she sees the wider world, its diversity, and its common values and underlying need for harmony. For many of the people we talked with, it was this kind of dual vision that had contributed most to their capacity to live in loyalty to one tradition while respecting the value of many others.

In a number of instances, learning to see with dual vision was significantly enhanced by the disjuncture people experienced between their home (or congregation) and their school. Although this disjuncture was often a source of conflict, it helped young people develop a more nuanced understanding of the world. At home, one learned to believe and practice in one specific way; at school, one discovered the necessity of getting along with people from many different backgrounds. An interesting example comes from a woman who had been raised outside the United States. Her parents were staunch Protestants who read the Bible at home every day and attended a Christian church every Sunday. At school, there were thirty-five students in her class, representing twenty-three different countries. She recalls, "We never even thought about discriminating against someone because of their race or beliefs or language or whatever."

In an extreme case like this, it is easy to compartmentalize childhood faith, separate it from the more relativistic atmosphere of school. However, we found that people have also learned to speak a double language in a way that helps them live in two worlds. For instance, this woman uses the language of discrimination to talk about classmates at school. She did not feel she had to agree with their beliefs but recognized the need to respect their rights. In her own tradition, she also finds support for the ideal of treating others fairly, and she has come to emphasize service to those around her, rather than preaching at them.

Although some of the people we talked with say they have abandoned their religious upbringing entirely and others say they have remained completely within it, the most common response is that they are still struggling in some measure to figure out the relationship between their faith and the rest of what they know about life. The religious stories and experiences of their childhood are too primordial to be dismissed out of hand, and yet unresolved questions are raised by these stories and experiences.

Elaine Margolis acknowledges that she has been trying for more than a quarter of a century to figure out the Christian idea of the atonement— Jesus' dying to atone for the sins of humanity. "I don't think I ever will un-

derstand it," she says, "and yet this is the linchpin around which Christianity revolves." She is unwilling to say it is just a silly notion, but she also
thinks it must be understood as some combination of divine truth, symbol-
ism, and human custom. A struggle like this puts her, in effect, between
two worlds. She still identifies deeply with the Christian tradition, yet en-
tertains the idea of a more inclusive understanding of the sacred. Both
worlds are part of her identity. She can appreciate the religious teachings
of her childhood but also identify with a broader subculture of other
people who take their own religious convictions seriously. In the process,
she is also capable of appreciating other kinds of cultural diversity.

Dual vision comes from dealing with family members, too. In virtually
all cases, the people we interviewed describe huge differences in the religious habits of their siblings. Despite their religious upbringing, some
people abandon religion, while their brothers or sisters remain involved.
Few of the latter are willing to cast aspersions on the former. Instead, they
construct accounts that permit them to view their siblings in the best light.
For example, an African American man in New York notes that his sister
had moved to California and "lived a very different lifestyle" that did not
include sending her children to church. Yet, he muses, "sometimes it's
better to find your own way and do things because you want to, rather than
having them thrust upon you."

Stephen Fukuyama has come to a similar view by a different route. His
wife's sister was raised in a Japanese American family that practiced Buddhism, and as an adult she has become a born-again Christian. She criti-
cizes Stephen for not being a good Christian, even though he teaches Sunday school, leads the worship service periodically, and considers himself
to be a follower of Christ. He senses that he is not as devout as his grandmother or his mother, so his sister-in-law's criticisms worry him. Nevertheless, he is able to reconcile variations in different kinds of religious expression with the following argument. "I practice Christianity differently
because I've been through lots of battles and I'm at peace with myself,
with my niche. When she starts whipping out verses at me, I say, 'You have
gained spirituality and I see you're very calm and you're a very happy person. That's great. Well, what makes me happy is I have my niche. This is
my way of being committed to God.'" Summarizing, he says, "I guess I'm
just a religious pragmatist."

At another level, our sense of what it means to live in a multicultural society is probably most deeply rooted in people's relationships with their parents. In one sense, parents are the main link people have with a particular, idiosyncratic tradition. Nevertheless, parents are also the launching pad from which people propel themselves into the more diverse world in which they will eventually live. *Ambivalence* toward parents propels people in this direction. In short, people become attached to their own tradition because they love and admire their parents, but they also gain respect for other traditions because they want to be independent from their parents.

Hal Meyerson's relationship with his father is a case in point. Samuel Meyerson, Hal says, was very difficult to have as a father. Everything Hal saw in his father was an unattainable standard. Hal played football, but his father had been an all-American. Hal made decent grades, but his father had a photographic memory and had never made less than an A in his life. Hal enjoyed going fishing and target shooting with his father, but his father always caught the bigger fish and got the higher score. In retrospect, Hal says that his fondest—and his worst—memories as a child are of his father. He loved his dad and enjoyed doing things with him. But he also competed and fought with his dad. He remembers one time pulling a butcher knife on his father. He says he would probably have hurt his father, but the older man was too quick.

This ambivalence has driven Hal both to affirm his childhood faith and to broaden his understanding of other people with different faiths. He not only learned how to pray from his father but also discovered that he could outdo his father religiously. For many years the older man seemed to lose interest in his faith and practiced it more from habit than from conviction. Hal became more active in his temple during this period and yearned to be more like his grandfather than his father.

Had Hal lived in a religiously monolithic society, he might have become a zealot. Exposed all his life to religious pluralism, however, he was able to use other traditions as an additional way of asserting his own identity in relation to his father. In high school, Hal ran with a bad crowd sometimes and did things that displeased his father. In college, he found it more sensible to mix with good people from other traditions than the ones his father knew. He was attracted to African Americans and to people from low-income backgrounds. He affirmed his own commitment to Judaism but prided himself on being able to learn from other faiths and subcultures as well.

Turning Communities into People

Harriet Sims is among the more reflective people we talked to about multiculturalism. After her divorce, she finished college and started teaching in an inner-city school. During these years, she became increasingly aware of her African American identity. She attributes this awareness to the fact that she was having to do more to secure resources for her own community than ever before. For example, after the FBI arrested Black Panther leaders, Harriet helped organize a breakfast program at her school to replace the one run by the Panthers. She also started attending a church headed by a woman pastor who was helping poor people in the neighborhood. Harriet has appropriated the pride she inherited from her great-grandmother, grandmother, and mother. Even though her religious involvements have been more varied, Harriet thinks her spirituality is basically the same as theirs.

Harriet's religious views give her insight into how to live peaceably in a multiethnic and multiracial society. She attends services now because they give her a spiritual home. She appreciates the familiarity of the ritual and the opportunity to have informal discussions with some of the other women. The church links her to African American traditions and to the African American neighborhood in which she lives. But it is also her bridge into the wider society. She senses an affinity with white people who share her Christian values and has been working with them lately to form an organization concerned with bringing Christian values into the public schools.

It worries her that people are not teaching their children Christian values the way her mother did. Dishonesty, materialism, and a lack of respect for others, she fears, are the inevitable result. She realizes that people are becoming more aware of racial and ethnic differences, but diversity in itself will only create divisions, she says, unless people recognize that there is value in diversity. Religion, in her view, holds the greatest potential for helping people recognize that value: "We all come from a common source, and that's through God, and we all are dependent on each other to maintain and sustain each other in this God-given environment."

From comments such as these, it is easier to understand why Americans are in such turmoil about how best to deal with the problems facing their society. People like Harriet Sims are divided, just as the nation is divided, over how much or how little can reasonably be expected of government. Some think government should be doing more for the poor, the elderly, for hungry children, and in general to support better education, health care, and urban development. Many think government programs are a waste of money, if not an outright blight on their neighborhood. They want churches, synagogues, parents, and community groups to do more to preserve society's future. But both views are deeply rooted in the perception that religion used to be the mainstay of American life and that this mainstay is in serious decline.

Harriet Sims is outspoken in calling on churches to do more, rather than relying on government. In fact, she thinks the growth of government in recent decades is one reason the churches are deteriorating. "We used to depend on each other and the churches. The mothers would have meetings at the churches, they would have prayer service at the church. If not in the churches, the church spirit and bodies would be in the communities, visiting homes, and they don't do that anymore. We don't circulate among the homes any longer." And yet she knows there is too much fear in her neighborhood to expect people to participate in churches like they did when she was a girl.

Clearly, caution needs to be exercised in determining public policy on the basis of personal perceptions of what it was like to have grown up religious. Although our interviews show that growing up religious is an important formative experience for many Americans, there is also a kind of nostalgia in these memories that must be taken into account. Some of the nostalgia is linked to the fact that many people's memories are of the 1950s, a time when mothers stayed at home to raise their children and churches flourished on the volunteer labor of these women. In part, the nostalgia is also rooted in memories of grandparents who may have seemed more religious than they really were, or in memories of holidays rather than daily practices.

There is, nevertheless, wisdom in the perception that spirituality has been a significant feature of the American past and that it remains so for many people, albeit in different versions than those of their parents and grandparents. Spirituality has been most effective in shaping the values of children when it has been practiced at home as well in formal organizations. In the past, people practiced spirituality at home under the most diverse (and adverse) conditions. The lesson from this history should be that spirituality is likely to survive as a feature of American childhood—*if parents and grandparents are committed to its importance.*

Notes

Introduction

1. To put Hal Meyerson's family history in perspective, it is helpful to know that a national study of American Jews in the 1970s showed that only 20 percent listed both their parents as being born in the United States; another 21 percent were themselves foreign born, leaving nearly six in ten for whom one parent was foreign born (Bernard Lazerwitz and M. Harrison, "American Jewish Denominations: A Social and Religious Profile," *American Sociological Review* 44 [1979], pp. 656–66). The same study showed that approximately one third of American Jews were college graduates and one third were employed in the professions.

2. The experience of Hal Meyerson's parents was similar in many respects to that of Jews in Park Forest, Illinois, as described in Herbert J. Gans, "The Origin of a Jewish Community in the Suburbs," in *The Jewish Community in America*, edited by Marshall Sklare (New York: Behrman House, 1974), pp. 19–41.

3. Madeleine L'Engle, in *The Summer of the Great-Grandmother* (New York: Seabury, 1979), p. 234, observes: "To the ancient Hebrew the ultimate hell consisted in being forgotten, erased from the memory of family and tribe, from the memory of God. Your life, your being, your *ousia*, is of no value whatsoever. You are a tale told by an idiot; forgotten; annihilated."

4. Just as Mary Shannon identified herself as a Saint Patrick's girl, so Patricia Hampl, in *Virgin Time* (New York: Ballantine Books, 1992), p. 41, writes, "I *belonged* to St. Luke's. That was the lingo. Mothers spoke of daughters who were going to the junior-senior prom with boys 'from Nativity' or 'from St. Mark's' as if from fiefdoms across the sea."

5. For a lively account of Catholic upbringing, see Andrew Greeley, *Confessions of a Parish Priest: An Autobiography* (New York: Simon and Schuster, 1986); more whimsical is Ed Stivender, *Raised Catholic* (Little Rock: August House, 1992).

6. See Cheryl Jeanne Sanders, *Saints in Exile: The Holiness-Pentecostal Experience in African American Religion and Culture* (New York: Oxford University Press, 1996).
7. Shirley Spencer June, "The Role of the Home in the Spiritual Development of Black Children," in *The Black Family: Past, Present, and Future* (Grand Rapids, MI: Zondervan, 1991), pp. 99–112, is helpful as a broader discussion; on African American churches more generally, see C. Eric Lincoln and Lawrence H. Mamiya, *The Black Church in the African American Experience* (Durham, NC: Duke University Press, 1990).
8. Randall Balmer, in *Grant Us Courage: Travels Along the Mainline of American Protestantism* (New York: Oxford University Press, 1995), profiles churches like the one in which Bruce Gallahue was raised.
9. The wider relevance of this observation is suggested by Jody Shapiro Davie, *Women in the Presence: Constructing Community and Seeking Spirituality in Mainline Protestantism* (Philadelphia: University of Pennsylvania Press, 1995), p. 135, who describes "a discernible pattern of prohibition against openness" among her Presbyterian subjects.
10. For studies of childhood religiosity, see especially Robert Coles, *The Spiritual Life of Children* (Boston: Houghton Mifflin, 1990), and David Heller, *The Children's God* (Chicago: University of Chicago Press, 1986); see also David J. Ludwig, Timothy Weber, and Douglas Iben, "Letters to God: A Study of Children's Religious Concepts," *Journal of Psychology and Theology* 2 (1974), pp. 31–35.
11. I distinguish "ordinary" from "typical" or "representative" but insist on the value of listening to ordinary people, especially at a time when so much of popular culture is dominated by the voices of elites; Barbara J. Scot, in *Prairie Reunion* (New York: Farrar Straus Giroux, 1995), p. 228, expresses the useful view that "the more ordinary one's experience is, the more that experience reflects the essence of the human condition."
12. For an extended treatment of the idea of practices, see Stephen Turner, *The Social Theory of Practices: Tradition, Tacit Knowledge, and Presuppositions* (Chicago: University of Chicago Press, 1994); my idea of embeddedness is similar to that in Mark Granovetter, "Economic Action and Social Structure: The Problem of Embeddedness," *American Journal of Sociology* 91 (1985), pp. 481–510, although my use of the term is also intended to point toward the material and symbolic culture of specific locations.
13. Previous research shows strong generational continuity between parental religiosity and adolescent religiosity, as well as in self-reported data from adults about their parents' religiosity; David Caplovitz and Frederick Sherrow, *The Religious Drop-Outs: Apostasy among College Graduates* (Beverly Hills: Sage, 1977); Dean Hoge and Gregory Petrillo, "Determinants of Church Participation and Attitudes among High School Youth," *Journal for the Scientific Study of Religion* 17 (1978), pp. 359–80; Raymond H. Potvin and Douglas M. Sloane, "Parental Control, Age, and Religious Practice," *Review of Religious Research* 27 (1985), pp. 3–14. Disinterest in religious socialization among scholars in recent years may be attributable to the assumption that these effects are relatively straightforward; in any case, C. Daniel Batson, Patricia Schoenrade, and

W. Larry Ventis, *Religion and the Individual: A Social-Psychological Perspective* (New York: Oxford University Press, 1993), which is a leading text, includes less than a page on the effects of parents' religion. One of the few books that includes an entire chapter on "growing up religious" is Andrew Greeley, *The Denominational Society: A Sociological Approach to Religion in America* (Glenview, IL: Scott Foresman, 1972).

14. My emphasis on listening to ordinary people differs from the professional expertise approach, perhaps best expressed in a scholarly article on religious education that concluded, "The information we have increasingly points to evermore complex phenomena in dealing with families and individuals. The mastery requires considerable training and graduate education" (Samuel M. Natale, "A Family Systems Approach to Religious Education and Development," *Religious Education* 74 [1979], 245–53). My own view is that such training is worthless if it does not start with the lived experience of ordinary people.

15. Charlotte Linde, *Life Stories: The Creation of Coherence* (New York: Oxford University Press, 1993).

16. A focus on adults' memories of their childhood necessarily contrasts with the literature concerned with identifying developmental stages in the religious maturation of children, adolescents, and adults; see James Fowler, *Stages of Faith* (San Francisco: Harper and Row, 1981); James Fowler, *Becoming Adult, Becoming Christian* (San Francisco: Harper and Row, 1984); and Steve Fortosis, "A Developmental Model for Stages of Growth in Christian Formation," *Religious Education* 87 (1992), pp. 283–98.

17. Peter L. Berger and Thomas Luckmann, *The Social Construction of Reality: A Treatise in the Sociology of Knowledge* (Garden City, NY: Doubleday, 1966), p. 22.

18. Frances FitzGerald, *Cities on a Hill: A Journey through Contemporary American Cultures* (New York: Simon and Schuster, 1986), p. 43.

19. These characteristics are emphasized especially in Wade Clark Roof, *A Generation of Seekers: The Spiritual Journeys of the Baby Boom Generation* (San Francisco: Harper San Francisco, 1993); see also Dean R. Hoge, Benton Johnson, and Donald A. Luidens, *Vanishing Boundaries: The Religion of Mainline Protestant Baby Boomers* (Louisville: Westminster/John Knox Press, 1994).

20. Madeleine L'Engle, *The Irrational Season* (New York: Seabury Press, 1979), pp. 16–17.

21. Nancy Lewis, "The Silent Partner," *Washington Post* (March 31, 1995), D1.

22. The term is apparently severed sufficiently from its religious roots that journalists recognize the need to explain it; for example, see David Kucharsky, *The Man from Plains: The Mind and Spirit of Jimmy Carter* (New York: Harper & Row, 1976), p. 14.

Chapter 1: Family Rituals

1. There have, nevertheless, been a number of denominational efforts in recent years to renew interest in the religious training of children; for example, see the joint statement of the Family Life Bureau of the United States Catholic Conference, the Commission on Marriage and Family of the National Coun-

cil of the Churches of Christ, and the Committee on the Family of the Syna-
gogue Council of America entitled "Marriage and Family Life in the United
States," in *Let's Celebrate the Family*, edited by Vicki S. Allen (New York:
American Mothers Committee, 1976), pp. 8–10.

2. Philippe Ariès, *Centuries of Childhood: A Social History of Family Life* (New
York: Vintage, 1962), provides useful background.

3. The essays in *The Religion and Family Connection: Social Science Perspectives*, edited by Darwin L. Thomas (Provo: Religious Studies Center, Brigham
Young University, 1988) are helpful as background to the present discussion.

4. Given the tremendous interest in angels in recent years, it is not surprising
that many people also say they learned to believe in angels and even to pray to
them as children. One woman recalls verbatim the prayer she said every night
before she went to sleep: "Angel of God, my guardian dear to whom God's love
commits me here. Ever this day be at my side to light, to guard, to rule and to
guide. Amen."

5. This reference to prayer's being like saying multiplication tables is similar to
the story about "praying the ABCs" in Albert J. Raboteau, *A Fire in the Bones:
Reflections on African-American Religious History* (Boston: Beacon, 1995), pp.
1–16.

6. On memorization, Patricia Hampl, in *Virgin Time*, p. 41, remarks, "The sky-
blue Baltimore Catechism, small and square, read like an owner's manual for
a very complicated vehicle. There was something pleasant, lulling and rhyth-
mic, like heavily rhymed poetry, about the singsong Q-and-A format."

7. This conclusion is drawn from my analysis of data from the 1992 Economic
Values Survey (a copy of this survey is included in my book *God and Mammon
in America* [New York: Free Press, 1994], appendix).

8. A woman in her eighties remembers every word of the prayer her family said
at meals: "In Jesus' name we come to dine. To eat and drink according to thy
promises. To God be the glory. Ours be the gain. We receive our food in Jesus'
name. Amen." A Lutheran woman remembered, "We prayed the common table prayer, 'Come, Lord Jesus, be our guest and let these gifts to us be blessed.'
After we ate, then we said, 'O, give thanks unto the Lord, for he is good, for his
mercy endures forever.'"

9. The scholarly literature has generally recognized the importance of family rituals in the transmission of Jewish identity; for example, one scholar writes,
"Jewish family life is interwoven with ethnic practices, thus giving children
the immense psychological benefit of a number of meaningful rituals and cer-
emonies that mark religious observances, holidays, family events, and rites
of passage" (H. M. Sebald, *Adolescence: A Sociological Analysis* [New York:
Appleton-Century-Crofts, 1968], p. 290).

10. For readers who may not be familiar with the term, Anton E. Mickelsen, in
"The Bible Has a Place in Our Family," *International Journal of Religious Education* 38 (1962), pp. 13–14, offers another firsthand account. Family devotions
have a long history in Protestant circles. John Wesley's mother, Susannah, for
instance, writes in a letter to her son how she had conducted family devotions
when he was little: "The children of this family were taught, as soon as they
could speak, the Lord's Prayer, which they were made to say at rising and bed-

time constantly. . . . At five o'clock [P.M.] . . . the oldest took the youngest that could speak, and the second the next, to whom they read the Psalms for the day and a chapter in the New Testament; as, in the morning, they were directed to read the Psalms and a chapter in the Old; after which they went to their private prayers." Quoted in Richard P. Heitzenrater, *The Elusive Mr. Wesley: John Wesley as Seen by Contemporaries and Biographers* (Nashville: Abingdon Press, 1984), pp. 18–20.

11. My analysis of data from the Economic Values Survey conducted in 1992, using discriminant analysis involving the questions mentioned in the text, as well as saying table grace, praying for finances, and being sent to Sunday school; exact wordings of the questions are shown in the appendix of my book *God and Mammon in America*.

12. Historians have suggested that prayer books and other devotional guides were popular throughout most of American history, perhaps gaining importance during the nineteenth century and being used even more widely in the twentieth century. Our interviews reveal some use of prayer books, especially among people raised between the 1920s and the 1950s. Religious organizations were the main source of these guides; they supplied them through congregations and sometimes by direct-mail subscription. Prior to these decades and among families who could not afford to purchase books, people sometimes improvised. For instance, a woman raised before World War I in a very poor Eastern European immigrant family recalls that her father created his own prayer book. "He had all different prayers that he wrote in there for different occasions, which was very European style. He would read these prayers and would try to teach my brothers little prayers when they were small."

13. Barbara J. Scot, in *Prairie Reunion*, pp. 84–85, illustrates this kind of upbringing: "The insistence on complete honesty before God remained part of the Scotch Grove Presbyterian consciousness into my childhood. 'You must never lie,' said my mother. 'The Catholics have confession,' said the minister. 'But to be a Presbyterian is to approach God directly. He knows. If you are telling a lie, even by omission, He knows.' He knows. If I squat quickly behind the rosebush, He knows. If I touch myself there in the bath, He knows. He knows, He knows, He knows."

14. For another example, see Corrie ten Boom, *In My Father's House* (Old Tappan, NJ: Fleming Revell, 1976), p. 23.

15. Practical manuals have often been better at recognizing the importance of sacred objects than theories of religious development; for example, one manual counsels parents, "If it is at all possible, there should be set aside in the house a sort of sacred spot or dedicated place—a family altar, if you please. This is not a 'shrine'; it is simply a place that may become very special as it gathers about it the memories of quiet moments. . . . It may be marked by a religious picture or by the presence of the Bible and devotional literature. It may have a cross and other symbols" (Herman J. Sweet, *Opening the Door for God: A Manual for Parents* [Philadelphia: Westminster Press, 1943], p. 107).

16. Protestant, Catholic, and Jewish examples of sacred objects are discussed, respectively, in Colleen McDannell, *The Christian Home in Victorian America, 1840–1900* (Bloomington: Indiana University Press, 1986); Ann Taves, *The*

Household of Faith: Roman Catholic Devotions in Mid-Nineteenth-Century America (Notre Dame: University of Notre Dame Press, 1986); and Jenna Weissman Joselit, *The Wonders of America: Reinventing Jewish Culture, 1880–1950* (New York: Hill and Wang, 1994). See also Colleen McDannell, *Material Christianity: Religion and Popular Culture in America* (New Haven: Yale University Press, 1995).

17. For urban dwellers, such objects helped especially to sacralize the home (whole neighborhoods were sometimes considered sacred space, too). For rural inhabitants, the very land on which the family lived was often imbued with sacred significance as well. In her book about growing up on a farm in Iowa, *Prairie Reunion*, Barbara Scot, writes, "You and your progeny were part of a succession that was not only grounded in the Bible, it was meant to endure until Judgment Day. On the family farm" (p. 54). One of the men we interviewed illustrates the same connection. His grandfather had purchased the farm more than a century ago, he himself had been baptized in a creek running through the farm, and his nephew was farming the land now that the man himself was retired.

18. Sacred objects also remind people of their mortality: "My mother had a crucifix that had everything in it for the last rites. It's a wooden crucifix and you can snap the top off, and inside are the vials of holy water and the oil, in case someone in the house dies, for the priest to anoint you; it's all right there. Then there's a thing of instructions in it, that if there is no priest available, anyone can say the prayer for the dead. And I used to be so fascinated with that as a kid."

19. In *Autobiography: His Public Life and Services* (New York: Harper & Row, 1848), pp. 8–9, Benjamin Franklin writes of his Protestant ancestors in England during the reign of Mary: "They had an English Bible, and to conceal it, and place it in safety, it was fastened open with tapes under and within the cover of a joint-stool. When my great-grandfather wished to read it to his family, he placed the joint-stool on his knees, and then turned over the leaves under the tapes. One of the children stood at the door to give notice if he saw the apparitor coming, who was an officer of the spiritual court. In that case the stool was turned down again upon its feet, when the Bible remained concealed under it as before." My own grandfather treasured a Bible that, under similar conditions, had been concealed from English soldiers.

20. My emphasis on specifically religious objects is not meant to deny that other aspects of childhood experience may have served equally as symbols of the sacred; for example, Patricia Hampl, in *Virgin Time*, writes (p. 6), "Even the spring flowers of that Catholic past—window-box tulips, hyacinths the dog rooted up, . . . the alleys of lilac cloaking the garbage cans—were not just our improbable spring after the savage Minnesota winter. They belonged to Mary, our Mother."

Chapter 2: Home for the Holidays

1. On the interplay between commercial and religious themes, see especially Leigh Eric Schmidt, *Consumer Rites: The Buying and Selling of American Holidays* (Princeton: Princeton University Press, 1995).

2. Friedrich Holderlin, "Bread and Wine," Part 7 of *News of the Universe*, translated by Robert Bly (San Francisco: Sierra Club Books, 1980).

3. In contrast to the perspective presented in Edward Robinson, *The Original Vision* (New York: Seabury Press, 1983), few of the people we interviewed report childhood religious experiences that came totally out of the blue and that fundamentally reshaped them for the rest of their lives; to the extent that they experienced moments of grace, these experiences were densely interwoven with their family's religious practices.

4. Maya Angelou, in *I Know Why the Caged Bird Sings* (New York: Random House, 1969), p. 19, also illustrates the value of preserving things, writing, "The custom was to can everything that could possibly be preserved. During the killing season, after the first frost, all neighbors helped each other to slaughter hogs and even the quiet, big-eyed cows if they had stopped giving milk. The missionary ladies of the Christian Methodist Episcopal Church helped Momma."

5. Penne L. Restad, *Christmas in America: A History* (New York: Oxford University Press, 1995), is a useful secondary source.

6. The importance of regularity is also emphasized in some published accounts of holiday celebrations by religious leaders. For example, the evangelical Protestant writer Edith Schaeffer describes how she and her husband celebrated Christmas the same way for twenty-eight years: having a candle-lighting ritual at five o'clock on Christmas Eve, then trimming the tree and drinking iced ginger ale, hanging the stockings, opening presents on Christmas morning, and then having an elaborate dinner, always using the same tablecloth. She writes that it is important to have some activities that are always done the same in order to create museums of memory (Edith Schaeffer, *What Is a Family?* [Old Tappan, NJ: Fleming Revell, 1975]).

7. Waiting until late Christmas Eve to obtain trees free or cheaper was allegedly the custom of Senator Robert Dole's parents, too; see Jake H. Thompson, *Bob Dole: The Republicans' Man for All Seasons* (New York: Donald I. Fine, 1994), p. 17.

Chapter 3: Generations in the Spirit

1. The role of grandparents is captured nicely in a cartoon depicting a little girl sitting on her grandmother's lap, above the caption, "They told you *that*? Well, Grandma has known God longer than Mommy and Daddy have!"

2. On Jewish migration to California, see Deborah Dash Moore, *To the Golden Cities: Pursuing the American Jewish Dream in Miami and L.A.* (New York: Free Press, 1994).

3. On the role of grandparents and extended families in the religious upbringing of African Americans, see Wallace Charles Smith, *The Church in the Life of the Black Family* (Valley Forge, PA: Judson Press, 1985), especially chapters 4 and 5.

4. Accounts of actually having enjoyed reading Bible stories are likely to seem peculiar in an age of television, cartoons, and action adventure films. Yet they are not uncommon, sometimes even being compared favorably with more vi-

sual forms of entertainment. News anchor Dan Rather, for example, writes warmly of his grandmother's entertaining him with Bible stories when he was a child in Texas: "'Come, Danny, I'll read to you,' she would say. That was enough to make me come running. It meant story time. . . . Meaning no disrespect for Grandma's religious beliefs, I should clarify that her Bible offerings were meant less to serve the cause of piety than our need for entertainment. Joshua was my Sylvester Stallone, I guess" (*I Remember* [Boston: Little, Brown, 1991], p. 42).

5. Of course, Marcus Hansen's hypothesis about immigrants (that "what the son forgets, the grandson remembers") is well known because of its appropriation by Will Herberg in *Protestant-Catholic-Jew: An Essay in American Religious Sociology* (Garden City, NY: Doubleday, 1955), especially p. 186; the present discussion suggests that grandchildren may "remember" even without the immigrant experience's necessarily being a factor.

6. Devout grandparents figure prominently in some of the biographies and autobiographies of religious leaders; for example, see Rolf Zettersten, *Dr. Dobson: Turning Hearts Toward Home* (Dallas: Word, 1989), pp. 15–16.

7. Katharine Hepburn's grandfather, a flamboyant country preacher, appears to have been a strong influence in her family's stories; see Christopher Andersen, *Young Kate: The Remarkable Hepburns and the Childhood That Shaped an American Legend* (New York: Henry Holt, 1988).

8. Barbara Kingsolver, *High Tide in Tucson: Essays from Now or Never* (New York: HarperCollins, 1995), p. 91.

9. The role of mothers in religious socialization has also been demonstrated in a study that collected information directly from mothers and fathers, as well as from adolescents; see Roger L. Dudley and Margaret G. Dudley, "Transmission of Religious Values from Parents to Adolescents," *Review of Religious Research* 28 (1986), pp. 3–15; see also Alan C. Acock and Vern L. Bengtson, "On the Relative Influence of Mothers and Fathers: A Covariance Analysis of Political and Religious Socialization," *Journal of Marriage and the Family* 40 (1978), pp. 519–30.

10. James Hillman, "When the Father Is Absent," in *The Rag and Bone Shop of the Heart*, edited by Robert Bly, James Hillman, and Michael Meade (New York: HarperCollins, 1992), p. 269. The absent father as a source of the idea of God has of course been much discussed in the psychoanalytic literature; see Sigmund Freud, *Totem and Taboo* (New York: Norton, 1913); Sigmund Freud, *The Future of an Illusion* (New York: Doubleday, 1927); and Sigmund Freud, *Moses and Monotheism* (New York: Vintage, 1939).

11. William Jay Smith, "American Primitive," *Collected Poems: 1939–1989* (New York: Charles Scribners Sons, 1990).

12. Robert Bly, *Iron John: A Book about Men* (Reading, MA: Addison-Wesley, 1990).

Chapter 4: Houses of Worship

1. Among cognitive approaches to religious development, see especially David Elkind and Sally F. Elkind, "Varieties of Religious Experience in Young Ado-

lescents," *Journal for the Scientific Study of Religion* 2 (1962), pp. 102–12; Diane Long, David Elkind, and Bernard Spilka, "The Child's Conception of Prayer," *Journal for the Scientific Study of Religion* 6 (1967), pp. 101–9; and David Elkind, "The Origins of Religion in the Child," *Review of Religious Research* 12 (1970), pp. 35–42.

2. The poet Tomas Transtromer has also captured an important dimension of the precarious relationship between sacred buildings and sacredness itself, describing the church as "pillars and vaulting white as plaster, like the cast around the broken arm of faith" ("The Scattered Congregation," *Friends You Drank Some Darkness: Selected Poems of Ekelof, Martinson, and Transtromer,* translated by Robert Bly [Boston: Beacon Press, 1975]).

3. Stiff clothing also conjured up negative experiences of the sacred, of course; for instance, Kathleen Norris, in *Little Girls in Church* (Pittsburgh: University of Pittsburgh Press, 1995), p. 25, writes: "I've made friends with a five-year-old Presbyterian. She tugs at her lace collar. I sympathize. We're both bored."

4. Martin E. Marty, in "The Sunday School: Battered Survivor," *Christian Century,* June 4–11, 1980, pp. 634–36; William H. Willimon, in "Growing Up Christian in Greenville," *Christian Century,* June 4–11, 1980, pp. 637–38; and John H. Westerhoff III, in "The Sunday School of Tomorrow," *Christian Century,* June 4–11, 1980, pp. 639–41, offer some personal reflections on their own experiences in Sunday school.

5. Eudora Welty, in *One Writer's Beginnings* (Cambridge, MA: Harvard University Press, 1984), p. 31, writes similarly of such hymns as her favorite aspect of Methodist Sunday school.

6. The catechetical tradition emphasized the confession of faith through verbal repitition of memorized scriptural tenets as the best means of instructing children; it was closely supervised by clergy and was understood to be preferrable to object lessons, the use of images, or storytelling; see Peter Y. DeJong, "Calvin's Contributions to Christian Education," *Calvin Theological Journal* 2 (1967), pp. 162–201. Horace Bushnell's *Christian Nurture* (Cleveland: Pilgrim Press, 1994; originally published in 1861) has generally been regarded as the decisive effort to refocus childhood religious instruction on the retelling of biblical narratives and away from an emphasis on divine wrath.

7. Some research also lays blame on Sunday school teachers for not being sufficiently warm and supportive toward their students; for example, see Margaret M. Sawin, "How the Family Shapes Religious Believing and How Religious Education Can Shape the Family," *American Baptist Quarterly* 3 (1984), 53–62.

8. From a discriminant analysis of six childhood activities as predictors of saying that religion had been very important in one's family while one was a youth; the question wordings are found in my book *God and Mammon in America.* Of the six items, Sunday school was the weakest (discriminant function coefficients, respectively, were .509 for parents reading the Bible at home; .469 for having had family devotions; .436 for having said grace at meals; −.022 for having prayed about money; −.034 for parents' having read the Bible to them; and −.117 for being sent to Sunday school; discriminant structure matrix coefficients for these items, respectively, were .774, .744, .709, .465, .532, and .207).

9. William Blake, "Proverbs from Hell," quoted in *The Rag and Bone Shop of the Heart*, edited by Robert Bly, James Hillman, and Michael Meade (New York: HarperCollins, 1992), p. 15.

10. Maya Angelou, *I Know Why the Caged Bird Sings*, pp. 27–28.

11. "Albert Schweitzer is reported to have commented that it is important for children to attend worship with their families, not because they will understand every word, but because they will feel the reverence of their parents and become sensitive to the wonder of life" (William H. Genne, "Families Worship in Church," *International Journal of Religious Education* 37 [1961], p. 12).

12. Advice books for parents in the 1940s and 1950s tend to idealize children's attraction to formal church services but occasionally capture this sense of reverence and transcendence; for example, "From his experiences in church the child gets a sense of something big, something worthwhile, a feeling of Somebody so great, so powerful . . . that people come together to . . . talk about him" (Robbie Trent, *Your Child and God* [New York: Harper & Brothers, 1952], p. 124).

13. A similar argument can be made for a balance between paternal and material images of God; for example, see Mark D. Keyser and Gary R. Collins, "Parental Image and the Concept of God: An Evangelical Protestant-Catholic Comparison," *Journal of Psychology and Theology* 4 (1976), pp. 69–80.

Chapter 5: The Ties That Bind

1. Gerhard Lenski's *The Religious Factor: A Sociological Study of Religion's Impact on Politics, Economics, and Family Life* (Garden City, NY: Doubleday, 1961), emphasizes the "communal" aspect of religion, and Glock, in his five dimensions of religiosity, includes attention to the role of community in his "ritual dimension" (see Charles Y. Glock and Rodney Stark, *Religion and Society in Tension* [Chicago: Rand McNally, 1965], p. 28). The function of "belonging" has especially been emphasized in Greeley's *The Denominational Society*, pp. 31–37.

2. This perspective on congregations is emphasized in much of the recent literature, but see especially Dorothy C. Bass, "Congregations and the Bearing of Traditions," in *American Congregations: New Perspectives in the Study of Congregations*, vol. 2, edited by James P. Wind and James W. Lewis (Chicago: University of Chicago Press, 1994), chapter 5.

3. Of church picnics, Maya Angelou, in *I Know Why the Caged Bird Sings*, pp. 115–16, writes, "The summer picnic fish fry in the clearing by the pond was the biggest outdoor event of the year. Everyone was there. All churches were represented. . . . The amount and variety of foods would have found approval on the menu of a Roman epicure."

4. One of the people quoted in Scot, *Prairie Reunion*, p. 197, voices a similar lament: "In the old days [the church] was really the heart, and things spread out from there—why, people who didin't belong to the church came to the dinners—it was a social center, you know. Now everything's so fluid."

5. On the history of Easter celebrations in the United States, see Schmidt, *Consumer Rites*, chapter 4; one of the few sociological investigations of Easter is Theodore Caplow and Margaret Holmes Williamson, "Decoding Middletown's Easter Bunny: A Study in American Iconography," *Semiotica* 32 (1980), pp. 221–32.

6. Theodore Roethke, "In a Dark Time," *Collected Poems of Theodore Roethke* (New York: Doubleday, 1960).

7. For an example of a Catholic funeral that graciously portrays the relationship between an inward language of grief and an outward language of order, see John Grady, "Full Military Honors," in *The Next Parish Over: A Collection of Irish-American Writing*, edited by Patricia Monaghan (Minneapolis: New Rivers Press, 1993), pp. 109–20.

8. Frederick Buechner, in *The Sacred Journey* (New York: Harper & Row, 1982), p. 57, writes, "Moments of grace come ultimately from farther away than Oz and deeper down than doom, holy because they heal and hallow."

Chapter 6: Learning to Be a Leader

1. Alexis de Tocqueville, *Democracy in America*, 2 vols (New York: Vintage Books, 1945; originally published in 1835).

2. On the history of the Sunday school movement, see Anne M. Boylan, *Sunday School: The Formation of an American Institution, 1790–1880* (New Haven: Yale University Press, 1988); and on Sunday schools in American Judaism, see Lloyd P. Gartner, "Jewish Education in the United States," in *The Jewish Community in America*, edited by Marshall Sklare (New York: Behrman House, 1974), pp. 221–48.

Chapter 7: Points of Departure

1. Rainer Maria Rilke, "I Live My Life," *Selected Poems by Rainer Maria Rilke*, translated by Robert Bly (New York: Harper Collins, 1981).

2. Barbara Kingsolver, *High Tide in Tucson: Essays from Now or Never*, p. 50.

3. Gerald Vann, *To Heaven with Diana!* (London: Collins, 1960), pp. 51–52.

4. Paul Tournier, *The Adventure of Living* (London: SCM, 1966), pp. 38–39.

5. Steve Turner, *Up to Date: Poems 1968–1982* (London: Hodder & Stoughton, 1983), p. 166.

6. Kathleen Norris, *Dakota: A Spiritual Geography* (New York: Ticknor and Fields, 1993), p. 92. See also John P. O'Hara, "A Research Note on the Sources of Adult Church Commitment among Those Who Were Regular Attenders During Childhood," *Review of Religious Research* 21 (1980), pp. 462–67.

7. Joseph Raz, in "Multiculturalism: A Liberal Perspective," *Dissent* 41 (Winter 1994), p. 71, writes that "a policy that forcibly detaches children from the culture of their parents not only undermines the stability of society by undermining people's ability to sustain long-term intimate relations, it also threatens one of the deepest desires of most parents, the desire to understand their children, share their world, and to remain close to them."

Chapter 8: Remembering the Past

1. Mevlana Celaleddin Rumi, *Crazy as We Are: Selected Rubais from Divan-i Kebir*, translated by Nevit O. Ergin (Prescott, AZ: Hohm Press, 1992), p. 44.
2. Frederick Buechner, *The Sacred Journey* (New York: Harper & Row, 1982), p. 21.
3. Although people have different pasts to remember, remembering encourages most of the people we interviewed to realize more clearly their need to move on. They discover, as Patricia Hampl does in writing about her Catholic upbringing in Minnesota (*Virgin Time*, p. 8), that "the grass of remembrance is never quite green" and that all the people have "turned to wax." Like her, some who are "fused with fascination to their past" find themselves "taking planes to distant places."
4. C. Pollack and B. Steele, "A Psychiatric Study of Parents Who Abuse Infants and Small Children," in *The Battered Child*, edited by R. Helfer and C. H. Kempe (Chicago: University of Chicago Press, 1968).
5. Kathryn Neufeld, "Child-Rearing, Religion, and Abusive Parents," *Religious Education* 74 (May–June 1979), 234–44.
6. As a vivid example of child-rearing practices that now seem abusive, Mary McCarthy writes of the bedtime ritual she endured as a child, "Adhesive tape that, to prevent mouth-breathing, was clapped upon our lips the moment the prayer was finished, sealing us up for the night, and that was removed, very painfully, with the help of ether, in the morning" (*Memories of a Catholic Girlhood* [New York: Harcourt Brace, 1955], p. 39). She also writes of abusive punishment: "We were beaten all the time, as a matter of course, with the hairbrush across the bare legs for ordinary occasions, and with the razor strop across the bare bottom for special occasions" (p. 64).
7. On abuse within religious contexts, see also Randy Frame, "Child Abuse: The Church's Best Kept Secret?" *Christianity Today*, February 15, 1985, pp. 32–34; and Louis J. Cozolino, "Ritualistic Child Abuse, Psychopathology, and Evil," *Psychology and Theology* 18 (1990), pp. 218–27.
8. Sharon Olds, "Saturn," *The Dead and the Living* (New York: Knopf, 1983).

Chapter 9: The Move to Spiritual Practice

1. My discussion of practices is indebted to the Valparaiso Project on the Education and Formation of People in Faith and especially to conversations with Dorothy Bass, who conceives of practices as shared, patterned, and ongoing activities.
2. Anna Fynn, *Mr. God, This Is Anna* (London: Collins, 1974), p. 118.
3. Joseph Raz, in "Multiculturalism: A Liberal Perspective," *Dissent* 41 (Winter 1994), p. 67, writes, "Moral knowledge is practical in a special sense: it is embodied in our practices and acquired by habituation." The same can be said of spiritual knowing.
4. James Hillman, *We've Had a Hundred Years of Psychotherapy—And the World's Getting Worse* (San Francisco: Harper San Francisco, 1992), p. 50;

Hillman writes of soul making as "a discipline—a religious devotion with rituals, symbols, teachings, kind submissions, obediences, sacrifices." See also Alan Jones, *Soul Making: The Desert Way of Spirituality* (New York: Harper & Row, 1985). Simone de Beauvoir ("A Very Easy Death," in *Mothers: Memories, Dreams and Reflections by Literary Daughters*, edited by Susan Cahill [New York: Penguin, 1983], p. 34) writes that prayer is "an exercise that called for concentration, thought and a certain condition of the soul." It was her mother's way of praying that taught her to view it this way.

5. Paul Tillich, "The Lost Dimension in Religion," in *The Religious Experience*, edited by George Brantl (New York: George Braziller, 1964), p. 586.
6. Quoted in Susan Ketchin, *The Christ-Haunted Landscape: Faith and Doubt in Southern Fiction* (Jackson: University Press of Mississippi, 1994), p. 81.
7. Edwin Muir, *An Autobiography* (London: Hogarth Press, 1954), p. 246.
8. The technique of visualization or imagining is also described in Frederick Buechner, *Now and Then* (San Francisco: Harper San Francisco, 1983), pp. 65–66.
9. Sherry B. Ortner, "Theory in Anthropology Since the Sixties," *Comparative Studies in Society and History* 26 (1984), p. 144.
10. Madeleine L'Engle, *The Summer of the Great-Grandmother*, p. 144.
11. Jelaluddin Rumi, *Feeling the Shoulder of the Lion: Selected Poetry and Teaching Stories from the Mathnawi*, translated by Coleman Barks (Putney, VT: Threshold Books, 1991), p. 35.
12. Jonathan Edwards, *Religious Affections*, edited by J. E. Smith (New Haven: Yale University Press, 1959), pp. 161–62.

Chapter 10: Bridging Diversity

1. On the broader question of religion as a source of unity or disunity in the contemporary United States, see the essays in *Reinventing the American People: E Pluribus in the Nineties*, edited by Robert Royal (Grand Rapids, MI: Eerdmans, 1995).
2. John Chrysostom, "An Address on Vainglory and the Right Way for Parents to Bring Up Their Children," translated by M. L. W. Laistner, in *Christianity and Pagan Culture in the Later Roman Empire*, edited by M. L. W. Laistner (Ithaca: Cornell University Press, 1951), pp. 94–95.

Chapter 11: Seeing with Four Eyes

1. A similar observation is made in Cecil Williams's *No Hiding Place: Empowerment and Recovery for Our Troubled Communities* (San Francisco: Harper San Francisco, 1992), p. 16.
2. See Christian Smith, *American Evangelicals: Embattled and Thriving* (Chicago: University of Chicago Press, 1998), for comparisons between self-identified fundamentalists, evangelicals, and mainline Protestants.